QUEENS OF THE STONE AGE

Published by
Hal Leonard

Exclusive Distributors:
Hal Leonard
7777 West Bluemound Road
Milwaukee, WI 53213
Email: info@halleonard.com

Hal Leonard Europe Limited
42 Wigmore Street
Marylebone, London, W1U 2RN
Email: info@halleonardeurope.com

Hal Leonard Australia Pty. Ltd.
4 Lentara Court
Cheltenham, Victoria, 3192 Australia
Email: info@halleonard.com.au

Order No. AM975832
ISBN 0-7119-9720-9

This book © Copyright 2002 by Hal Leonard

Music arrangements by Steve Cooper.
Music processed by The Pitts.

www.halleonard.com

SONGS FOR THE DEAF

GUITAR TABLATURE EXPLAINED

Guitar music can be notated three different ways: on a musical stave, in tablature, and in rhythm slashes.

RHYTHM SLASHES are written above the stave. Strum chords in the rhythm indicated. Round noteheads indicate single notes.

THE MUSICAL STAVE shows pitches and rhythms and is divided by lines into bars. Pitches are named after the first seven letters of the alphabet.

TABLATURE graphically represents the guitar fingerboard. Each horizontal line represents a string, and each number represents a fret.

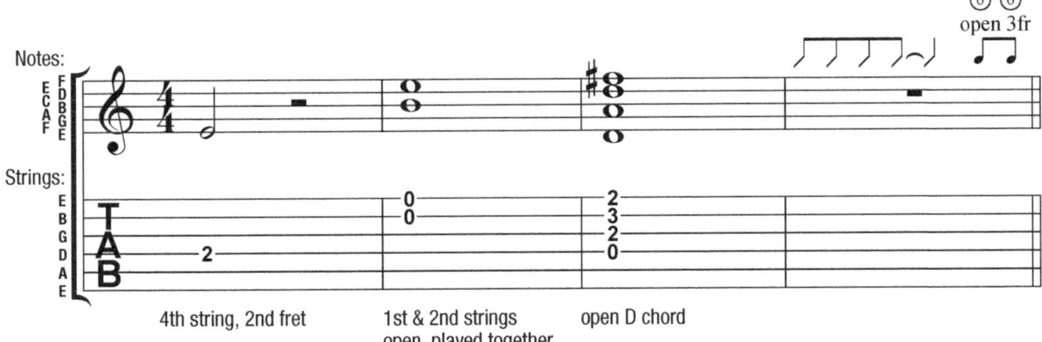

DEFINITIONS FOR SPECIAL GUITAR NOTATION

SEMI-TONE BEND: Strike the note and bend up a semi-tone (1/2 step).

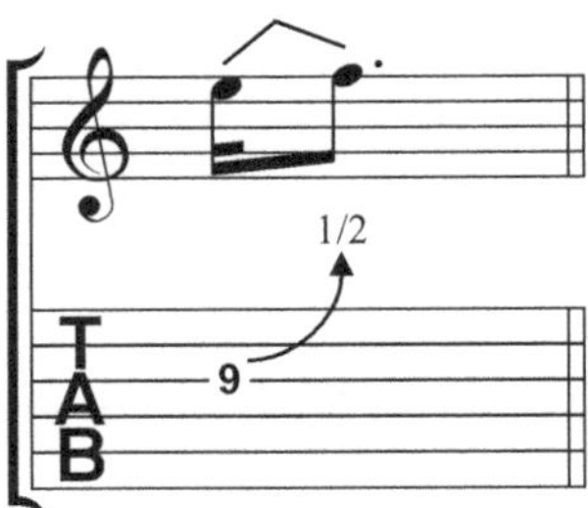

WHOLE-TONE BEND: Strike the note and bend up a whole-tone (whole step).

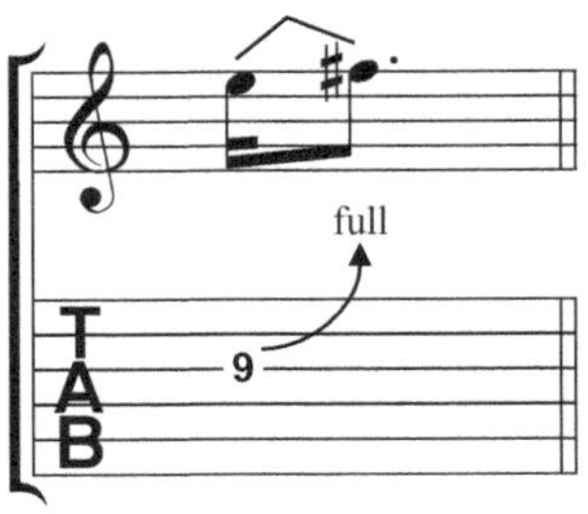

GRACE NOTE BEND: Strike the note and bend as indicated. Play the first note as quickly as possible.

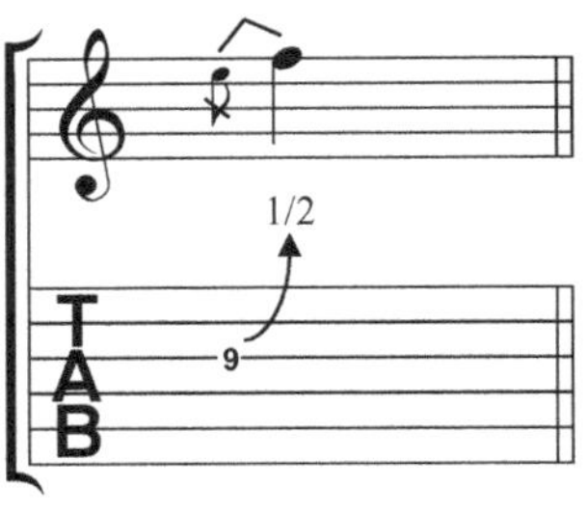

QUARTER-TONE BEND: Strike the note and bend up a 1/4 step.

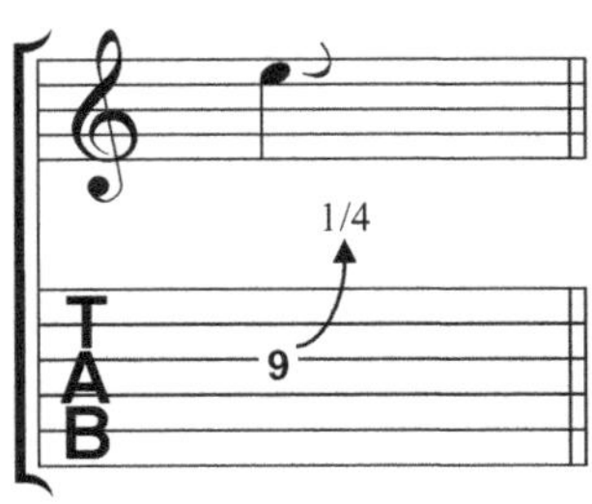

BEND & RELEASE: Strike the note and bend up as indicated, then release back to the original note.

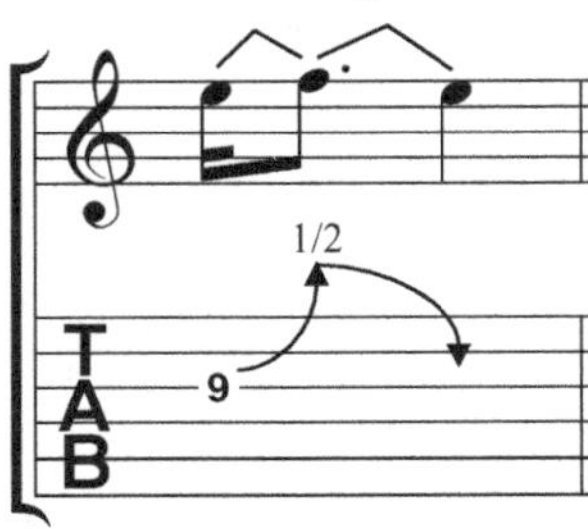

COMPOUND BEND & RELEASE: Strike the note and bend up and down in the rhythm indicated.

PRE-BEND: Bend the note as indicated, then strike it.

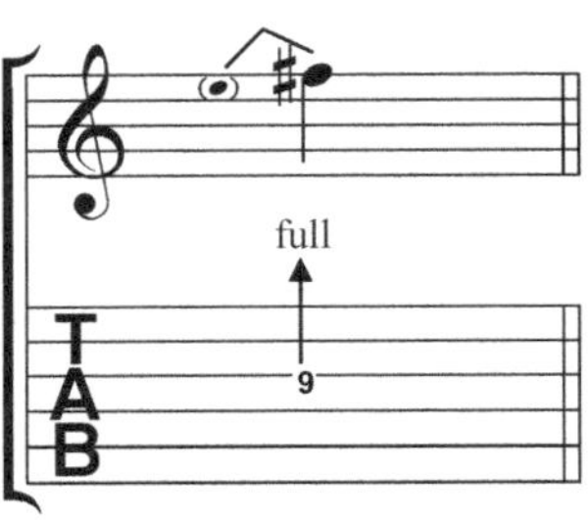

PRE-BEND & RELEASE: Bend the note as indicated. Strike it and release the note back to the original pitch.

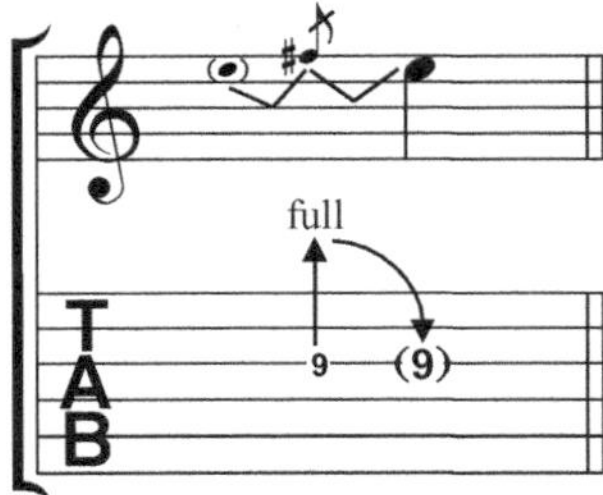

UNISON BEND: Strike the two notes simultaneously and bend the lower note up to the pitch of the higher.

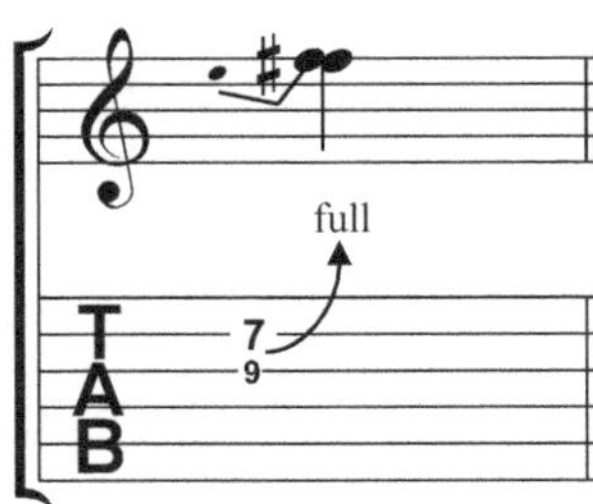

BEND & RESTRIKE: Strike the note and bend as indicated then restrike the string where the symbol occurs.

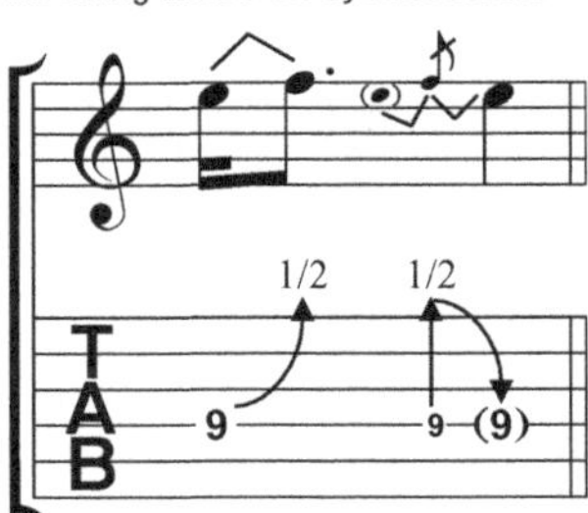

BEND, HOLD AND RELEASE: Same as bend and release but hold the bend for the duration of the tie.

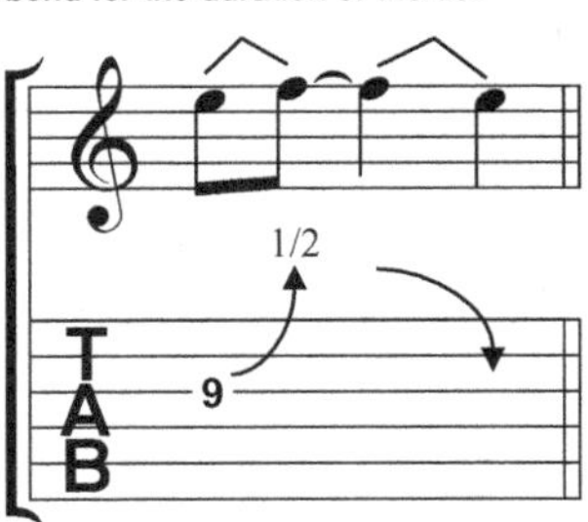

BEND AND TAP: Bend the note as indicated and tap the higher fret while still holding the bend.

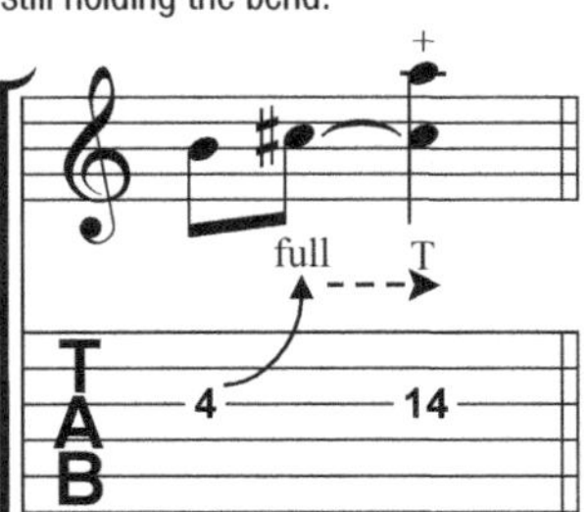

VIBRATO: The string is vibrated by rapidly bending and releasing the note with the fretting hand.

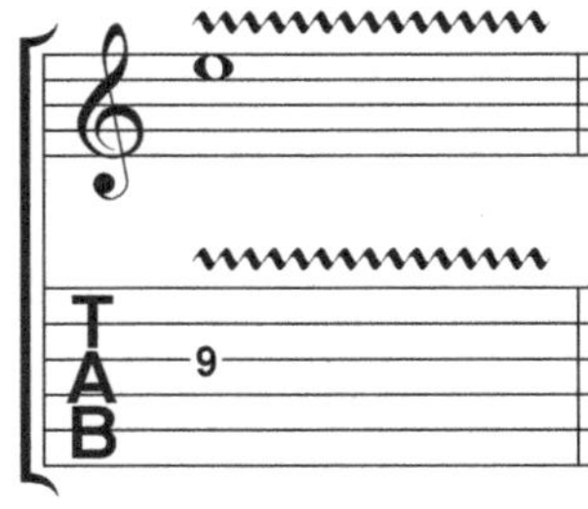

HAMMER-ON: Strike the first note with one finger, then sound the second note (on the same string) with another finger by fretting it without picking.

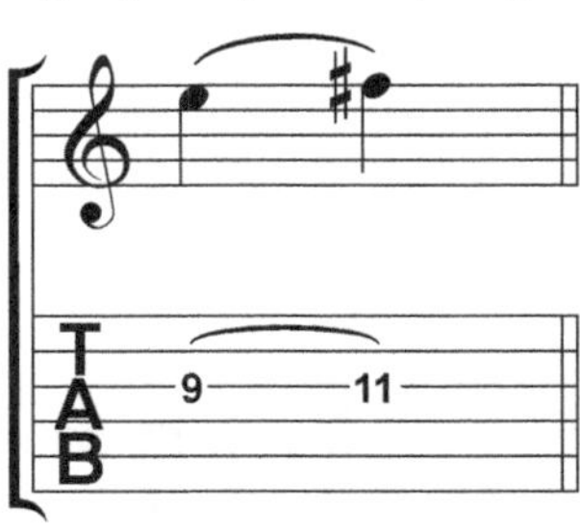

PULL-OFF: Place both fingers on the notes to be sounded, strike the first note and without picking, pull the finger off to sound the second note.

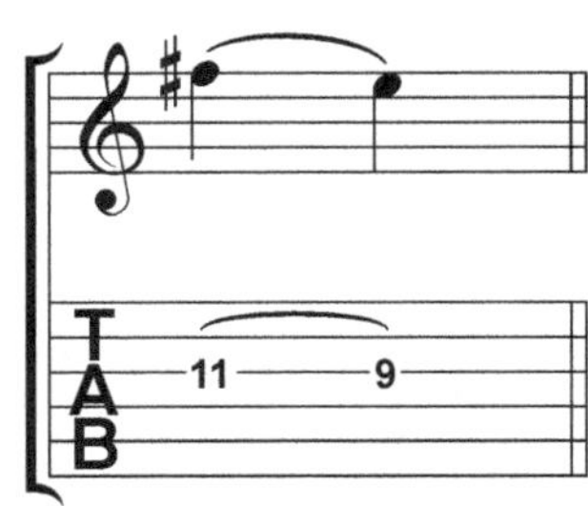

LEGATO SLIDE (GLISS): Strike the first note and then slide the same fret-hand finger up or down to the second note. The second note is not struck.

SHIFT SLIDE (GLISS & RESTRIKE): Same as legato slide, except the second note is struck.

MUFFLED STRINGS: A percussive sound is produced by laying the fret hand across the string(s) without depressing, and striking them with the pick hand.

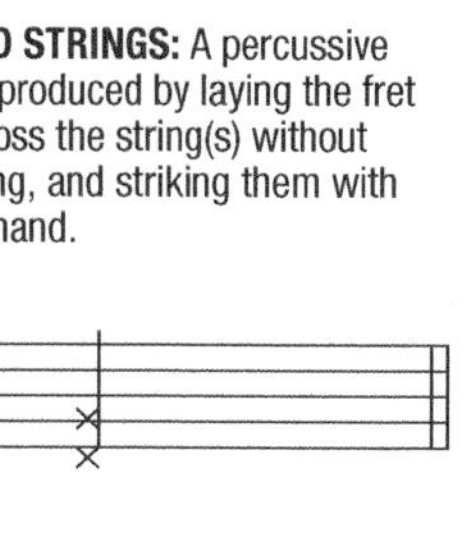

PALM MUTING: The note is partially muted by the pick hand lightly touching the string(s) just before the bridge.

SWEEP PICKING: Rhythmic downstroke and/or upstroke motion across the strings.

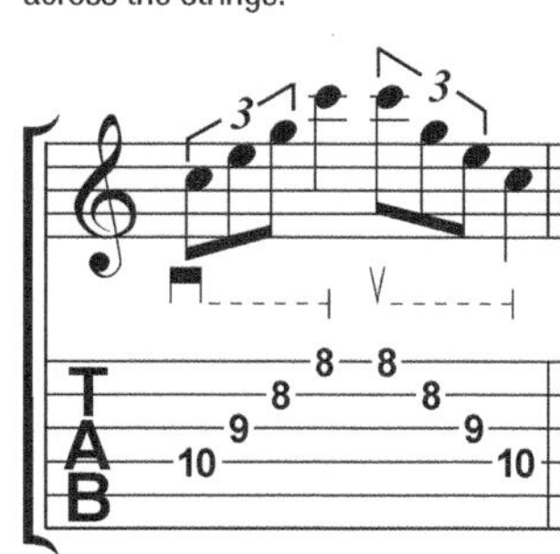

TRILL: Very rapidly alternate between the notes indicated by continuously hammering on and pulling off.

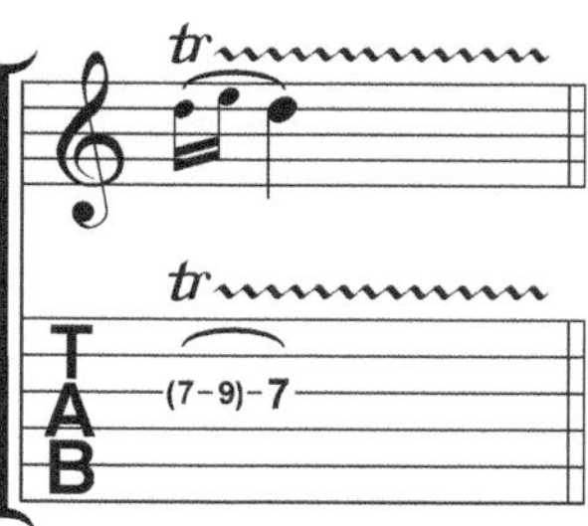

NATURAL HARMONIC: Strike the note while the fret-hand lightly touches the string directly over the fret indicated.

RAKE: Drag the pick across the strings indicated with a single motion.

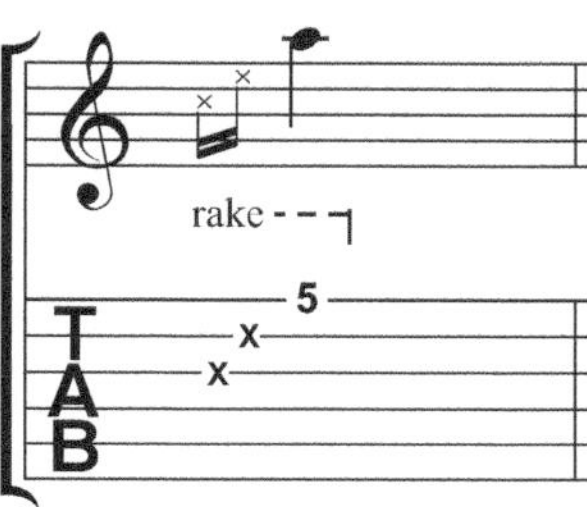

VIBRATO DIVE BAR AND RETURN: Thepitch of the note or chord is dropped a specific number of steps (in rhythm) then returned to the original pitch.

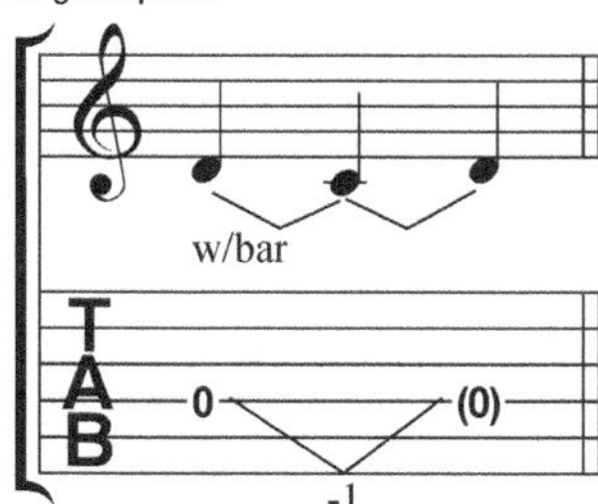

TAPPING: Hammer ("tap") the fret indicated with the pick-hand index or middle finger and pull off to the note fretted by the fret hand.

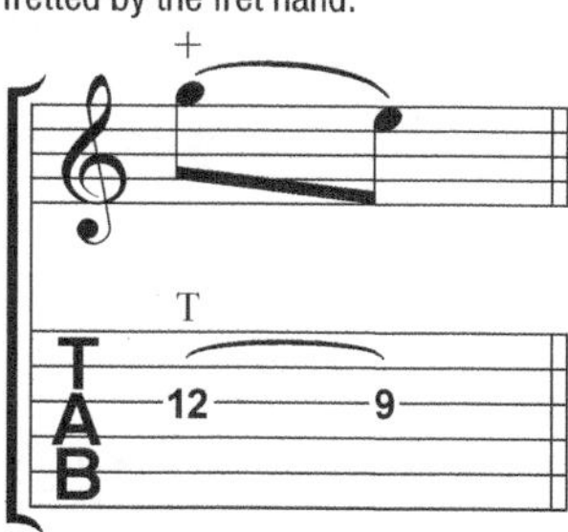

PINCH HARMONIC: The note is fretted normally and a harmonic is produced by adding the edge of the thumb or the tip of the index finger of the pick hand to the normal pick attack.

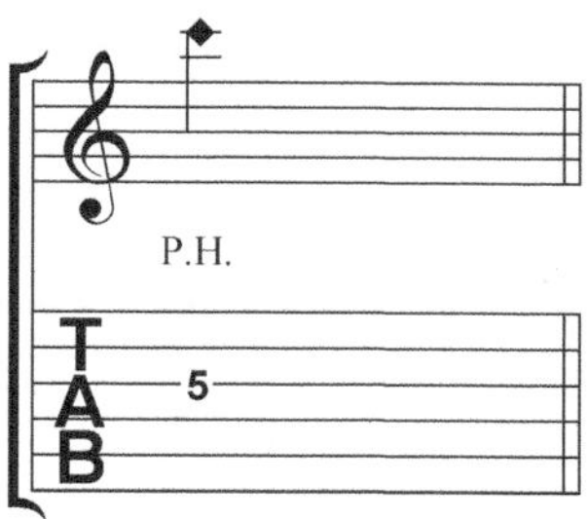

TREMOLO PICKING: The note is picked as rapidly and continuously as possible.

VIBRATO BAR SCOOP: Depress the bar just before striking the note, then quickly release the bar.

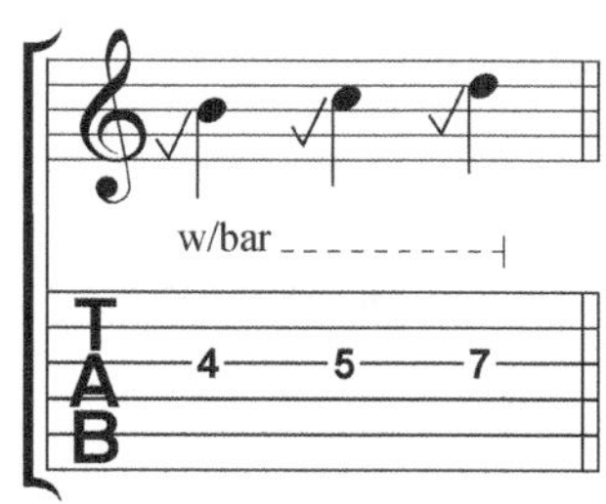

PICK SCRAPE: The edge of the pick is rubbed down (or up) the string, producing a scratchy sound.

HARP HARMONIC: The note is fretted normally and a harmonic is produced by gently resting the pick hand's index finger directly above the indicated fret (in brackets) while plucking the appropriate string.

ARPEGGIATE: Play the notes of the chord indicated by quickly rolling them from bottom to top.

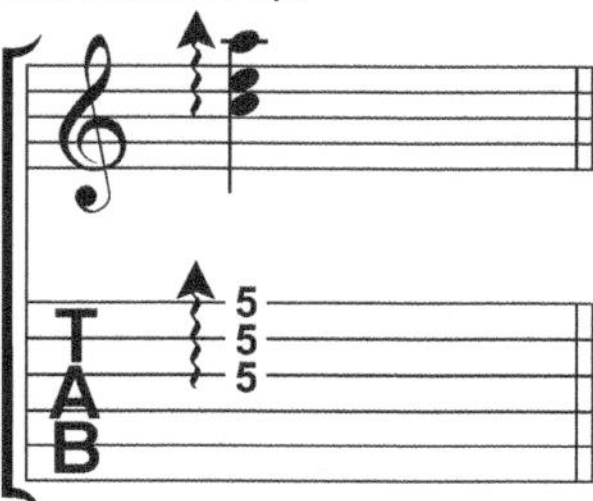

VIBRATO BAR DIP: Strike the note and then immediately drop a specific number of steps, then release back to the original pitch.

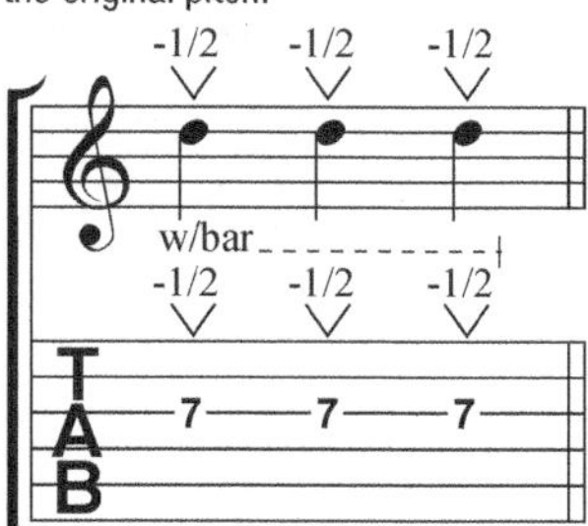

ADDITIONAL MUSICAL DEFINITIONS

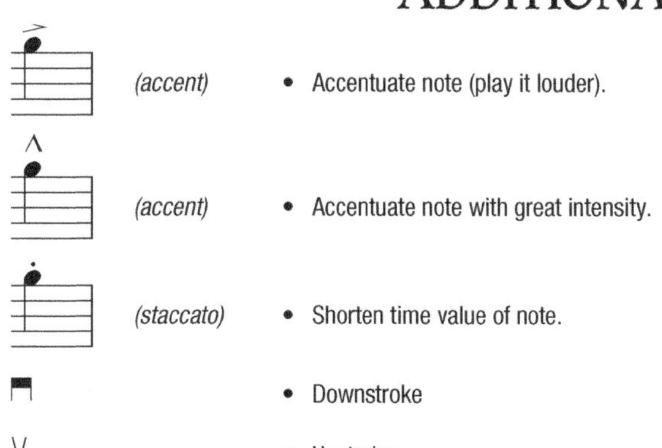

(accent)	•	Accentuate note (play it louder).
(accent)	•	Accentuate note with great intensity.
(staccato)	•	Shorten time value of note.
▬	•	Downstroke
V	•	Upstroke

D.%. al Coda — • Go back to the sign (%), then play until the bar marked *To Coda* ⊕ then skip to the section marked ⊕ *Coda*.

D.C. al Fine — • Go back to the beginning of the song and play until the bar marked *Fine*.

tacet — • Instrument is silent (drops out).

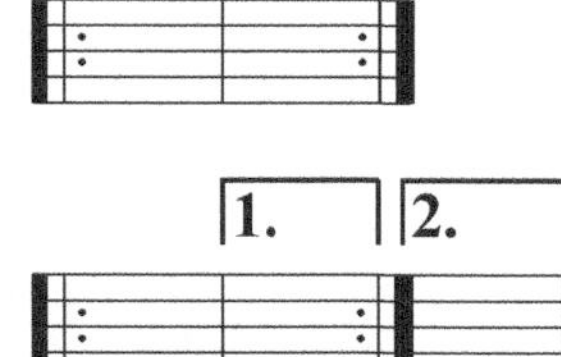

• Repeat bars between signs.

• When a repeated section has different endings, play the first ending only the first time and the second ending only the second time.

NOTE: Tablature numbers in brackets mean:
1. The note is sustained, but a new articulation (such as hammer on or slide) begins.
2. A note may be fretted but not necessarily played.

YOU THINK I AIN'T WORTH A DOLLAR, BUT I FEEL LIKE A MILLIONAIRE

Words & Music by Josh Homme, Nick Oliveri & Mario Lalli

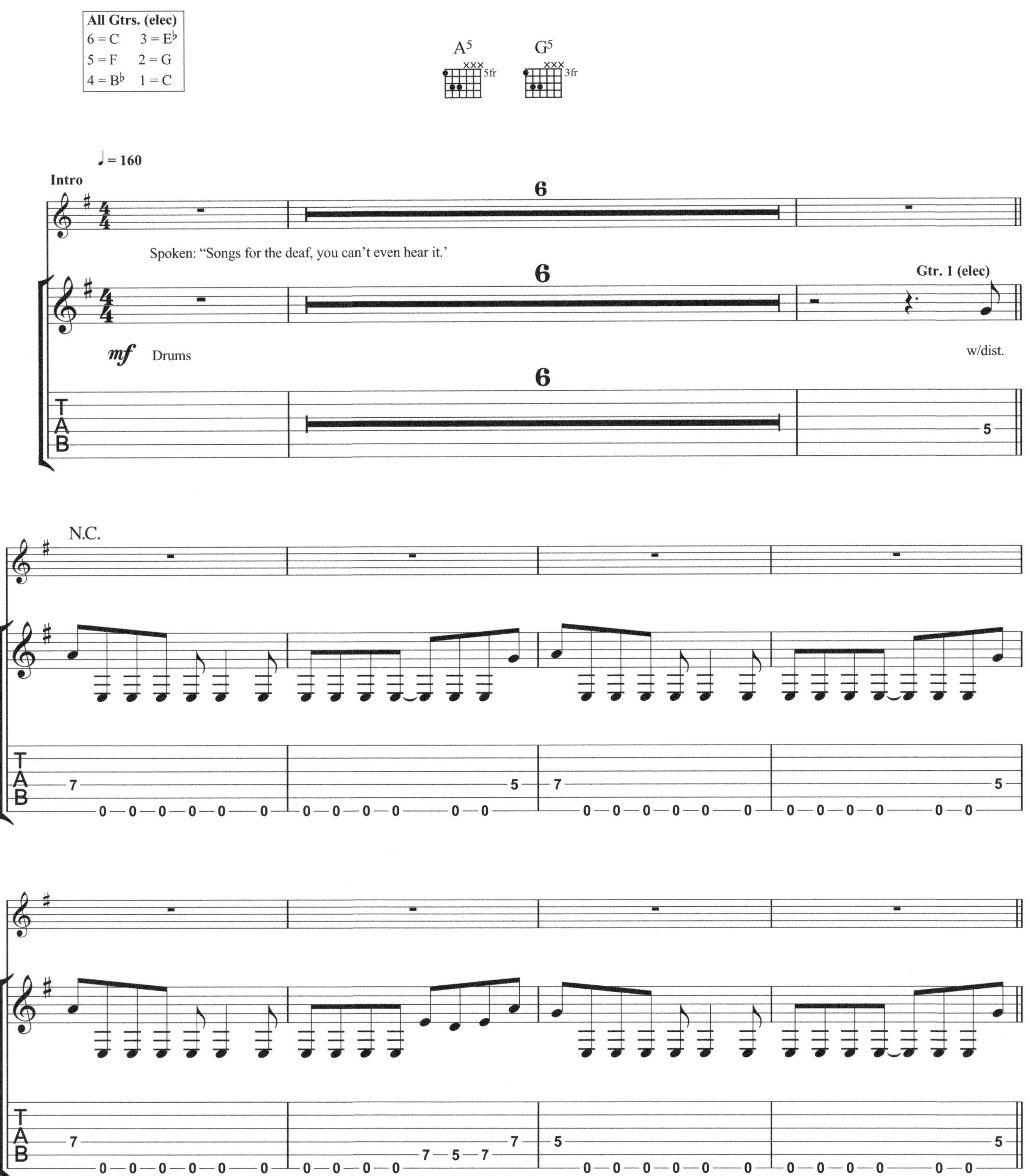

Verse
N.C.
1. Dead bull, with the life on the low, ___ I'll be mas - sive con -
Gtrs. 1+2 (elec)
f
w/dist.
3
quis - ta - dor. ___ Gim - me ___ soul, or show me the door. ___
Me - tal hea - vy, soft at the core, ___ gim - me to - ro,
gim - me some more. ___ Gim - me to - ro, gim - me some more. ___

Pres - sur - ised   and   neu - tra - lised,   deep - fried,
A5   G5   Bridge
gim - me   some   more.
A5   G5
Gtr. 3 (elec)
w/dist.
1/4
Gtr. 3 tacet

6

N.C.
play 3 times
Verse
N.C.
2. Space flun - ky, four on the floor __ forti - fied with the
li - quor store. __ This one's __ down, gim - me some more, __
gim - me to - ro, gim - me some more. _______ Give me to - ro,

A5
G5
gim - me some more. ___ Give me to - ro, gim - me some more. ___

Bridge
A5
G5
Gtr. 3
1/4

N.C.
let ring…

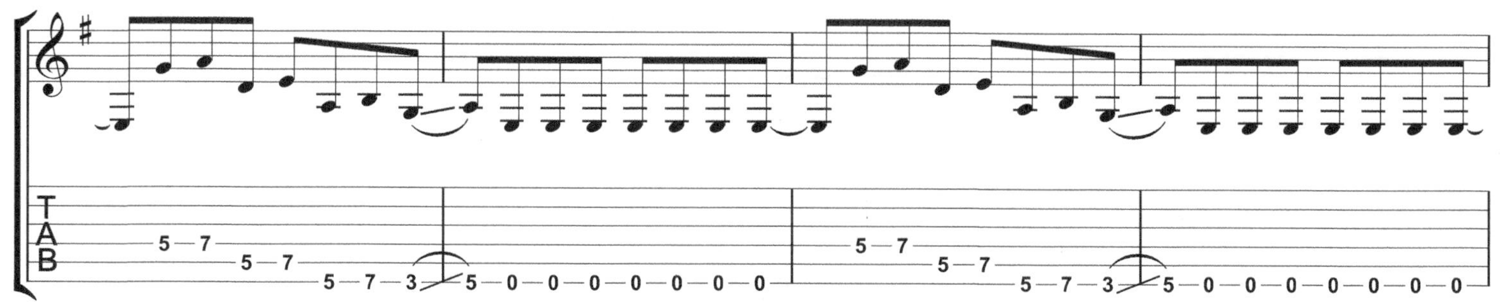
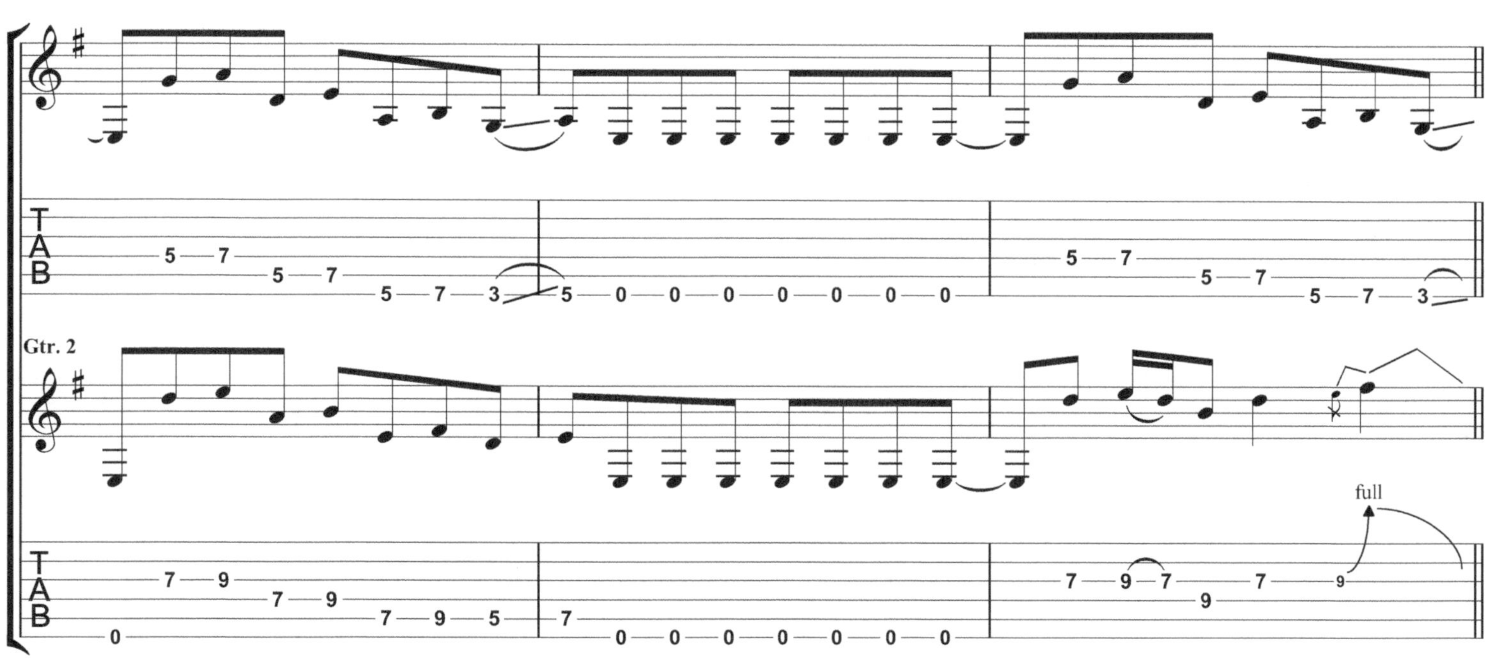

3. Shrun - ken head I love to a - dore, B - Mo - vie,

gim - me some gore. ___
Give me to - ro, ___
gim - me some more, ___
B - Mo - vie,
gim - me some gore. ___
A5
G5
Gtrs. 1+2
Gtr. 3
Gtr. 2 cont. in stave above
full

A5
G5
N.C.
TAB
5 5 5 5 7 7 7 5
5 5 5 5 7 7 7 5
3 3 3 3 5 5 5 3
5 5 5 5 5 5 5
5 5 5 5 5 5 5
3 3 3 3 3 3 3
5 5 7
5 7
5 7 3
TAB
12 - 14 - 12
15 17
14 16 12 14
12

Oh.
3/4
4/4
TAB
0
0
0 0 0 0 0 0 0 0 0 0 0 0
5
Gtr. 3 tacet
3/4
4/4
TAB
14

Give me to-ro, ___ gim - me some more. ___
Give me to-ro, ___
full
gim - me some more. ___ Give me to-ro, ___
gim - me some more. ___
full

A5
G5
Give me to - ro, __ gim - me some more. __
full
TAB
Gtr. 3

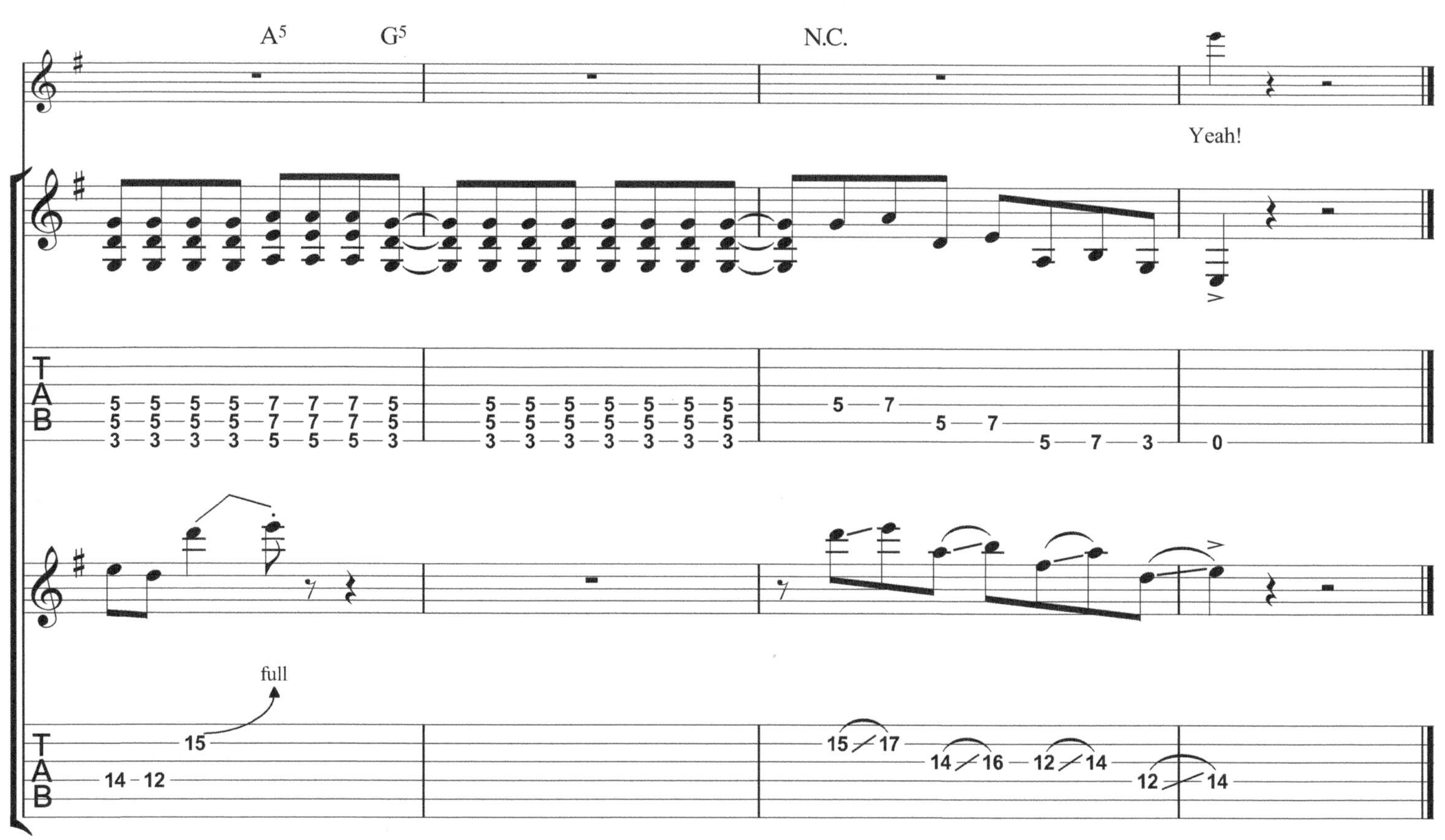

A5
G5
N.C.
Yeah!
TAB
full
TAB

NO ONE KNOWS

Words & Music by Josh Homme, Nick Oliveri & Mark Lanegan

that and this, these and those.
how they stick in your throat.
B
Eb
No one knows.
Taste like gold.
1.
Em
2.
Em
Oh, what you do

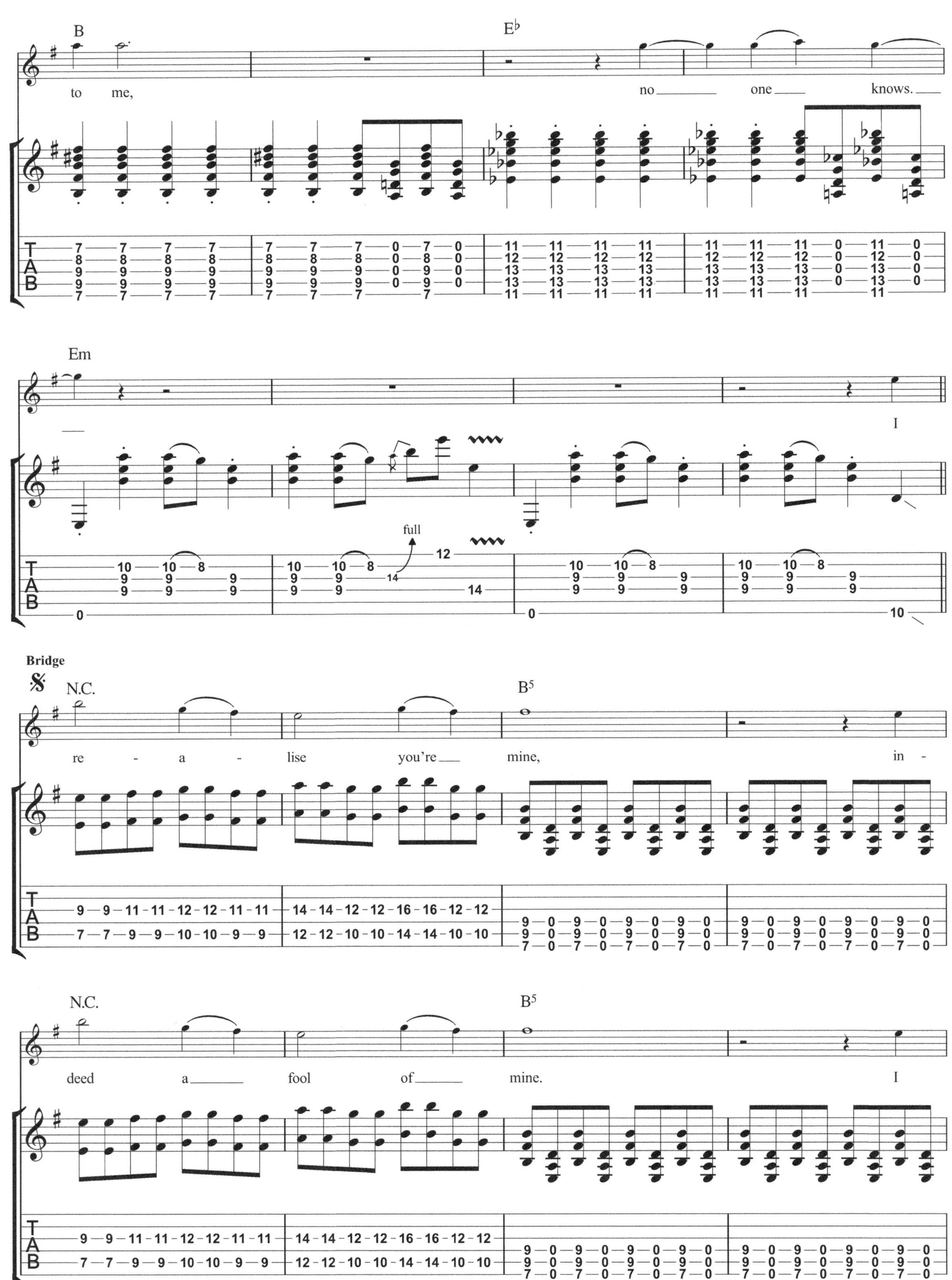

B
E♭
to me,
no one knows.
Em
I
Bridge
N.C.
B5
re - a - lise you're mine,
in -
N.C.
B5
deed a fool of mine.
I
full
16

re - a - lise you're mine, in -
deed a fool am I. Ah.
3. I jour - ney through the de - sert
Ah. Ah. Ah.

of the mind with no hope.
Ah. Ah. Ah. Ah.
B E♭
Ah.
I fol - low.
Em
Verse
Em
4. I drift a - long the o - - cean,
Ah. Ah. Ah.

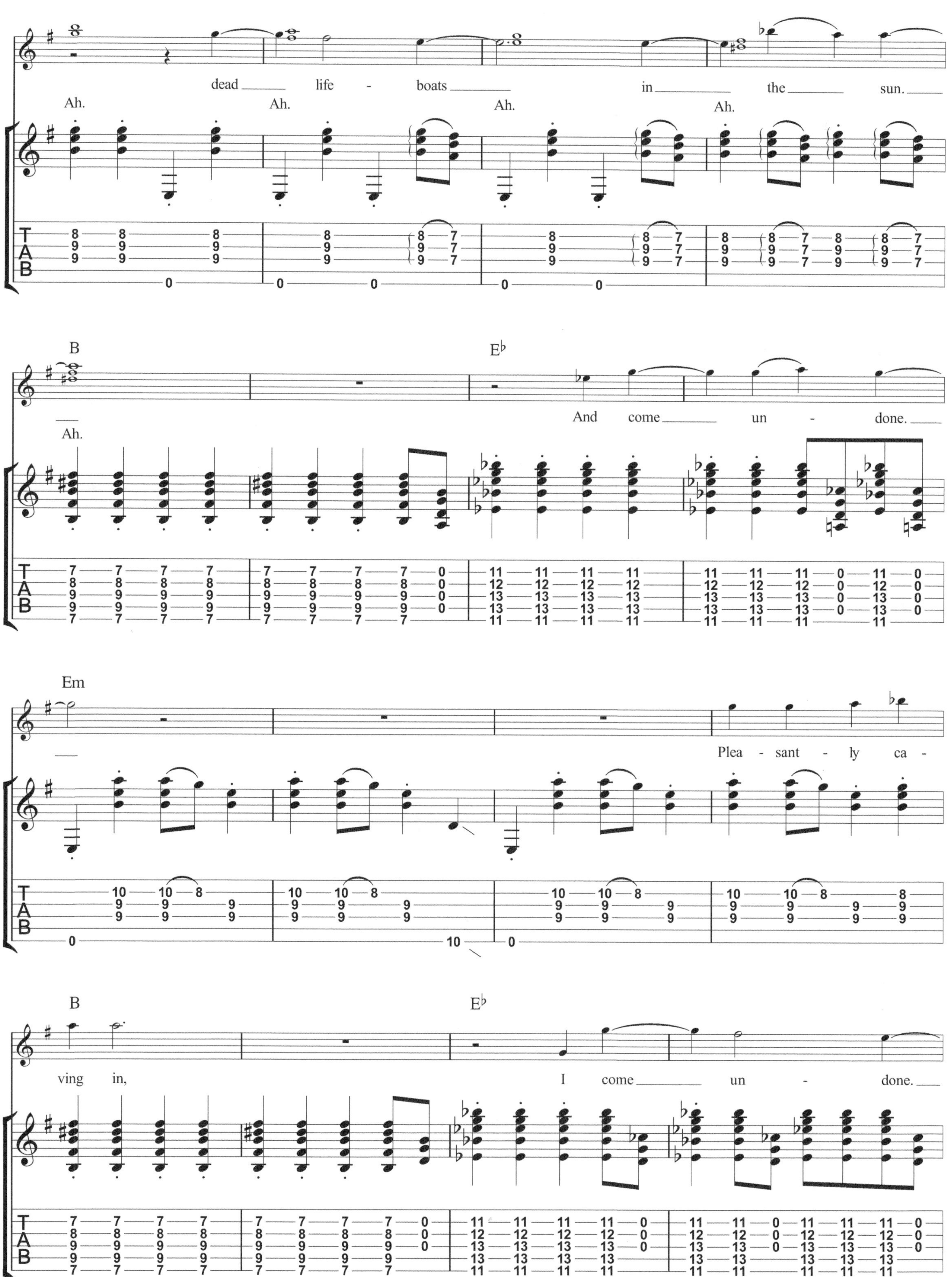

dead life - boats in the sun.
Ah. Ah. Ah. Ah.
B
Ah.
And come un - done.
Em
Plea - sant - ly ca -
B
ving in, I come un - done.

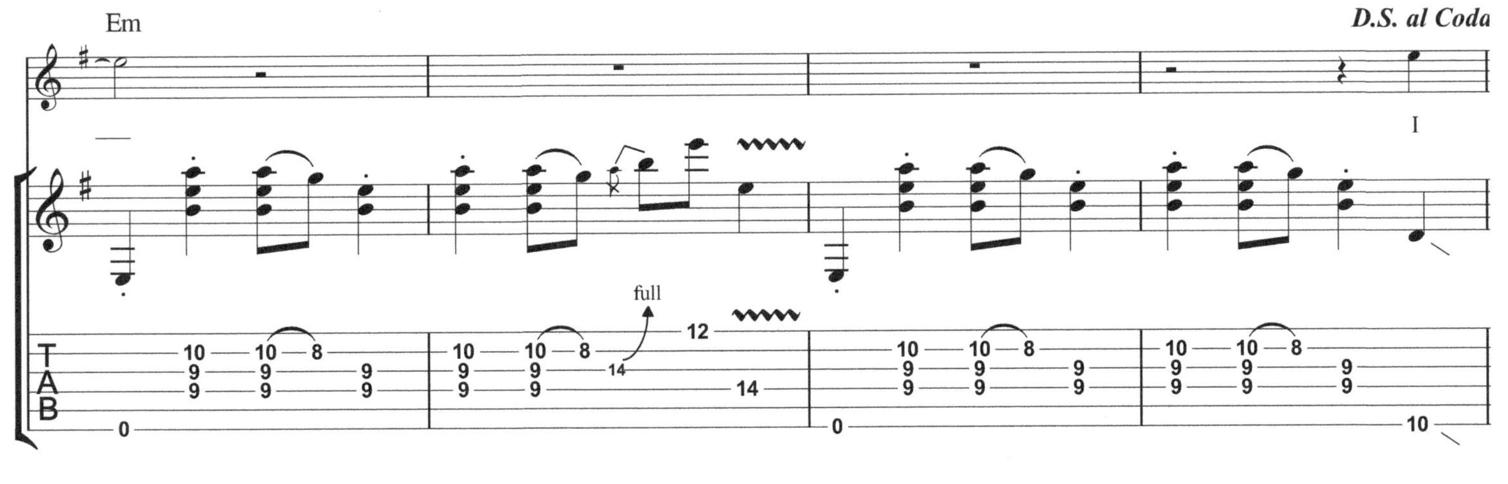
Em
D.S. al Coda
full
I

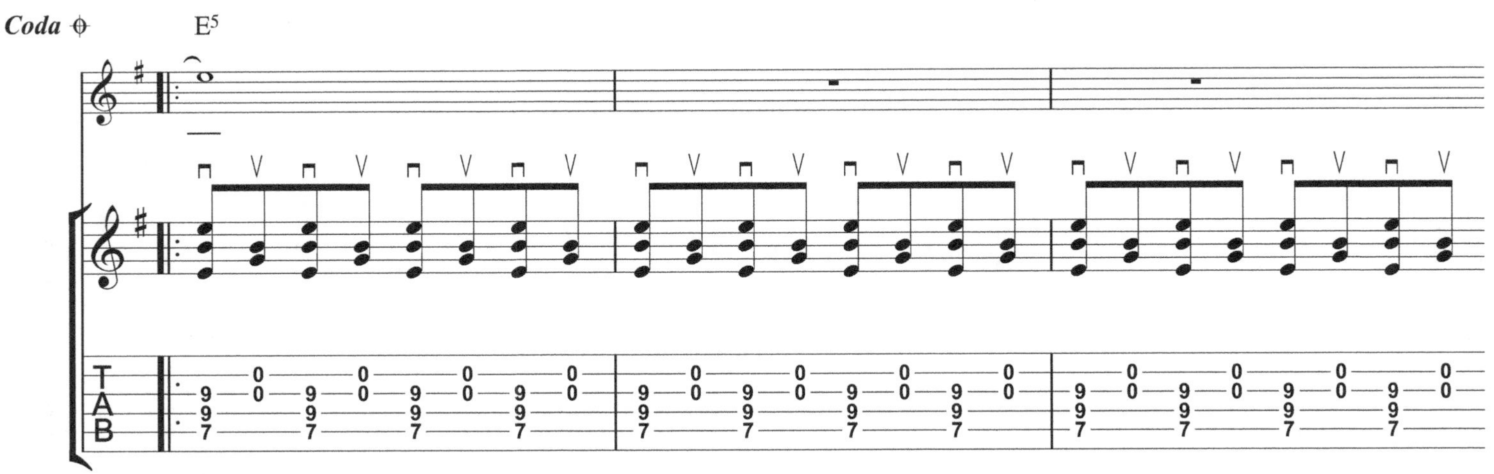
Coda
E5

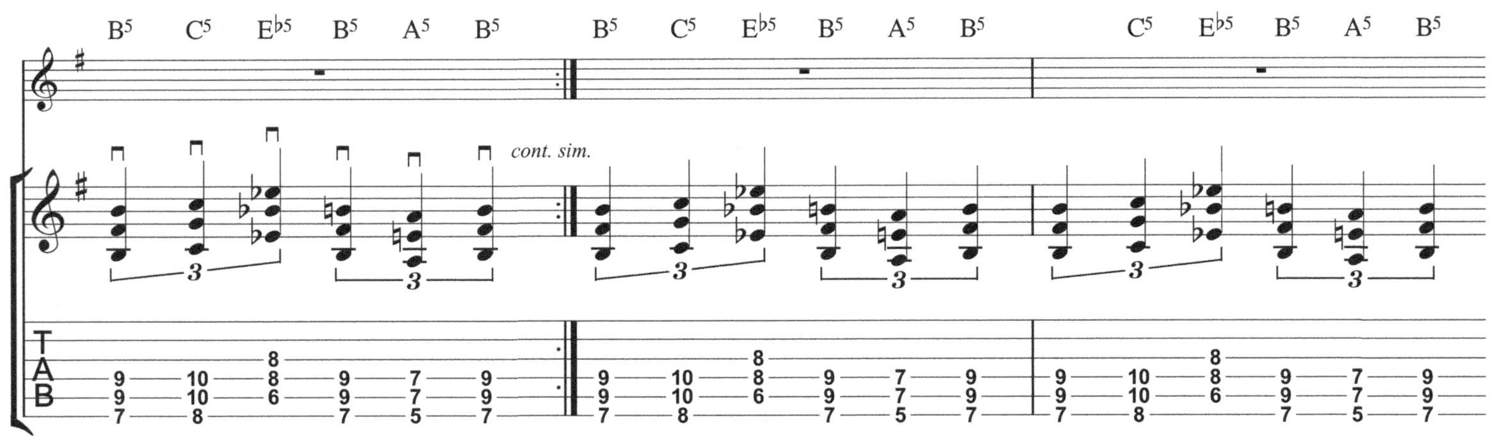
B5 C5 Eb5 B5 A5 B5
B5 C5 Eb5 B5 A5 B5
C5 Eb5 B5 A5 B5
cont. sim.

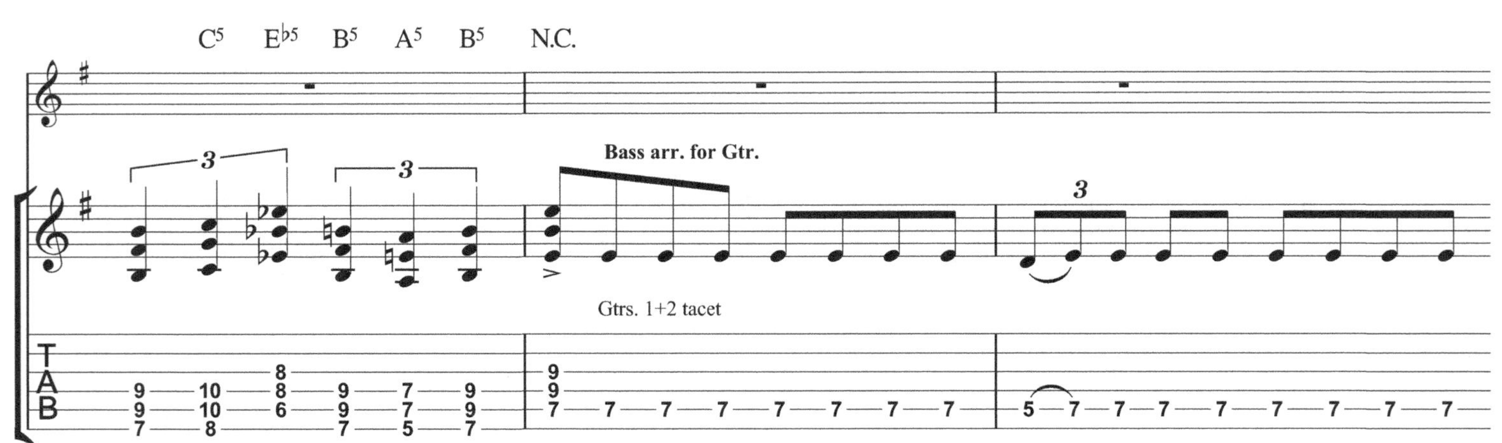
C5 Eb5 B5 A5 B5 N.C.
Bass arr. for Gtr.
Gtrs. 1+2 tacet

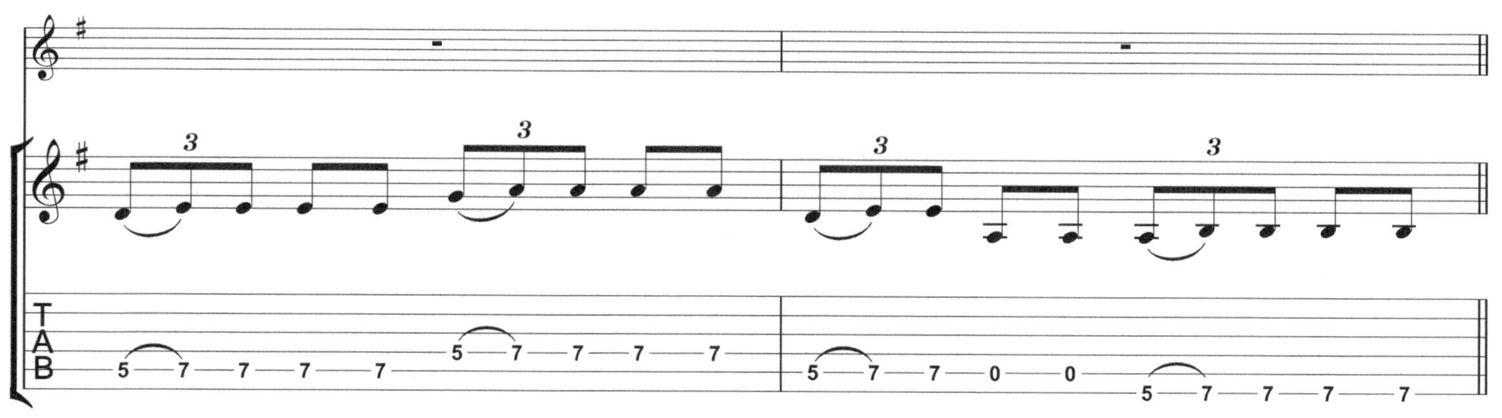

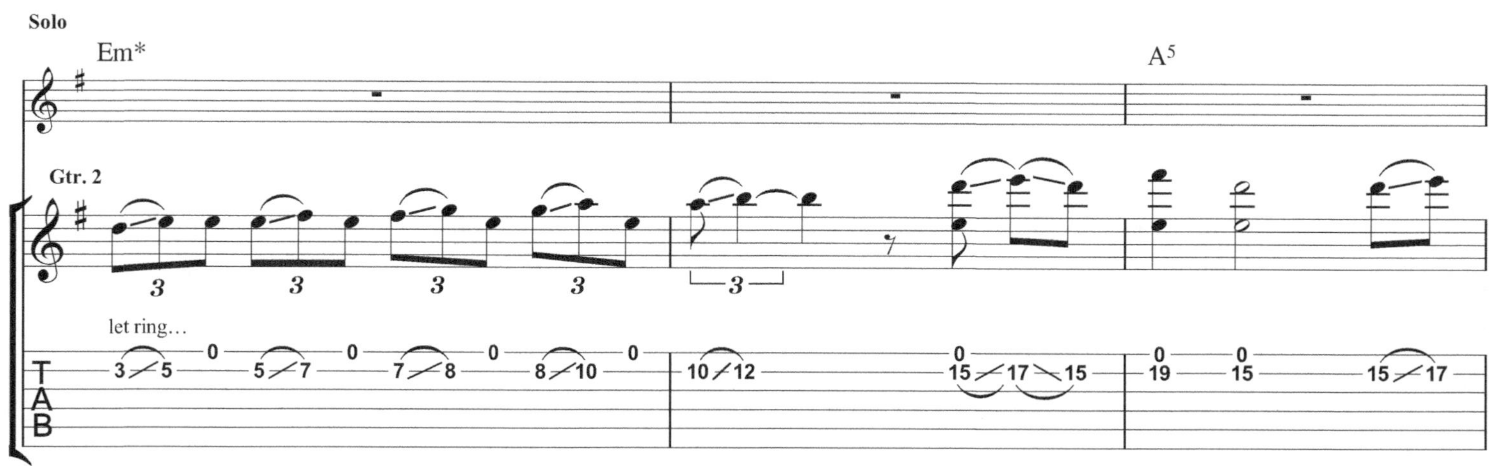
Solo
Em*
A5
Gtr. 2
let ring…

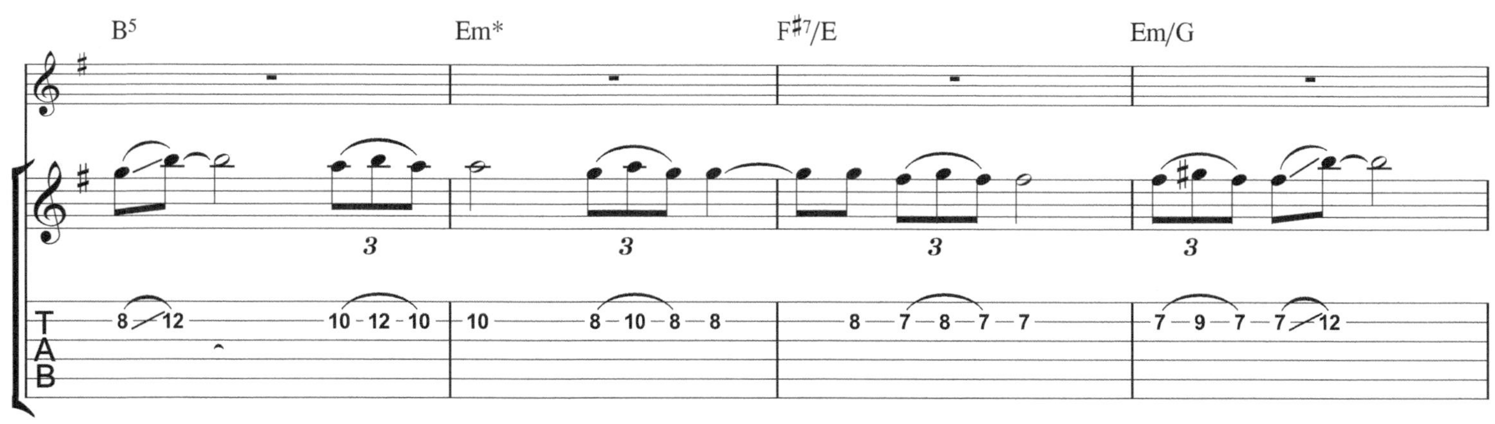
B5
Em*
F#7/E
Em/G

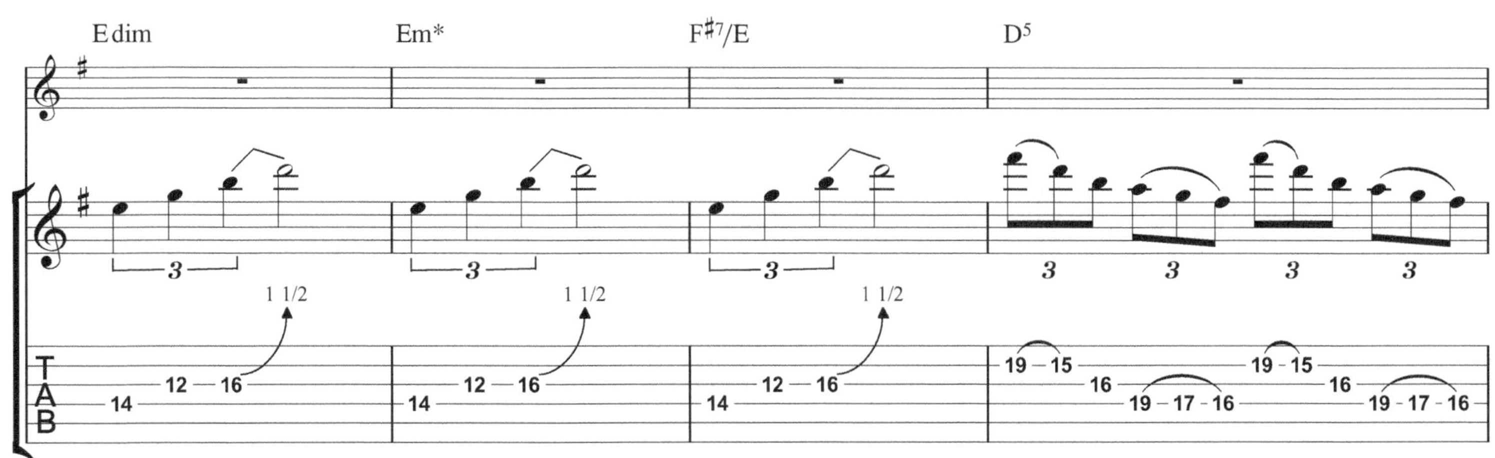
E dim
Em*
F#7/E
D5
1 1/2
1 1/2
1 1/2

D#5
E
Bass arr. for Gtr.
mf
3 3 3 3
N.C.
Hea - ven smiles
a - bove me, what a gift
Em
Gtr. 1
*strike strings behind bridge
here be - low.
B

E♭
Em
But no one knows.
(The) gift that you give
B
E♭
to me, no
Em
one knows.
23

A SONG FOR THE DEAD

Words & Music by Josh Homme, Nick Oliveri & Mark Lanegan

Gtrs. 1+2 (elec)
Play 4 times
N.C.
w/dist.

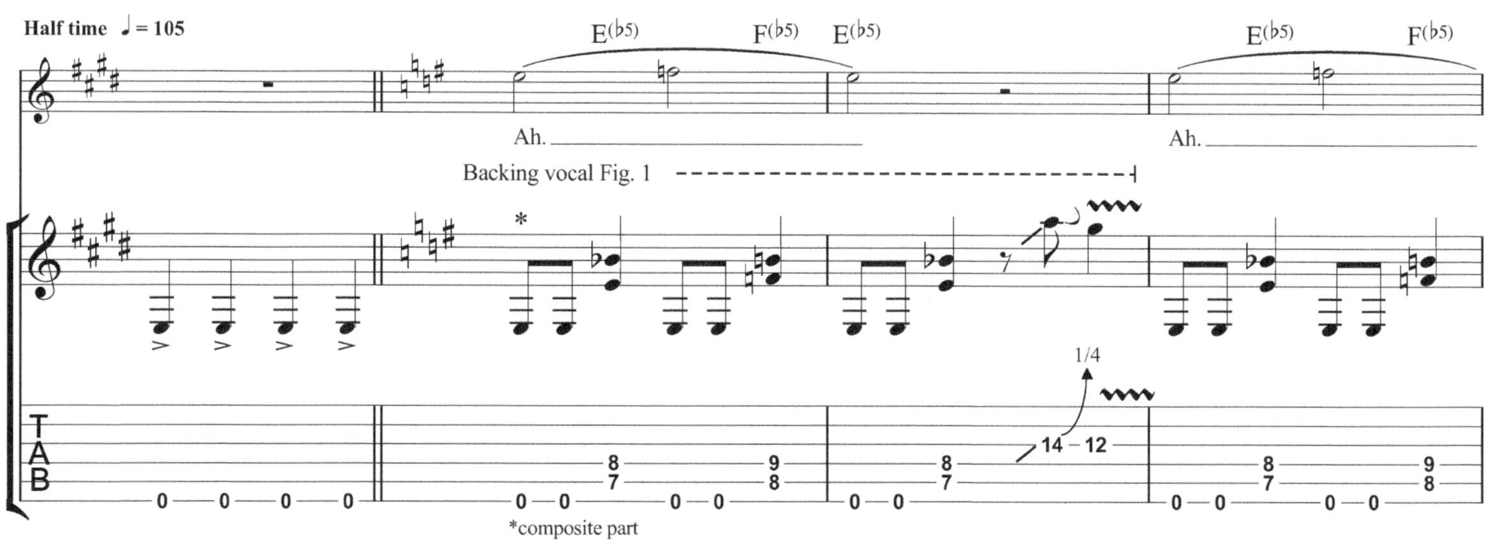

Half time = 105
E(b5)
F(b5)
E(b5)
E(b5)
F(b5)
Ah.
Backing vocal Fig. 1
*
1/4
*composite part

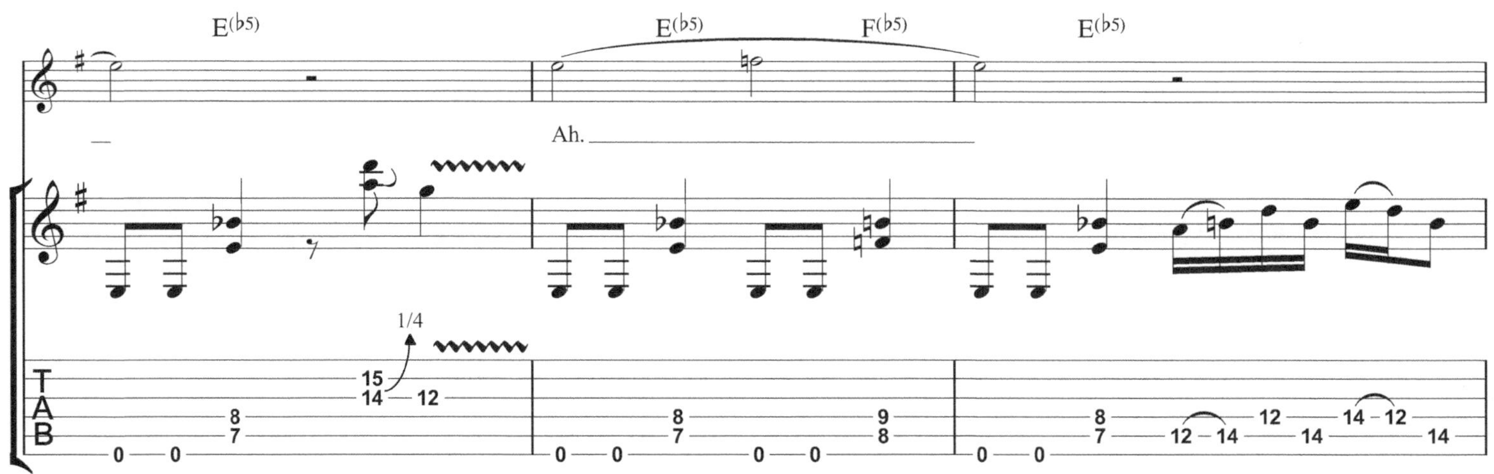

E(b5)
E(b5)
F(b5)
E(b5)
Ah.
1/4

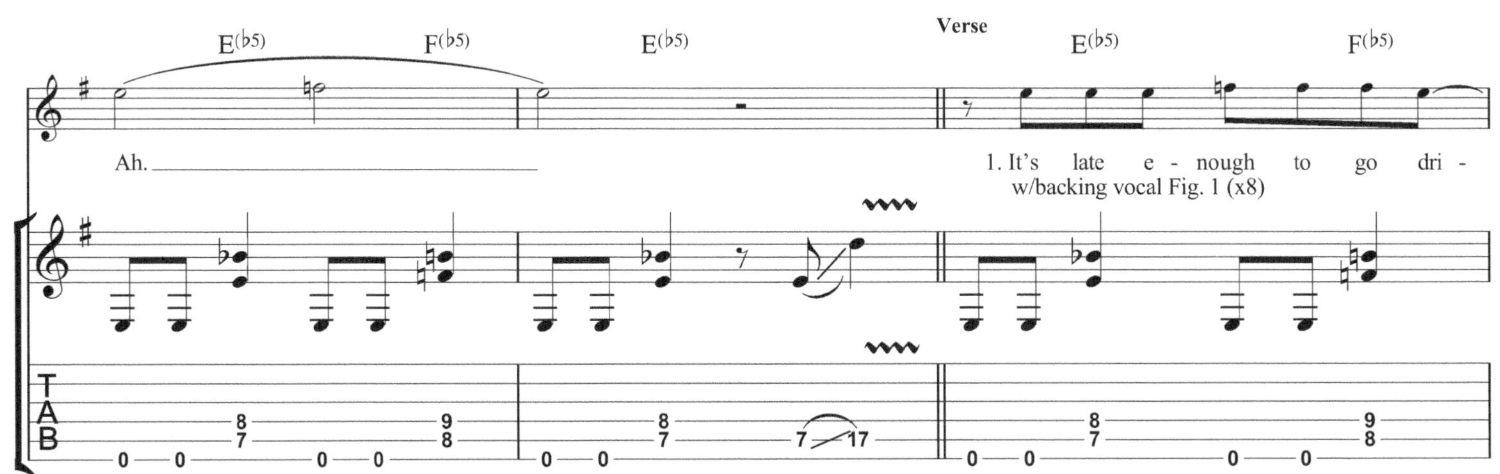

E(b5)
F(b5)
E(b5)
Verse
E(b5)
F(b5)
Ah.
1. It's late e - nough to go dri -
w/backing vocal Fig. 1 (x8)

-vin'
and see what's mine.
Life's the stu-dy of dy-ing,
how to do it right.
let ring
if you're a ho-ly rol-ler,
if you're bent in the loose.
If you're hang-ing a round

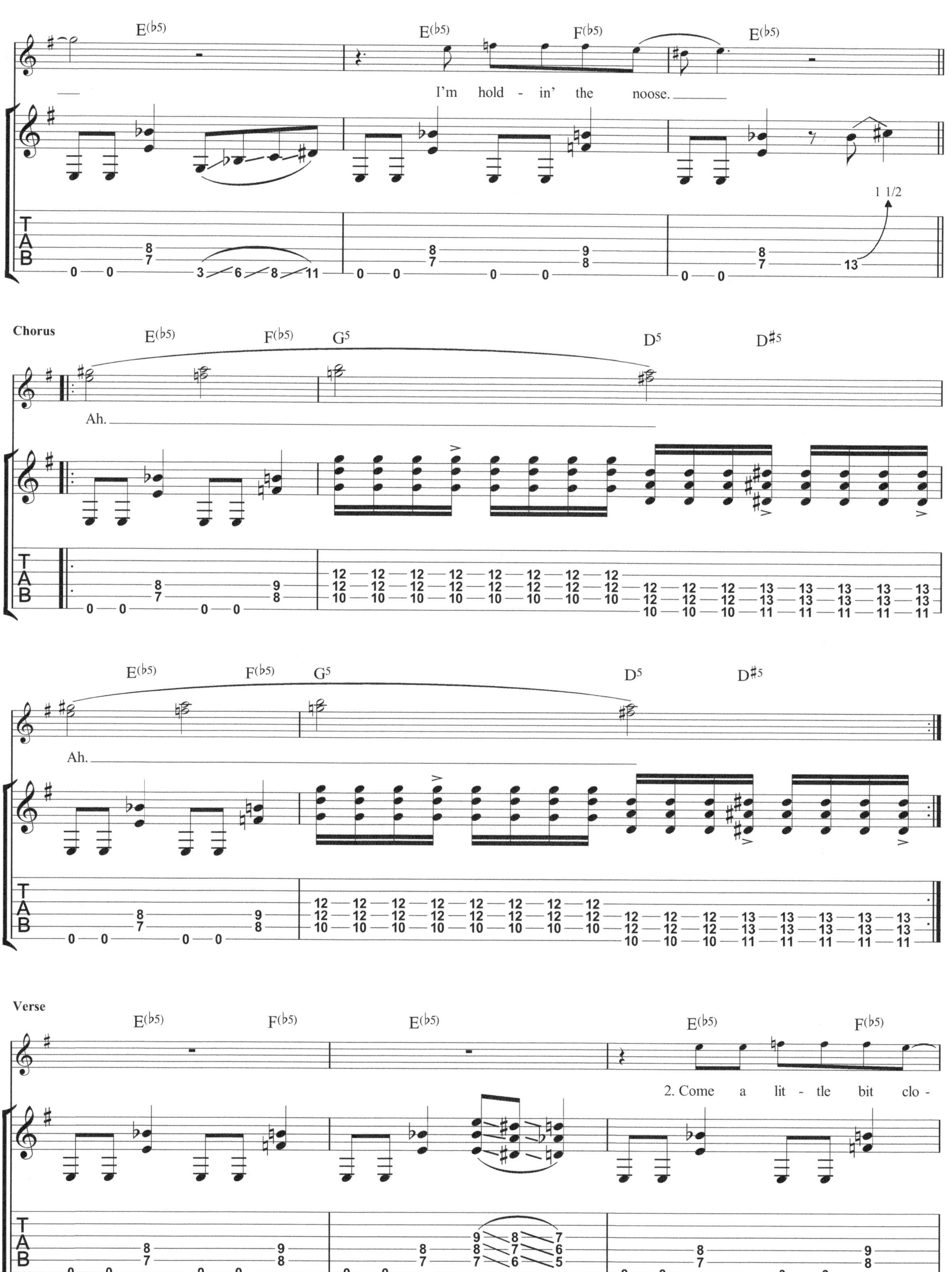

27

- ser
and get un - tied
in a hearse rol - lin' o - ver
just a track in the line.
Chorus
Ah.
Ah.

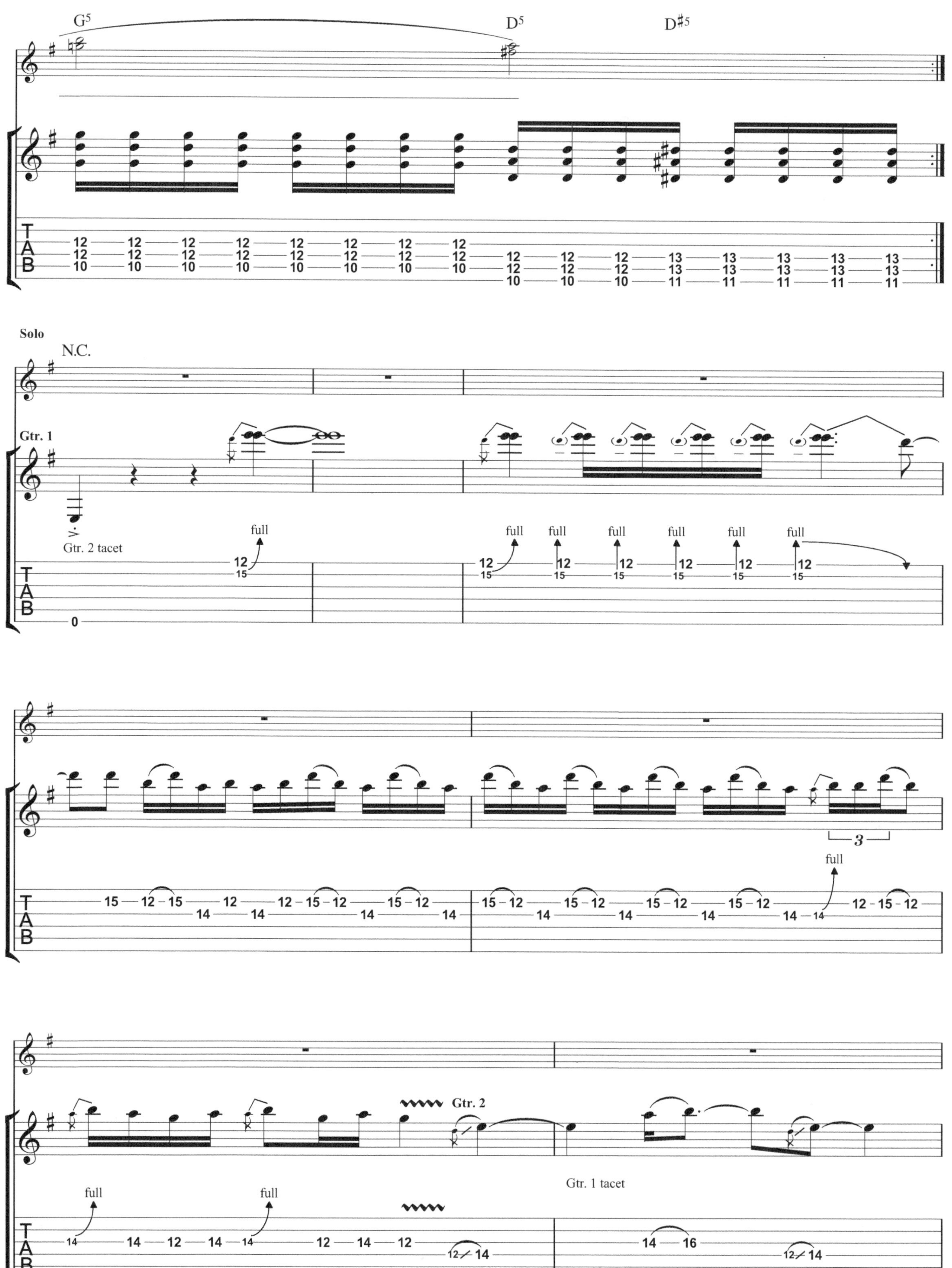

G5
D5
D#5
Solo
N.C.
Gtr. 1
Gtr. 2 tacet
full
full
full
full
full
full
full
full
3
full
full
full
Gtr. 2
Gtr. 1 tacet
full
full

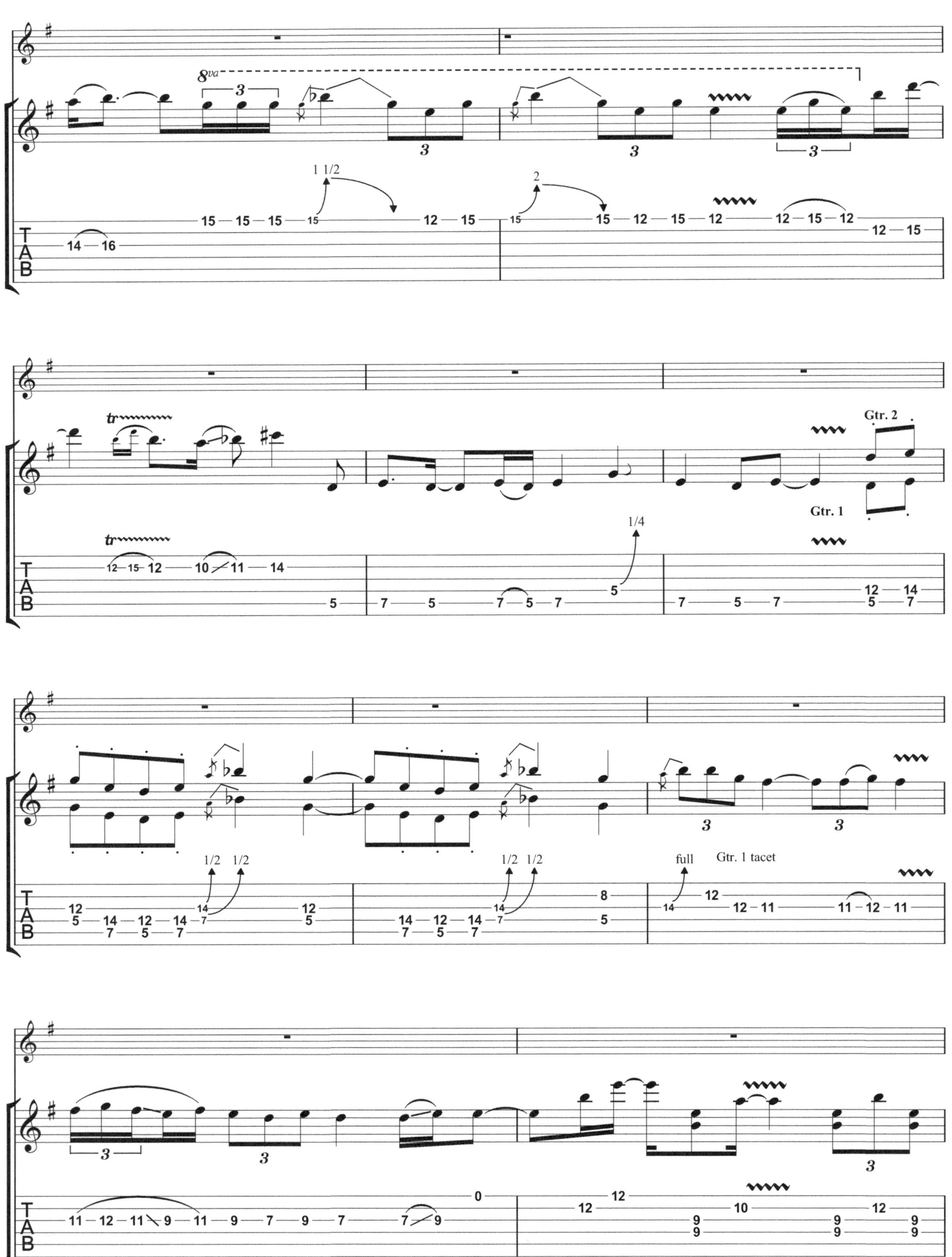

E(♭5)
F(♭5)
E(♭5)
Ah.
*Gtrs. 1+2
*composite part
tr
E(♭5)
F(♭5)
E(♭5)
E(♭5)
F(♭5)
E(♭5)
Ah.
Ah.
P.M.
1/2
E(♭5)
F(♭5)
E(♭5)
Ah.
3
3
3
3
3

E(b5)   F(b5)   E(b5)   F(b5)
Come on, let's go dri - vin', come, let's take a lit - tle
Backing vocals w/Fig. 1 (x4)
full
E(b5)   E(b5)   F(b5)   E(b5)
ride. __   Life's the stu - dy of dy - ing,
(Bass)
E(b5)   F(b5)   E(b5)
how to do it right. __
Chorus
E(b5)   F(b5)   G5   D5   D#5
Ah. __

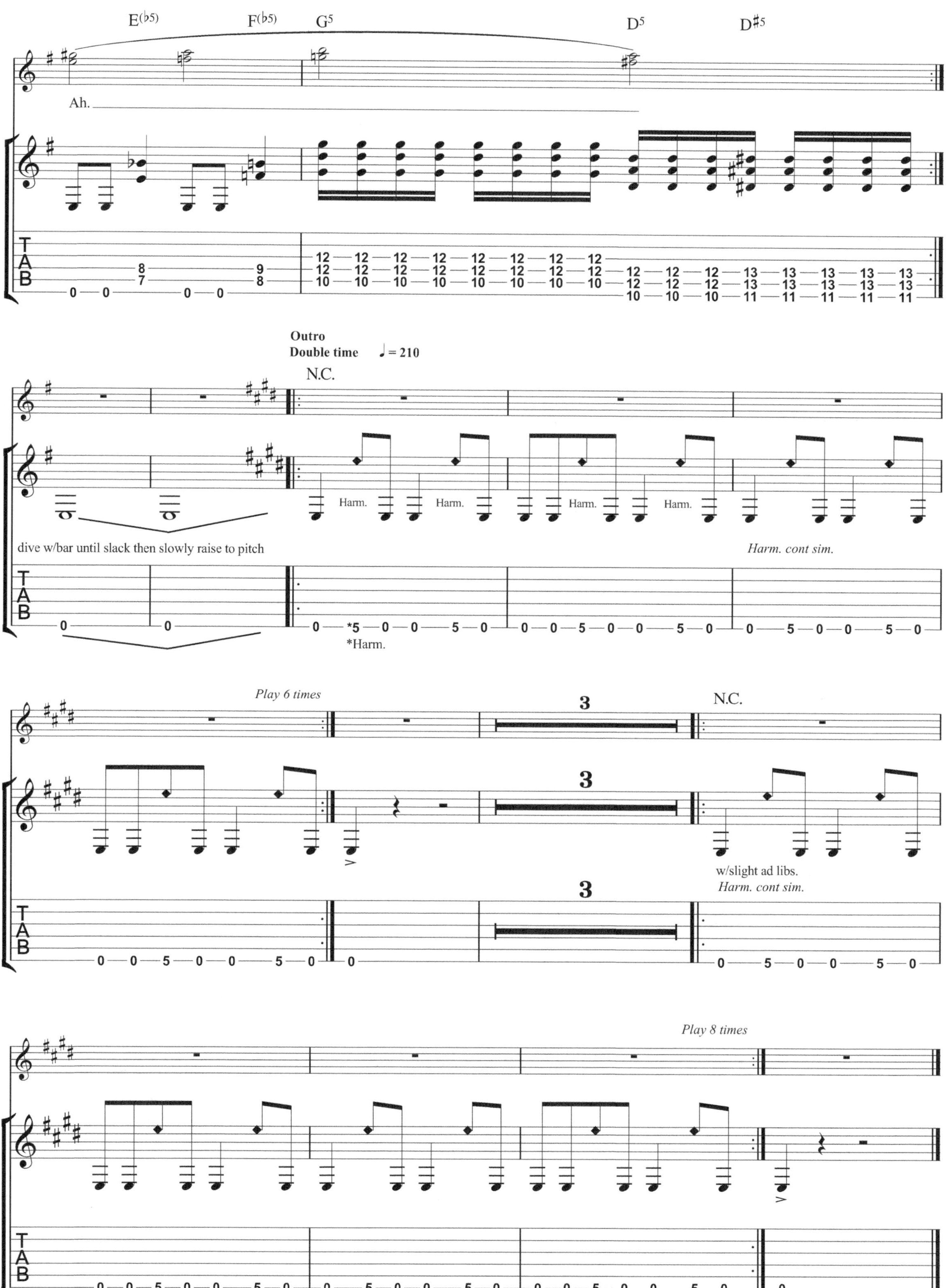

E(♭5)
F(♭5)
G5
D5
D#5
Ah.
8
7
0 0
9
8
0 0
12 12 12 12 12 12 12 12
12 12 12 12 12 12 12 12
10 10 10 10 10 10 10 10
12 12 12 13 13 13 13 13
12 12 12 13 13 13 13 13
10 10 10 11 11 11 11 11
Outro
Double time
♩ = 210
N.C.
dive w/bar until slack then slowly raise to pitch
Harm.
Harm.
Harm.
Harm.
Harm. cont sim.
0
0
0 *5 0 0 5 0 0 0 5 0 0 5 0 0 5 0 0 5 0
*Harm.
Play 6 times
3
N.C.
3
3
w/slight ad libs.
Harm. cont sim.
>
0 0 5 0 0 5 0 0
0 5 0 0 5 0
Play 8 times
>
0 0 5 0 0 5 0 0 5 0 0 5 0 0 5 0 0 5 0 0

THE SKY IS FALLIN'

Words & Music by Josh Homme & Nick Oliveri

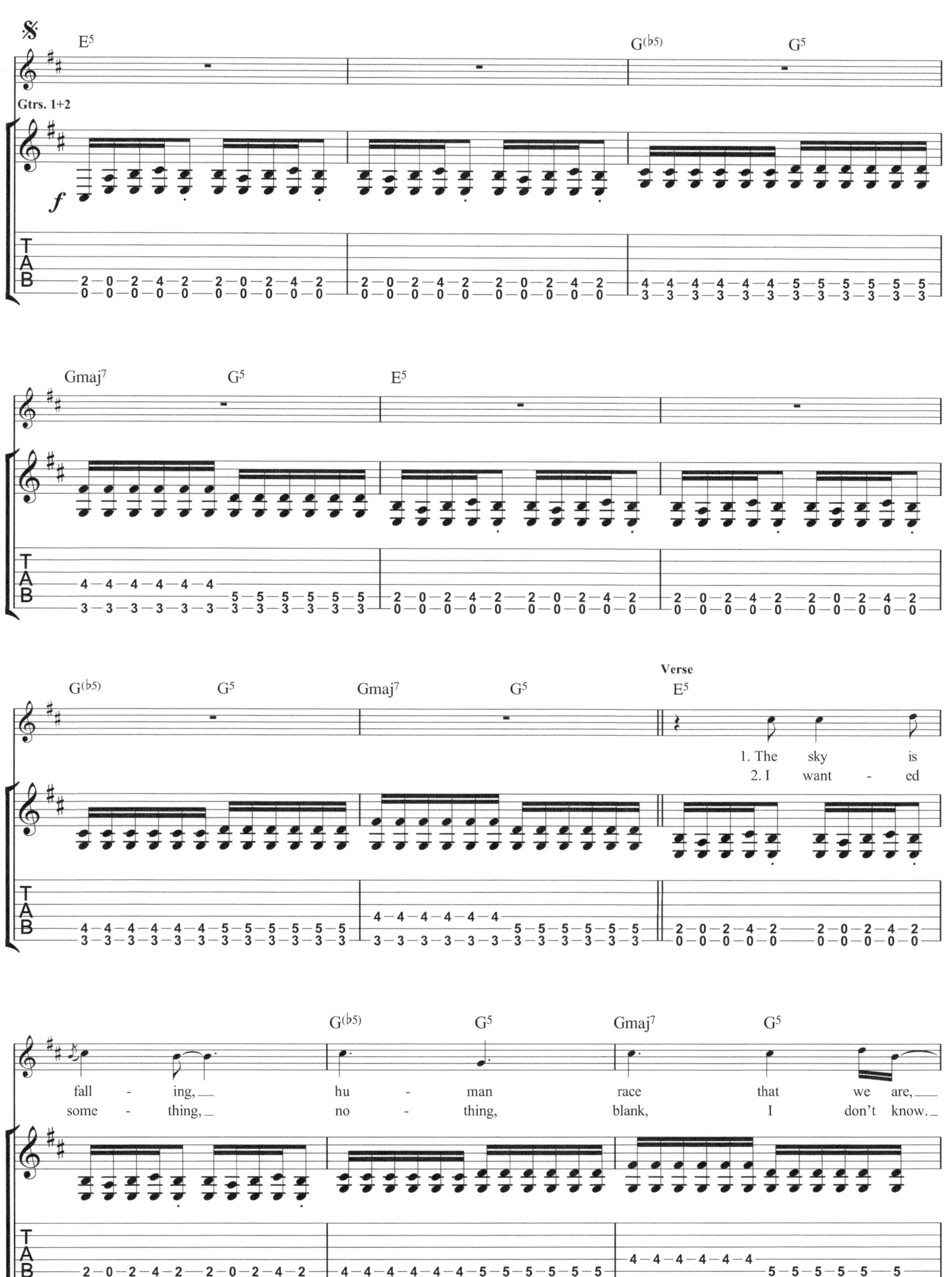

Gtrs. 1+2
1. The sky is
2. I want - ed
fall - ing, hu - man race that we are,
some - thing, no - thing, blank, I don't know.
Verse

E5   G(♭5)   G5
has left me craw - ling, __ star - ing
It's hard de - flec - ting, __ stones are
TAB
2—0—2—4—2—2—0—2—4—2 2—0—2—4—2—2—0—2—4—2 4—4—4—4—4—4—5—5—5—5—5—5
0—0—0—0—0—0—0—0—0—0 0—0—0—0—0—0—0—0—0—0 3—3—3—3—3—3—3—3—3—3—3—3—3—3

Gmaj7   G5   E5
straight at __ the sun. __ All in a mo - ment, I no - tice
ea - sy __ to throw. __ All in a mo - ment, I no - ticed
TAB
4—4—4—4—4—4   2—0—2—4—2—2—0—2—4—2 2—0—2—4—2—2—0—2—4—2
3—3—3—3—3—3—5—5—5—5—5—5 0—0—0—0—0—0—0—0—0—0 0—0—0—0—0—0—0—0—0—0

G(♭5)   G5   Gmaj7   G5   E5
ev - 'ry dog has his day. __ I paid at -
ho - urs, days left be - hind. __ One was - ted
TAB
4—4—4—4—4—4—5—5—5—5—5—5 4—4—4—4—4—4   2—0—2—4—2—2—0—2—4—2
3—3—3—3—3—3—3—3—3—3—3—3 3—3—3—3—3—3—5—5—5—5—5—5 0—0—0—0—0—0—0—0—0—0

G(♭5)   G5   Gmaj7   G5
ten - tion, __ cost me so much to hate.
use - less, __ self - less none of a kind. __
TAB
2—0—2—4—2—2—0—2—4—2 4—4—4—4—4—4—5—5—5—5—5—5 4—4—4—4—4—4
0—0—0—0—0—0—0—0—0—0 3—3—3—3—3—3—3—3—3—3—3—3 3—3—3—3—3—3—5—5—5—5—5

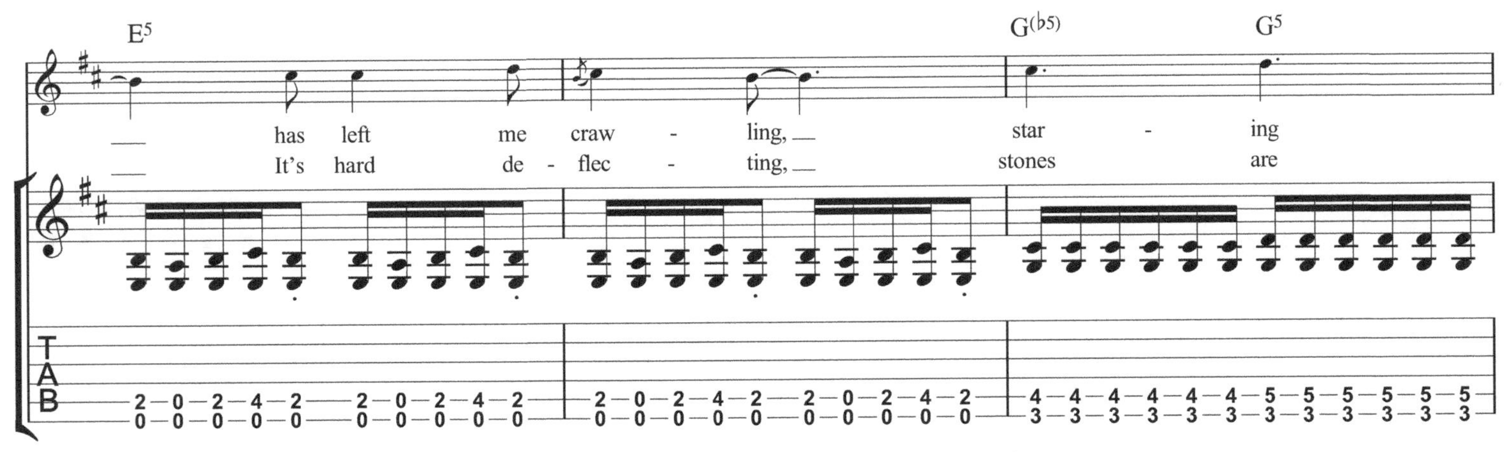

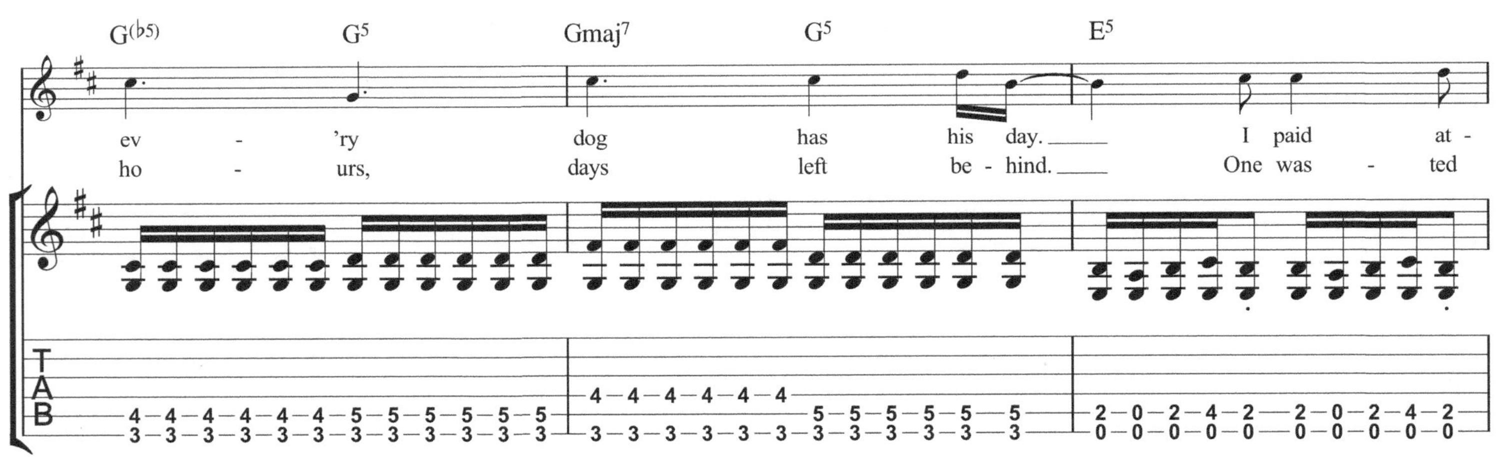

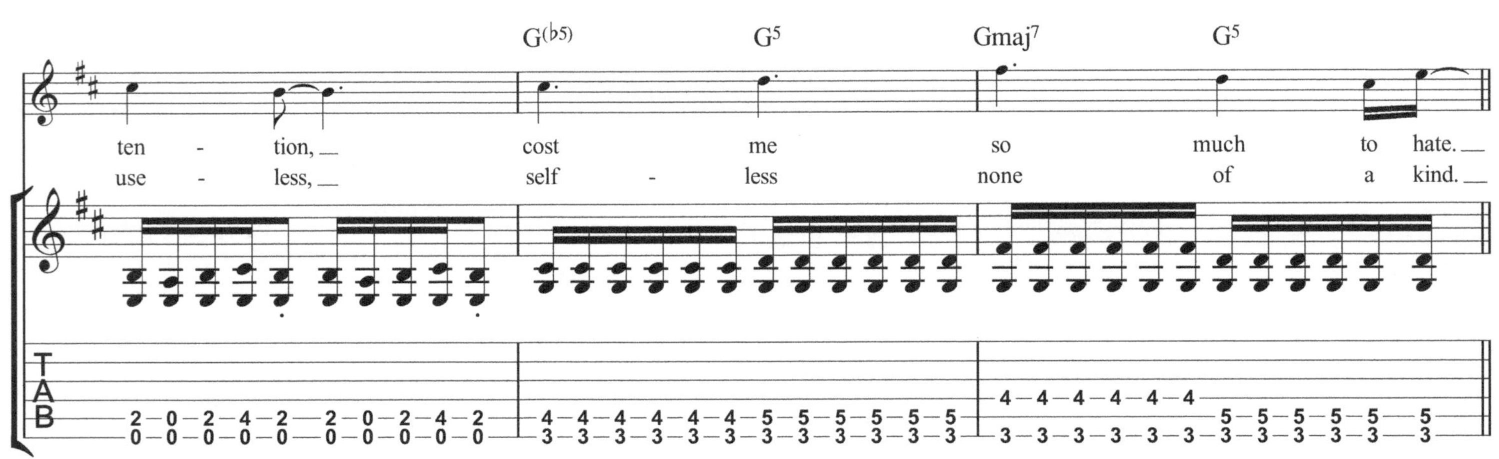

36

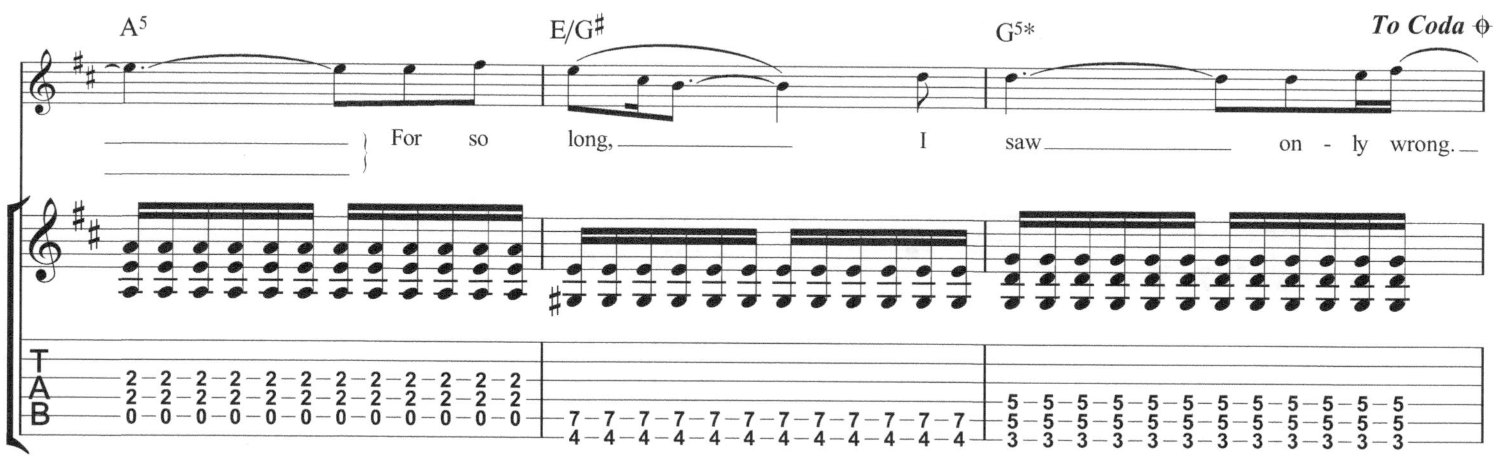

A5
E/G#
G5*
To Coda
For so long, I saw on - ly wrong.

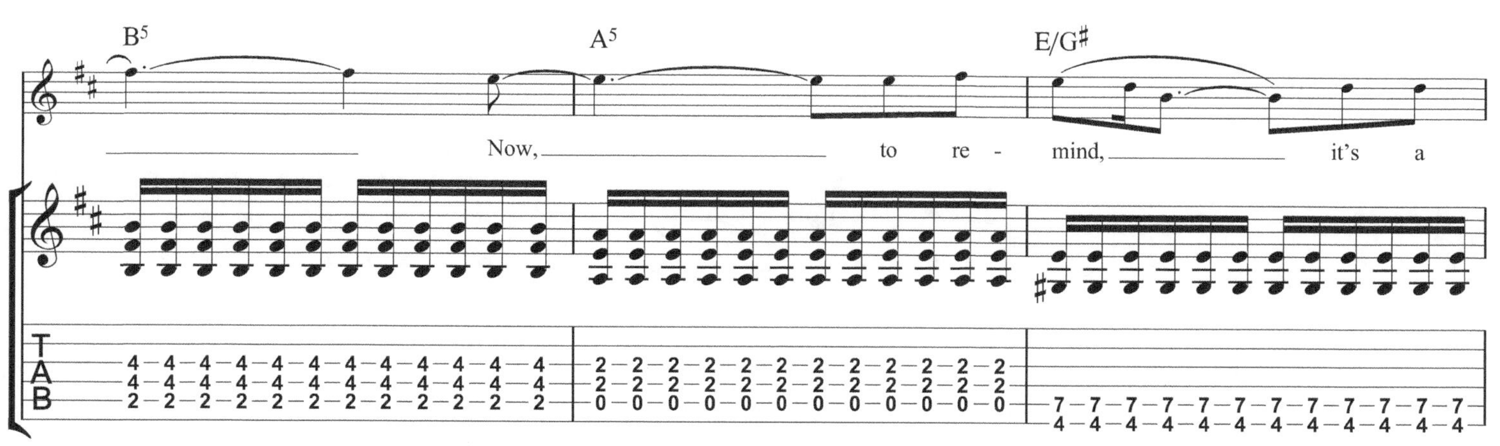

B5
A5
E/G#
Now, to re - mind, it's a

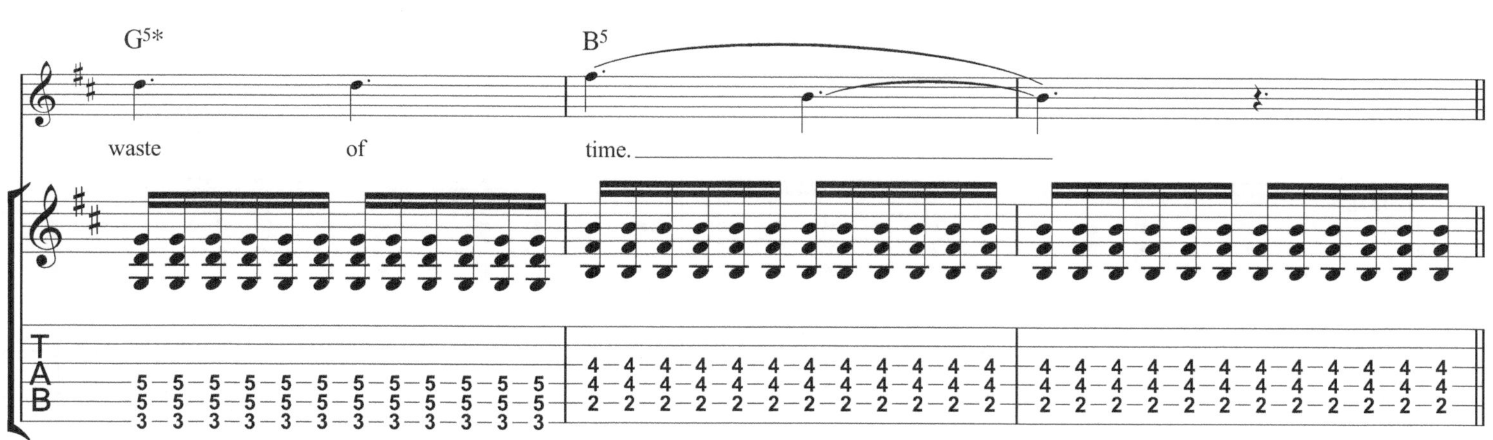

G5*
B5
waste of time.

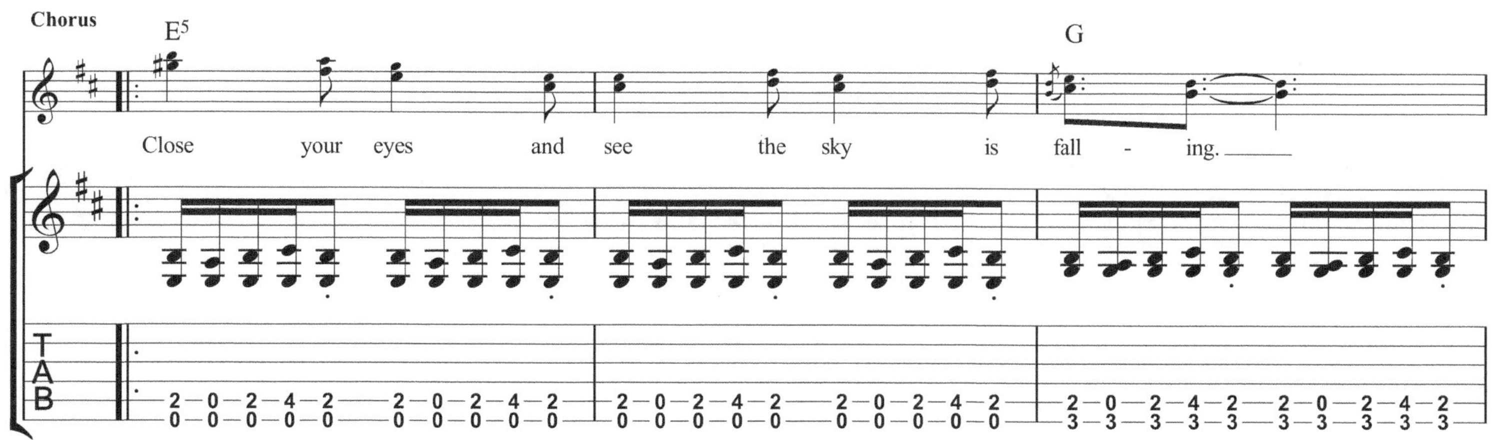

Chorus
E5
G
Close your eyes and see the sky is fall - ing.

37

N.C.
Ah.
mf
w/light dist.
TAB

D.S. al Coda
Ah.
cont. sim.
TAB

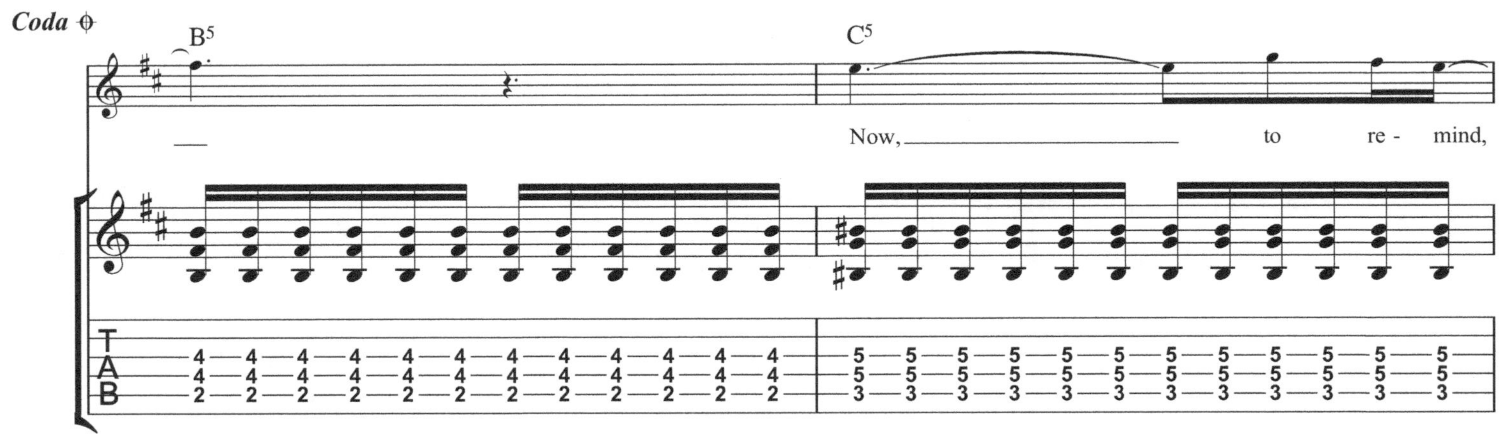

Coda
B5
C5
Now, to re - mind,
TAB

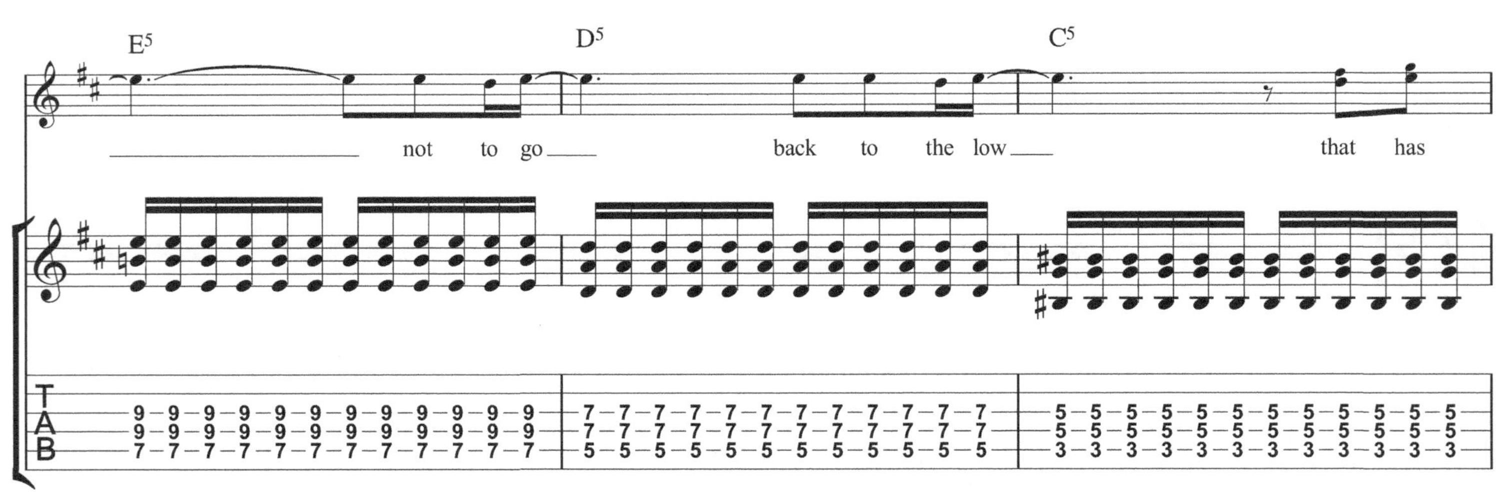

E5
D5
C5
not to go back to the low that has
TAB

G♭7(♯11)
G6
Cmaj7
drained   my   life   so   long.   That has
cont. sim.
F♯7(♯11)
G6
Cmaj7
drained   my   life   so   long.   That has
F♯(♯11)
G6
drained   my   life   so
Cmaj7
F♯7(♯11)
long.   That has   drained   my:

Chorus
E5
G
Close your eyes and see the sky is fall - ing.
E5*
Close your eyes and see the sky is
Fig. 1
G*
E5
fall - ing.
Gtr. 1
Close your eyes and
Gtr. 2 w/Fig. 1
G
see the sky is fall - ing.

Interlude
N.C.
Ah,
ah.
Gtr.1
mf
let ring…
T
A
B
Gtr. 2
mf
w/warm dist.
3
T
A
B
3
3
T
A
B

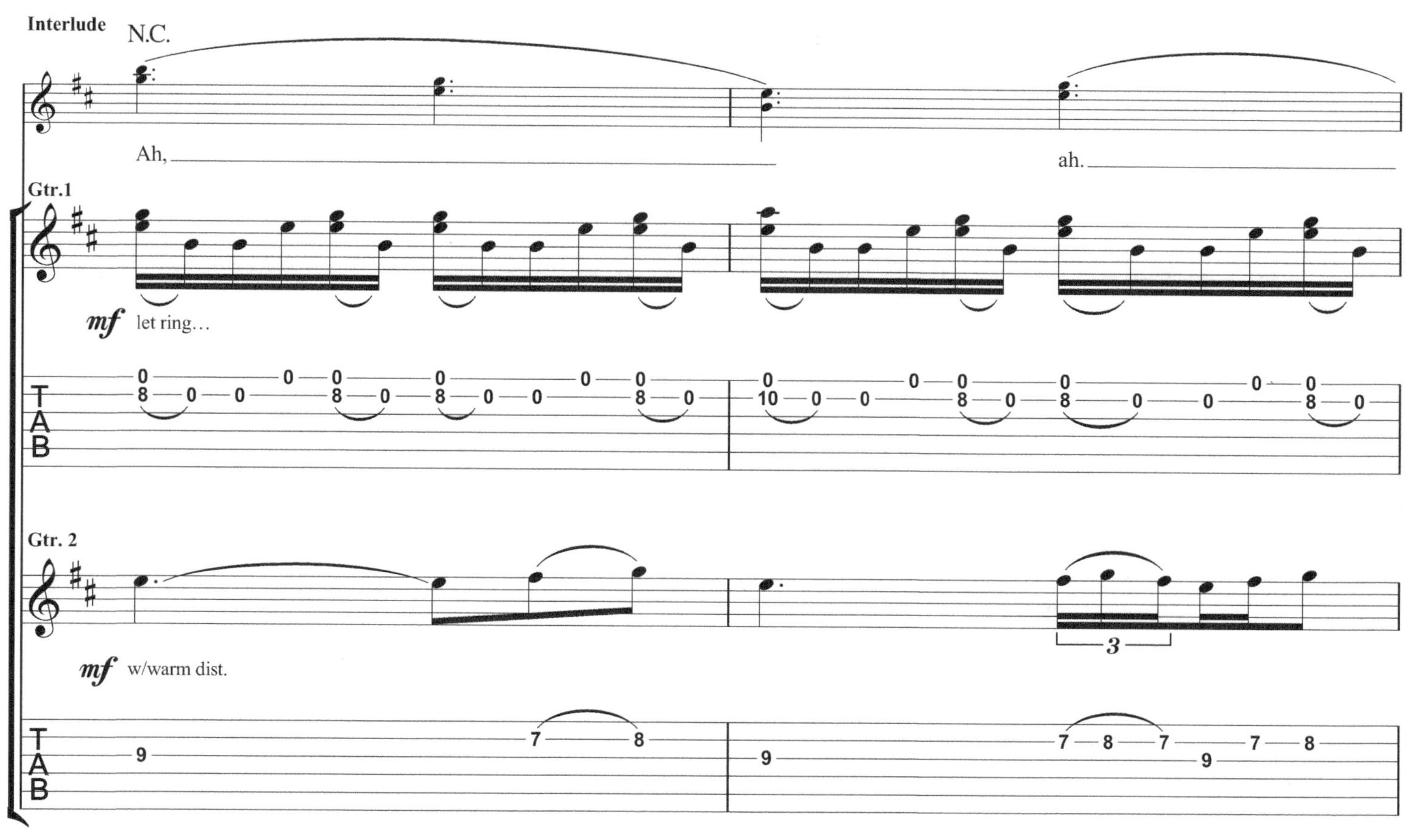

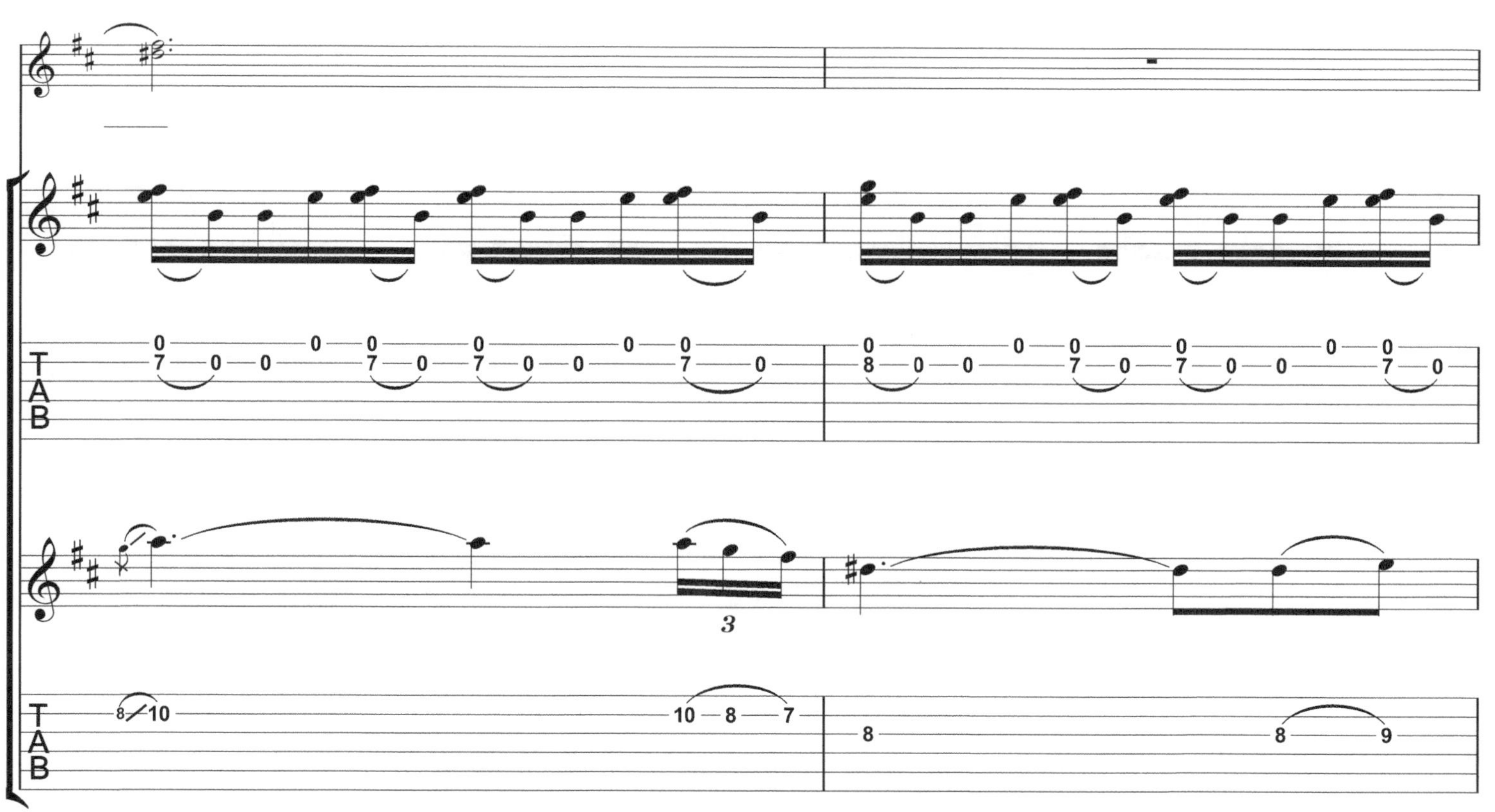

41

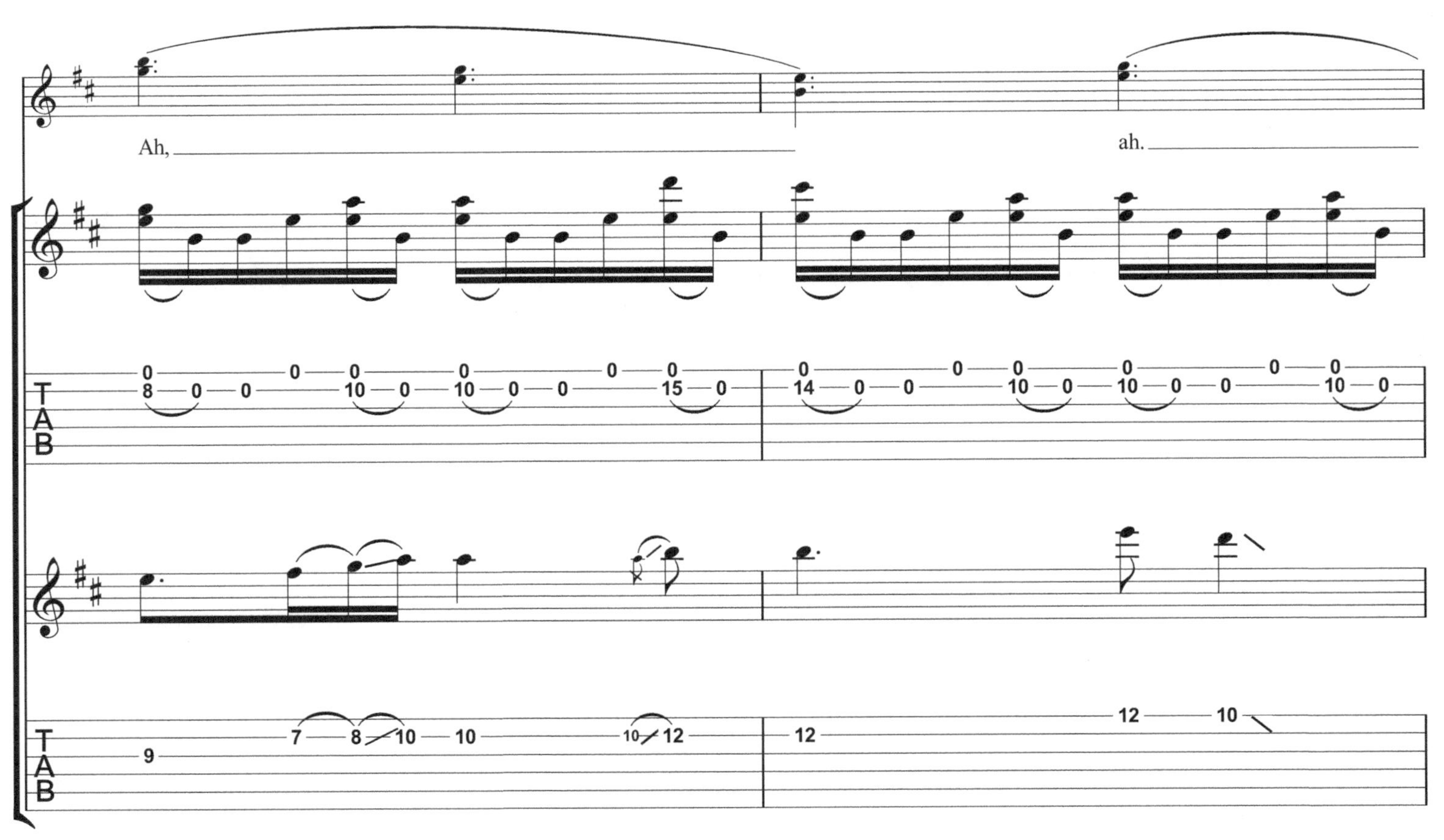

Ah,
ah.

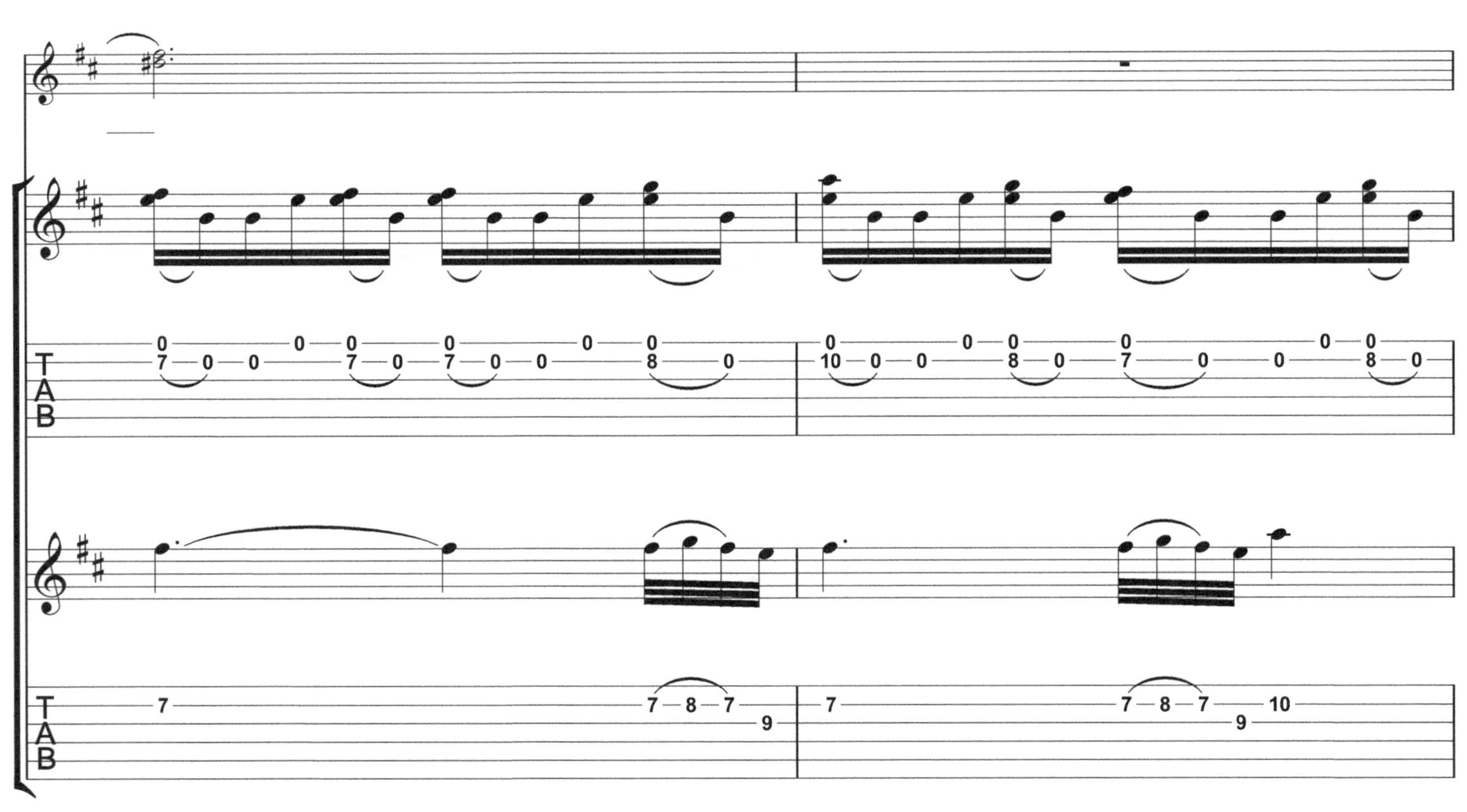

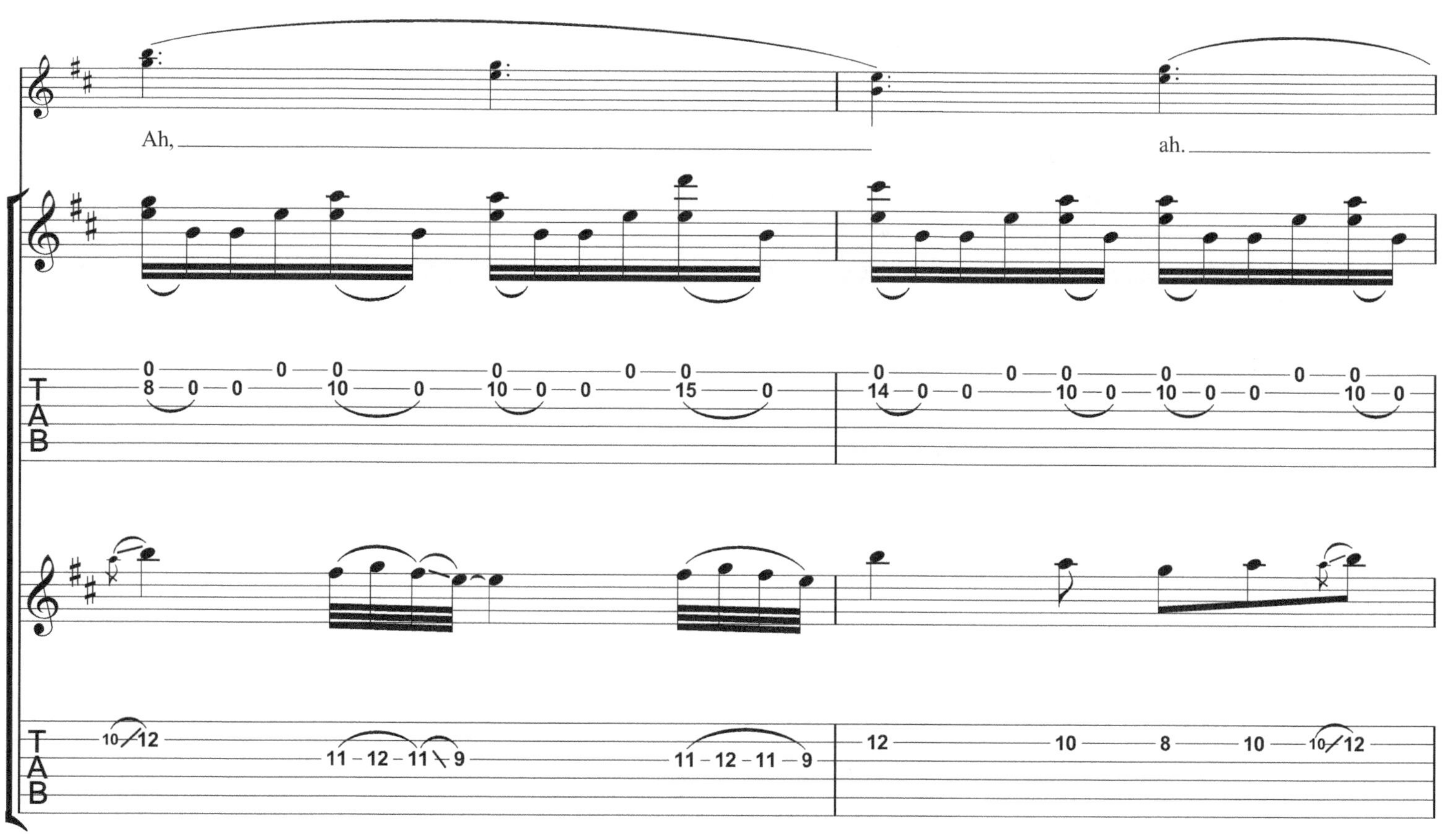

Ah,
ah.

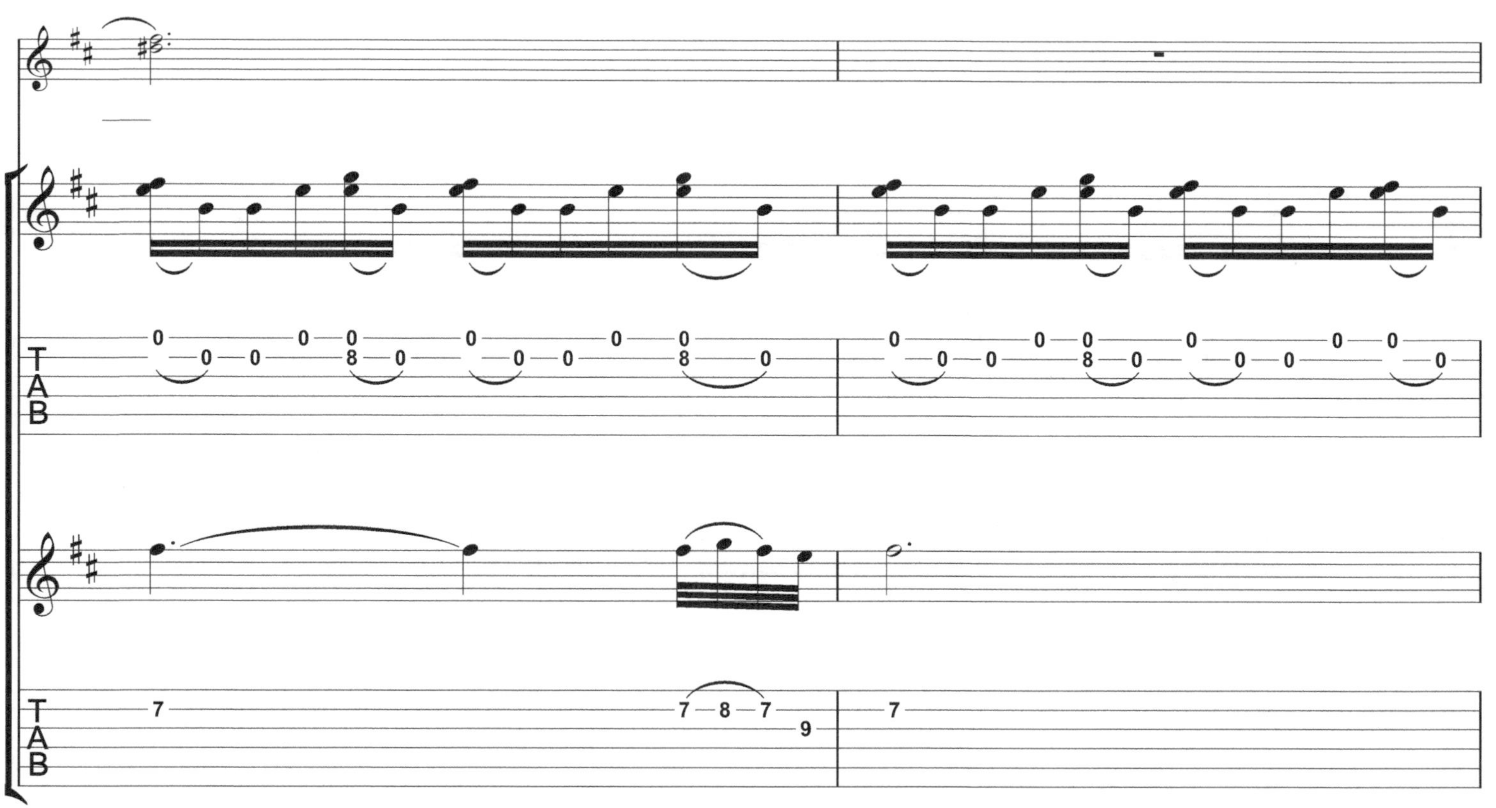

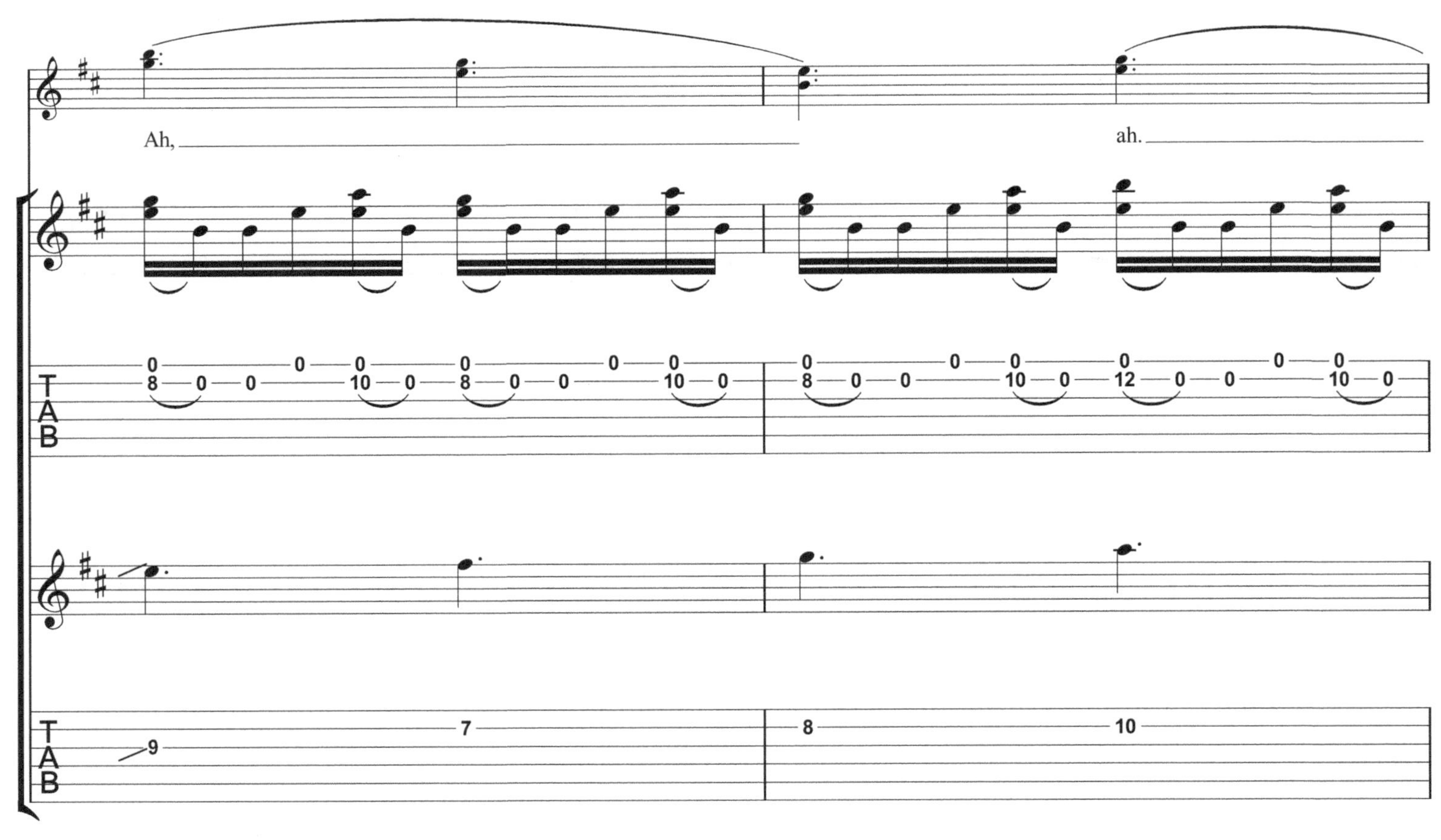

Ah,
ah.
T
A
B
T
A
B
9
7
8
10
0
8
0
0
0
10
0
8
0
0
0
10
0
0
8
0
0
0
10
0
12
0
0
0
10
0

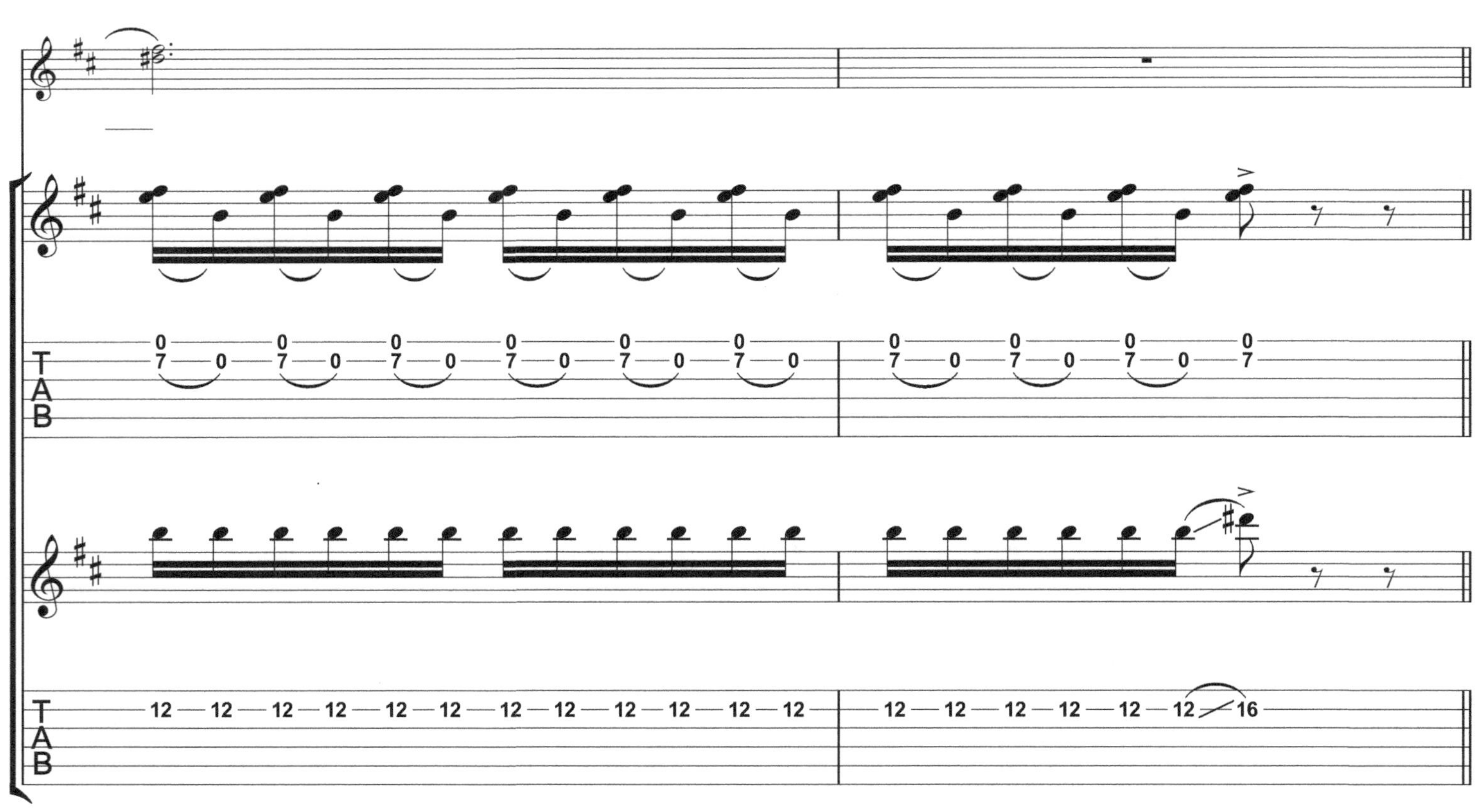

T
A
B
T
A
B
0
7
0
0
7
0
0
7
0
0
7
0
0
7
0
0
7
0
0
7
0
0
7
0
0
7
12
12
12
12
12
12
12
12
12
12
12
12
12
12
12
12
12
12
16

Chorus
E5
G
Gtr. 1+2
Close your eyes and see the sky is fall - ing.
T A B

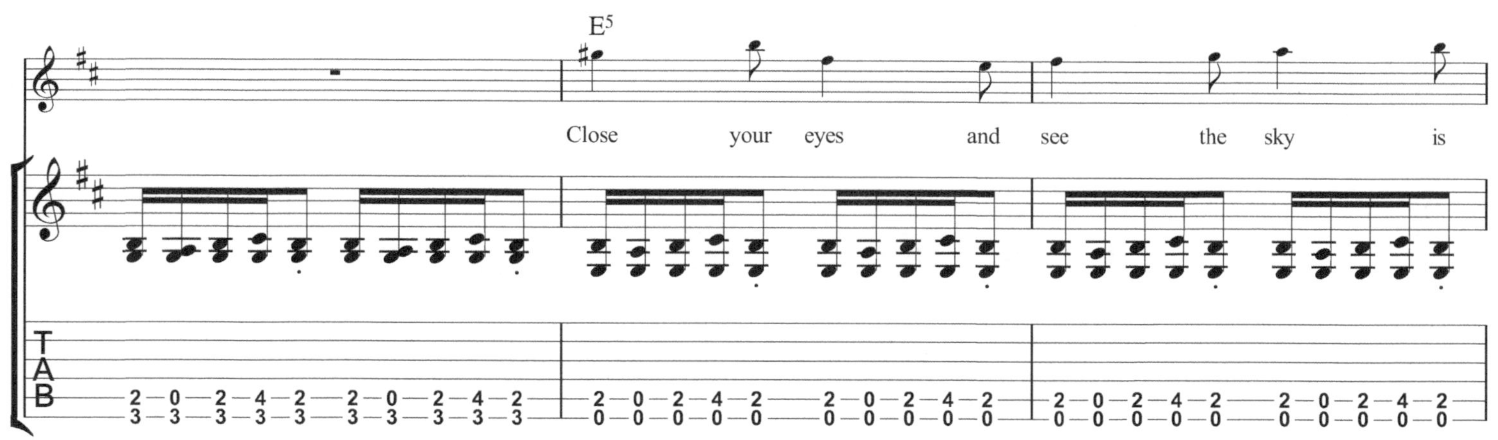

E5
Close your eyes and see the sky is
T A B

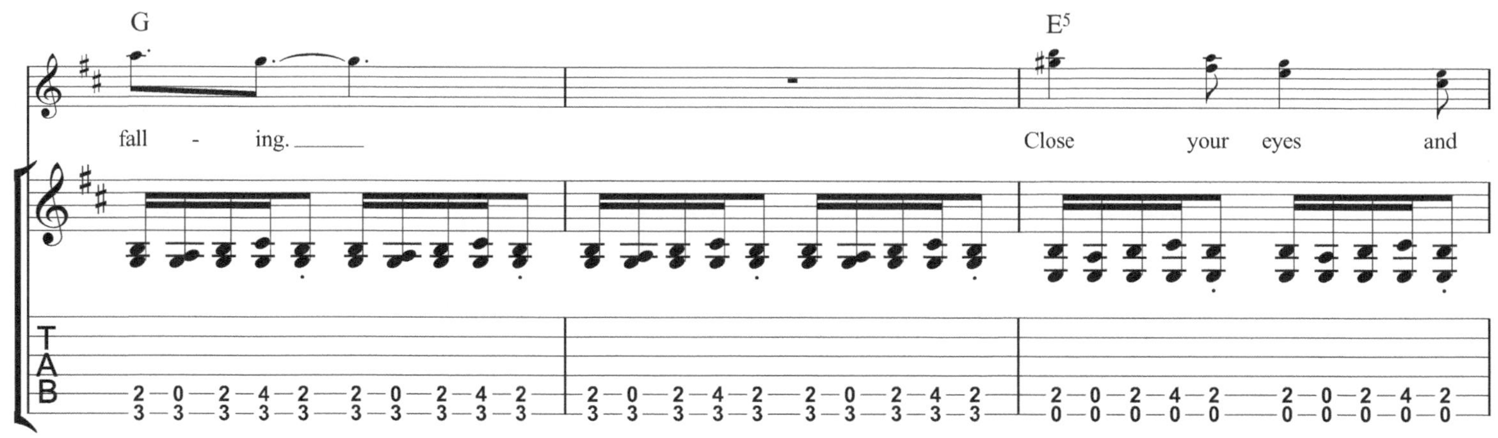

G
E5
fall - ing.
Close your eyes and
T A B

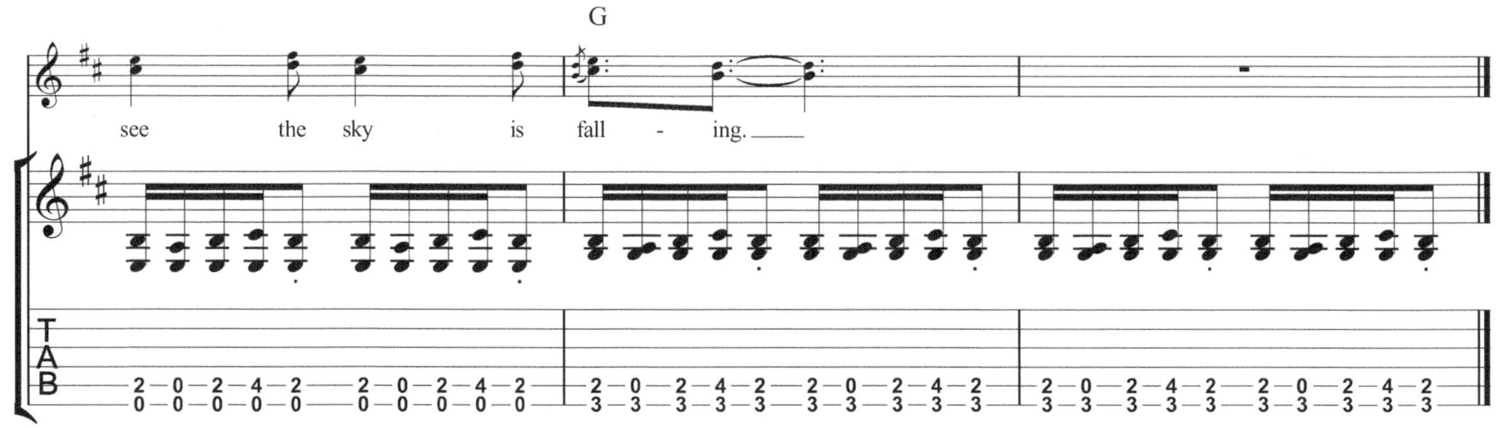

G
see the sky is fall - ing.
T A B

FIRST IT GIVETH

Words & Music by Josh Homme & Nick Oliveri

you're ___ in me, ___ I can tell. ___

You're so cruel, ___ more ___ than me, ___ it is true. ___

N.C.
Lo - yal too, ___ on - ly you, ___
Gtr. 1
Gtr. 2

up your sleeve.
I want some
(of) all of you, trick - ing me.
Chorus
D5
F5
First it gi - veth, then it ta - keth a - way.
Gtrs. 1+2

48

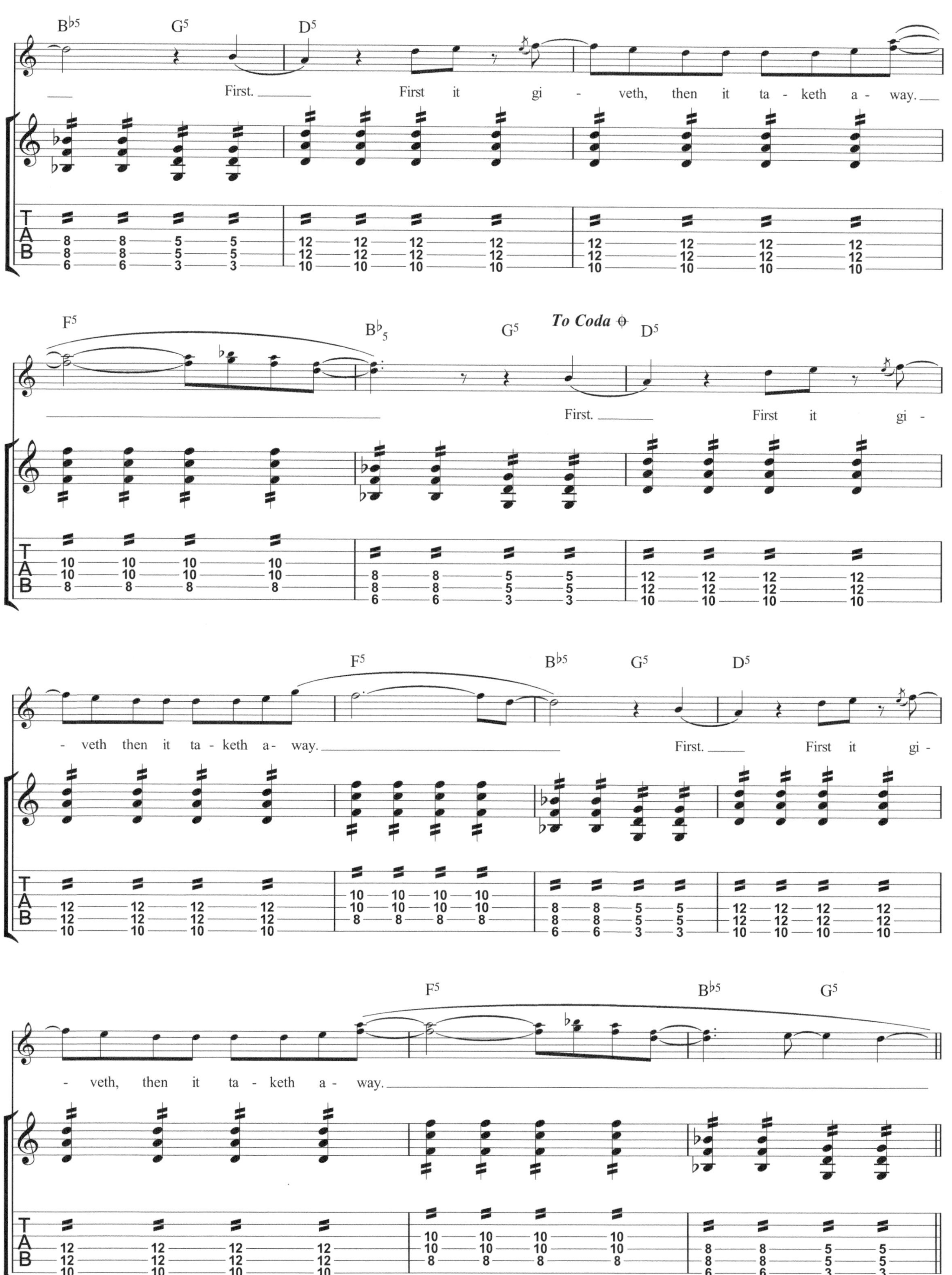

B♭5   G5   D5
First. _____ First it gi - veth, then it ta - keth a - way. ___
F5   B♭5   G5   To Coda   D5
First. _____ First it gi -
F5   B♭5   G5   D5
- veth then it ta - keth a - way. _____ First. _____ First it gi -
F5   B♭5   G5
- veth, then it ta - keth a - way. _____

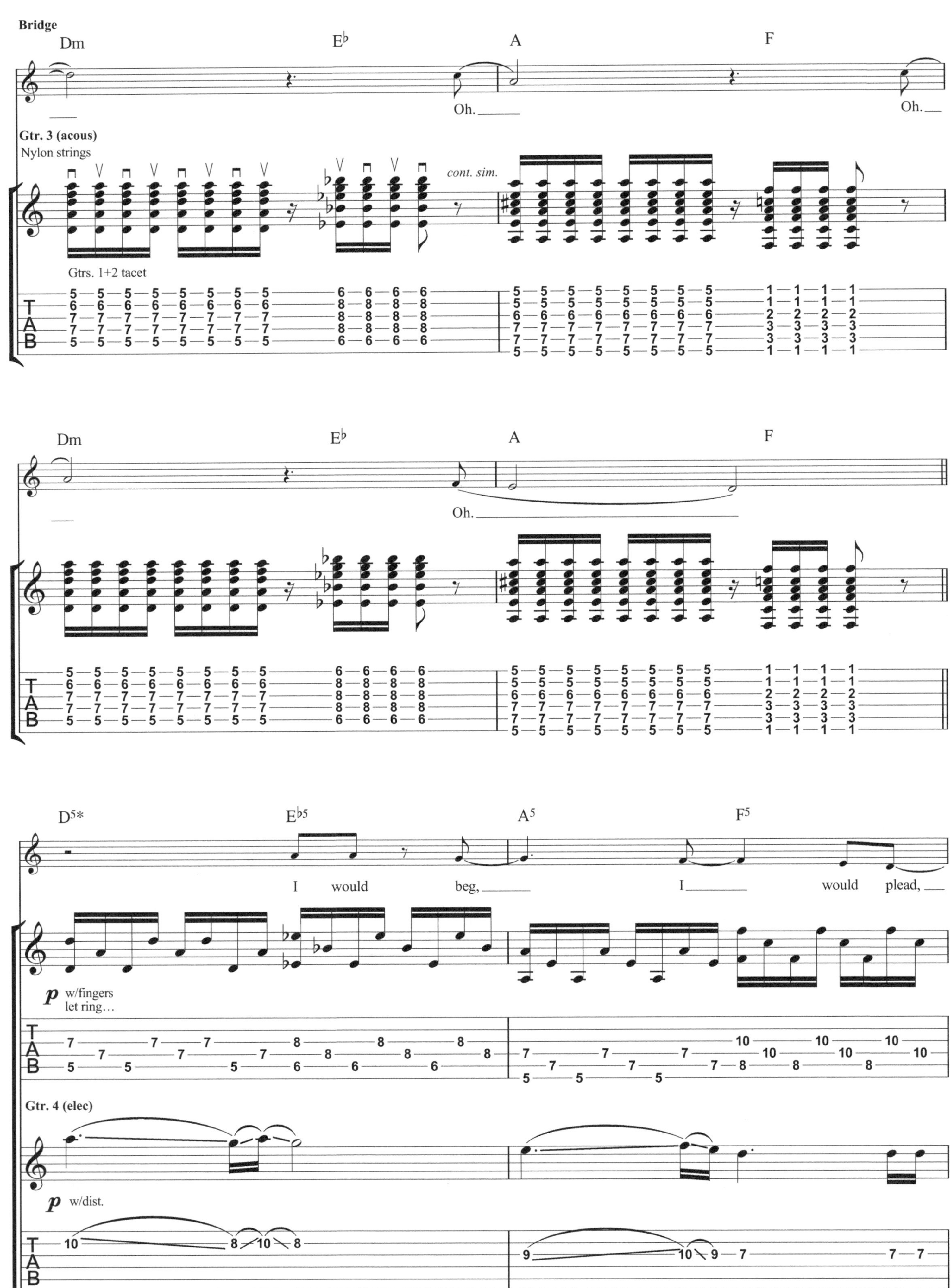

Bridge
Dm
Eb
A
F
Oh.
Oh.
Gtr. 3 (acous)
Nylon strings
cont. sim.
Gtrs. 1+2 tacet
TAB
Dm
Eb
A
F
Oh.
TAB
D5*
Eb5
A5
F5
I would beg,
I would plead,
p w/fingers
let ring…
TAB
Gtr. 4 (elec)
p w/dist.
TAB

D5
Eb5
A
I would shake.
7 7 7 7 8 8 8
5 5 7 5 7 6 8 6 8 6 8
6 6 6 6
7 7 7
5 5
10 8 10 8
6 14
Verse
N.C.
Gtrs. 1+2
cont. sim.
2. On a hook dan - gling by the way.
f Gtrs. 3+4 tacet
5 5 5 5 5 6 6
5 5 1 1 3
5 5 6 6
I'm so young, beau - ti - ful,
5 5 5 5
5 3 5 6 5 6
5 3 5 1 1
9 7 9 10 9 10
4 4 0 0

I'm no fool.
Time goes by,

D.S. al Coda

ta - bles turn,
now I know.

Coda
D5
F5
First it gi - veth, then it taket a - way.
Bb5
G5
D5
First.
First it gi - vet, then it ta - keth a - way,
F5
Bb5
G5
hmm.
Outro
D5
G5
F#5/C#
Bb5
First it gi - veth, then it ta - keth a - way.

C#5
D5
G5
F#5/C#
First.
First it gi - veth, then it ta - keth a - way,
Bb5
C#5
Bb5
a - way,
C#5
Bb5
C#5
a - way.
Ah.
Gtrs. 1+2 cont. in slashes
D5*
Eb5
Gtrs. 1+2
Oh!
Gtr. 3

SIX SHOOTER

Words & Music by Josh Homme & Nick Oliveri

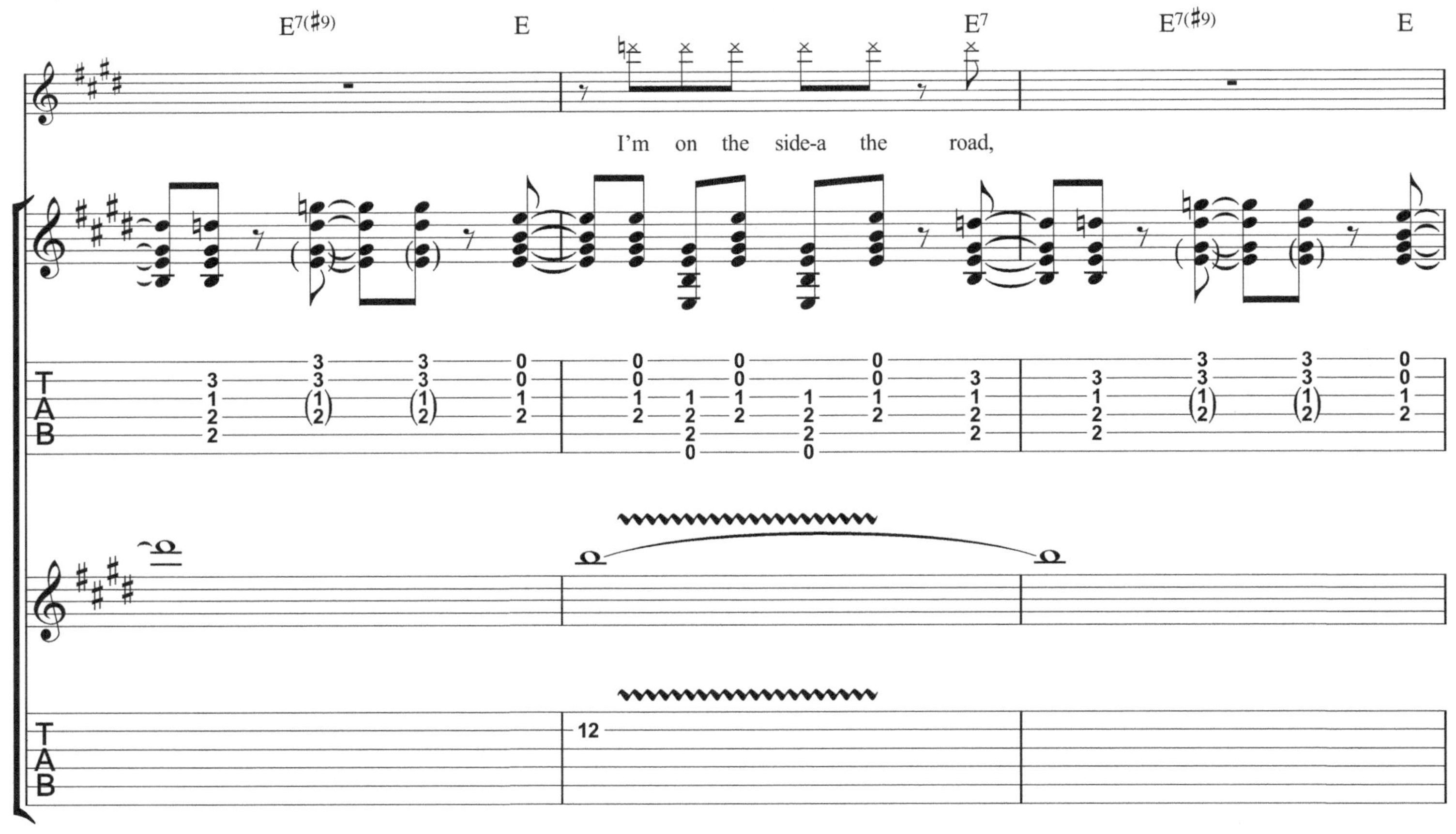

E7(#9)
E
E7
E7(#9)
E
I'm on the side-a the road,
Chorus
E7
E7(#9)
A5
B5
C5
you'll all fuck-in' die.
Yeah.
Yeah.

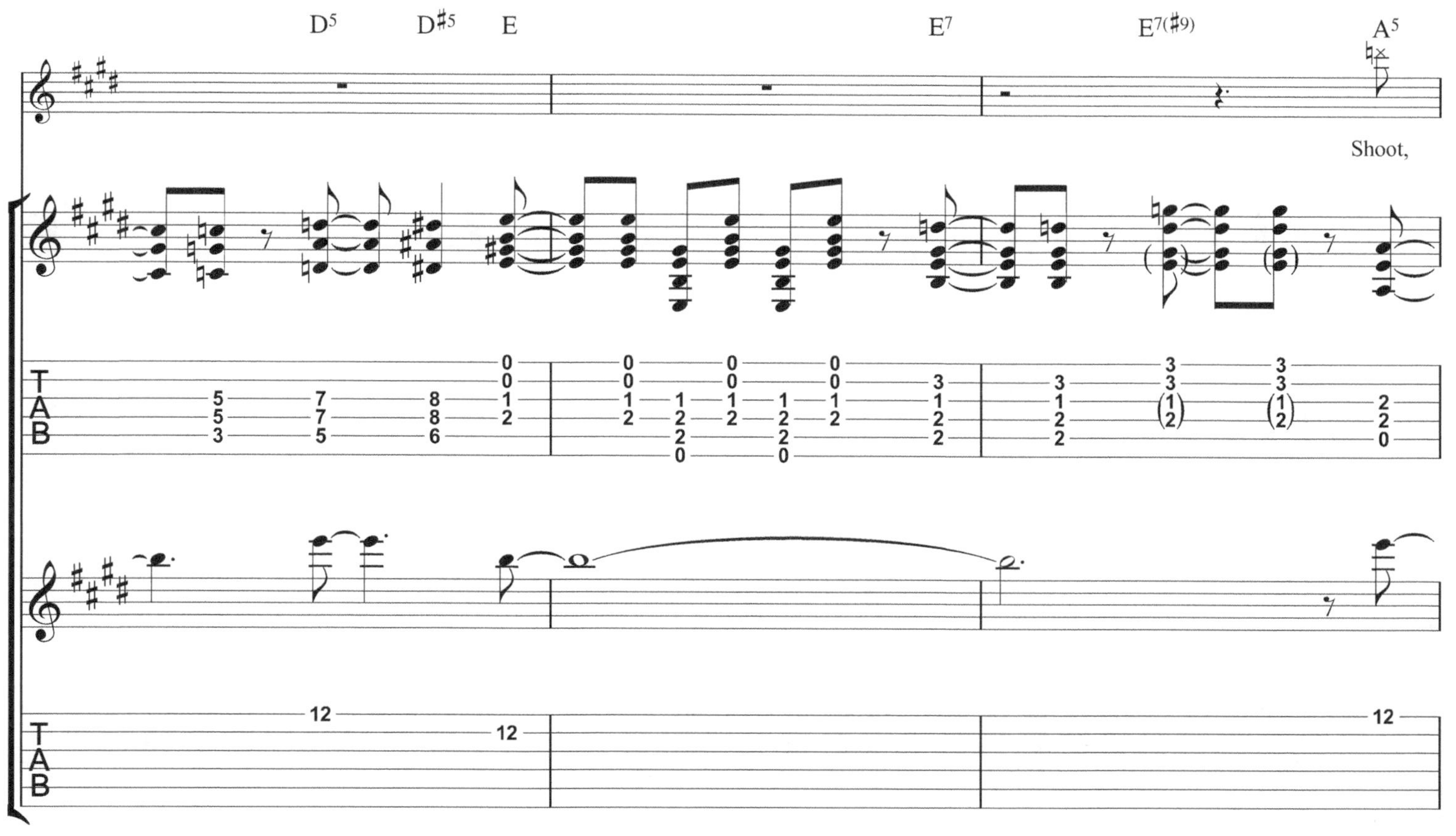

D5 D#5 E
E7 E7(#9) A5
Shoot,
B5 C5 D5 D#5 E
shoot, shoot, shoot. Pow!

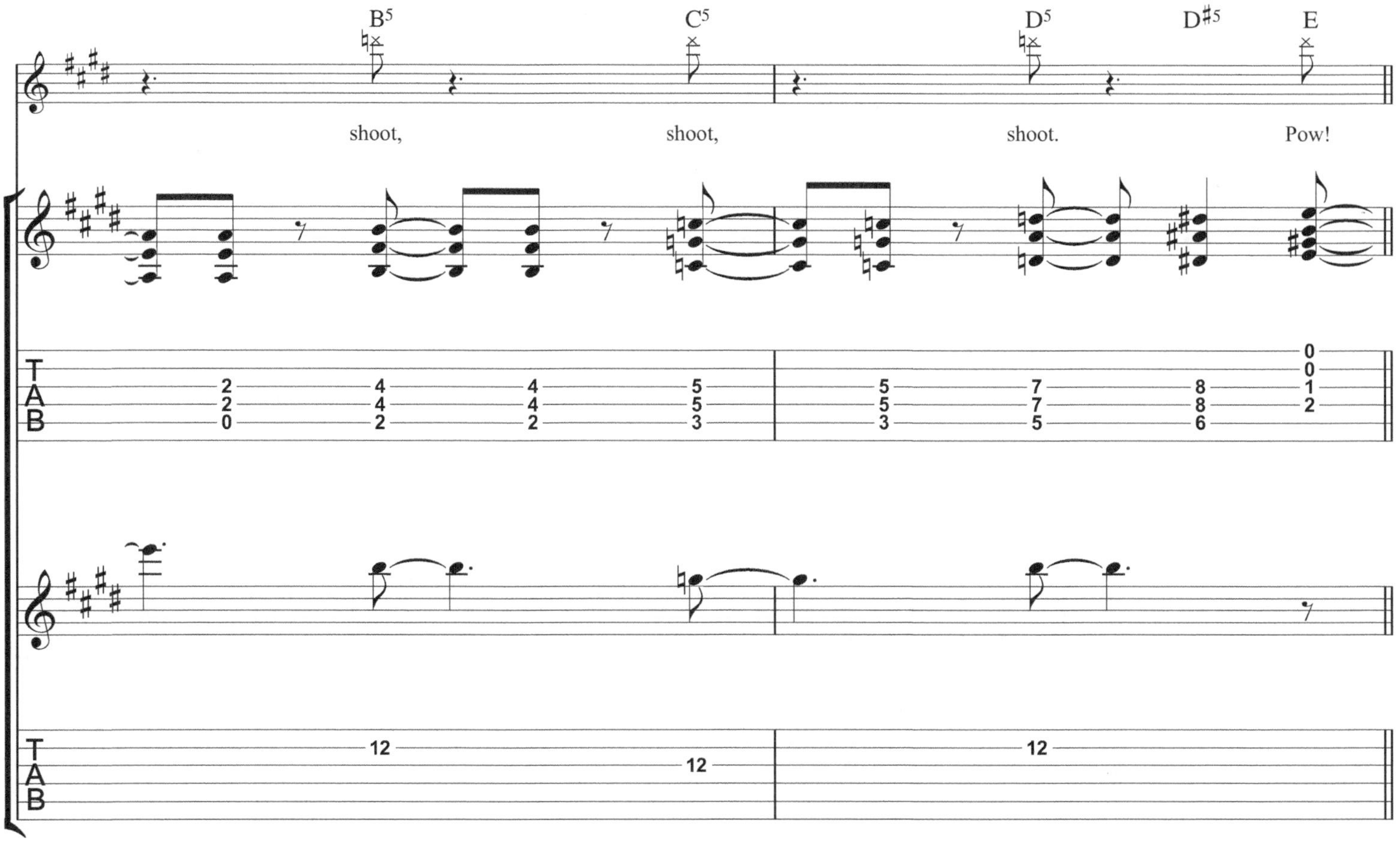

E7
E7(#9)
E
E7
Gtr. 2 w/ad lib. fills
TAB
E7(#9)
E
Verse
E7
E7(#9)
E
Pow!
2° only
2. Fuck this world,
E7
E7(#9)
E
E7
fuck you too,
I'll fuck - in' kill your best
E7(#9)
E
E7
E7(#9)
A5
friend.
What you fuck - in' gon - na do?
Shoot,

B5   C5   D5   D#5   E   E7
shoot, shoot, shoot, shoot, shoot, shoot.
E7(#9)   A5   B5   C5   D5   D#5   E
Shoot, shoot, shoot, shoot. Pow!
E7   E7(#9)   Play 3 times   E   E7
w/vocal ad libs.
Pow!
E7(#9)   A5   B5   C5   D5   D#5   E
Shoot, shoot, shoot, shoot, shoot, shoot. Pow!
w/echo

GO WITH THE FLOW

Words & Music by Josh Homme & Nick Oliveri

Verse

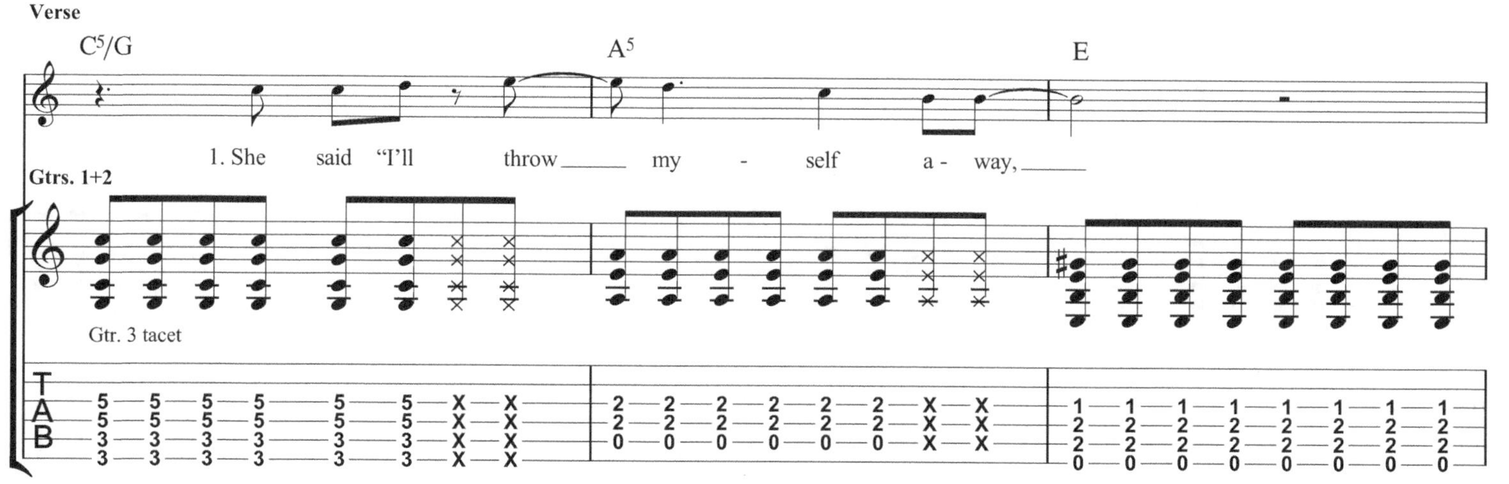

C5/G
A5
E
Gtrs. 1+2
Gtr. 3 tacet
1. She said "I'll throw my - self a - way,

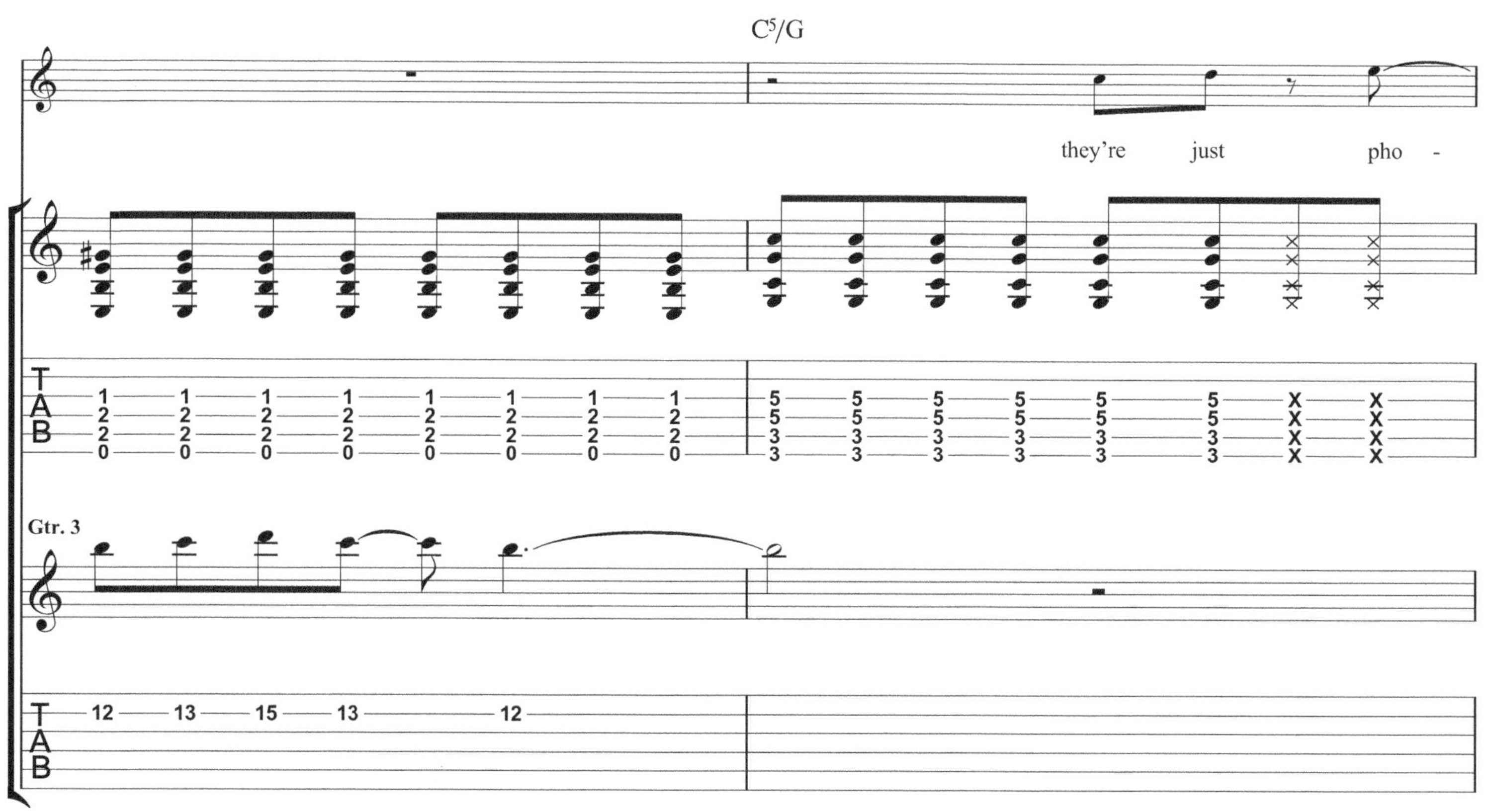

C5/G
Gtr. 3
they're just pho -

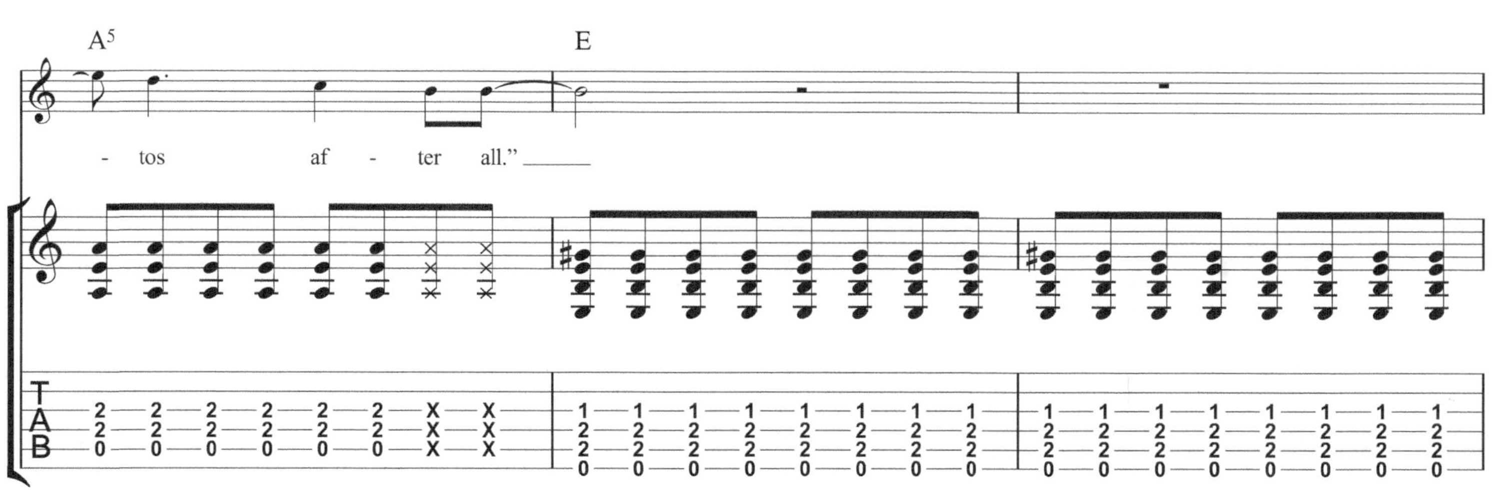

A5
E
- tos af - ter all."

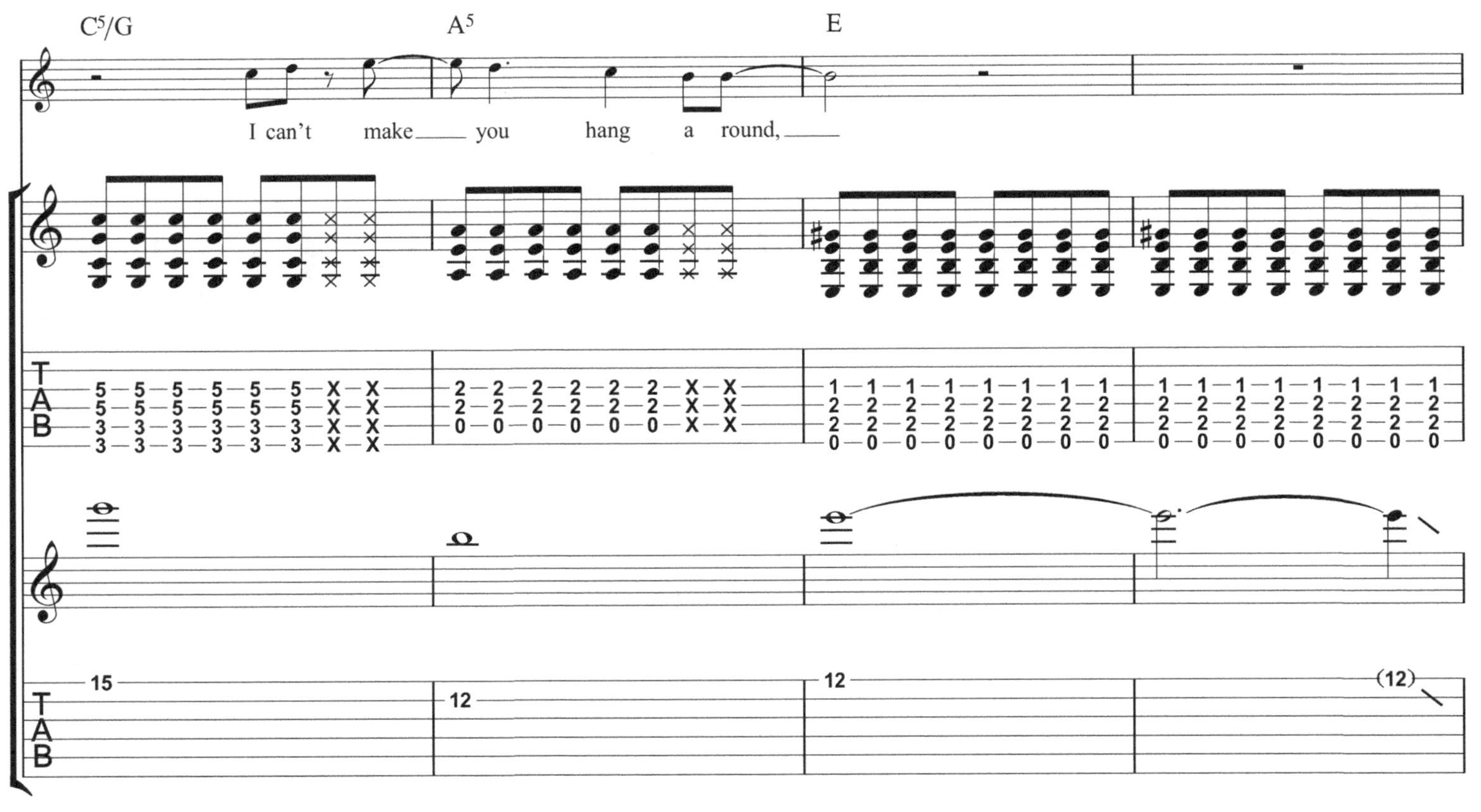

C5/G
A5
E
I can't make you hang a round,
TAB

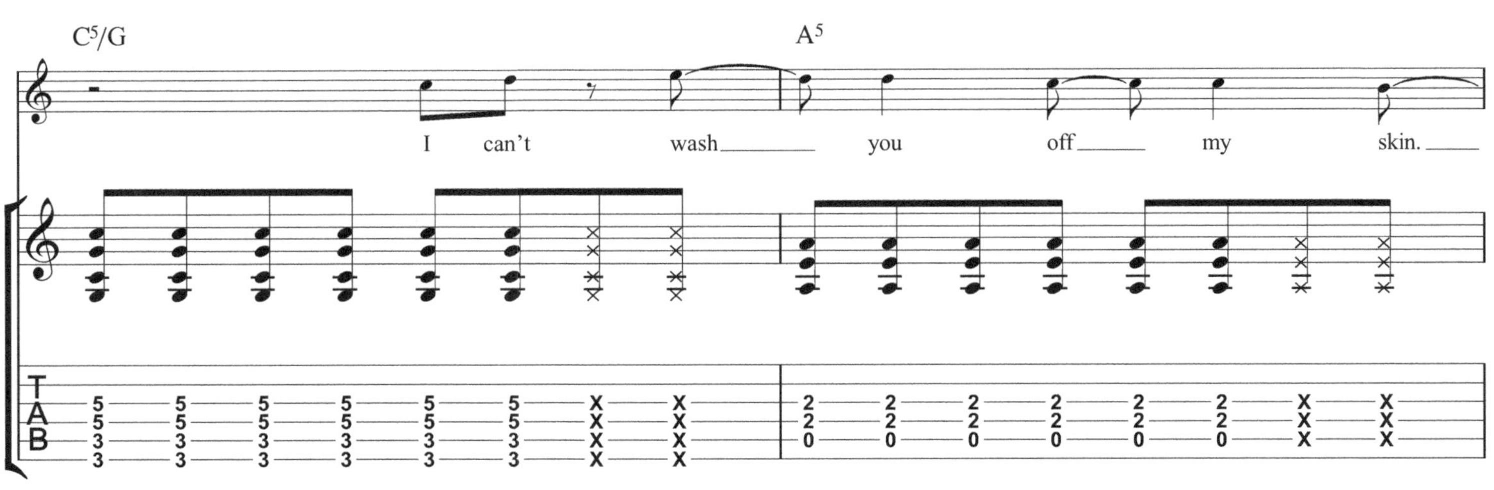

C5/G
A5
I can't wash you off my skin.
TAB

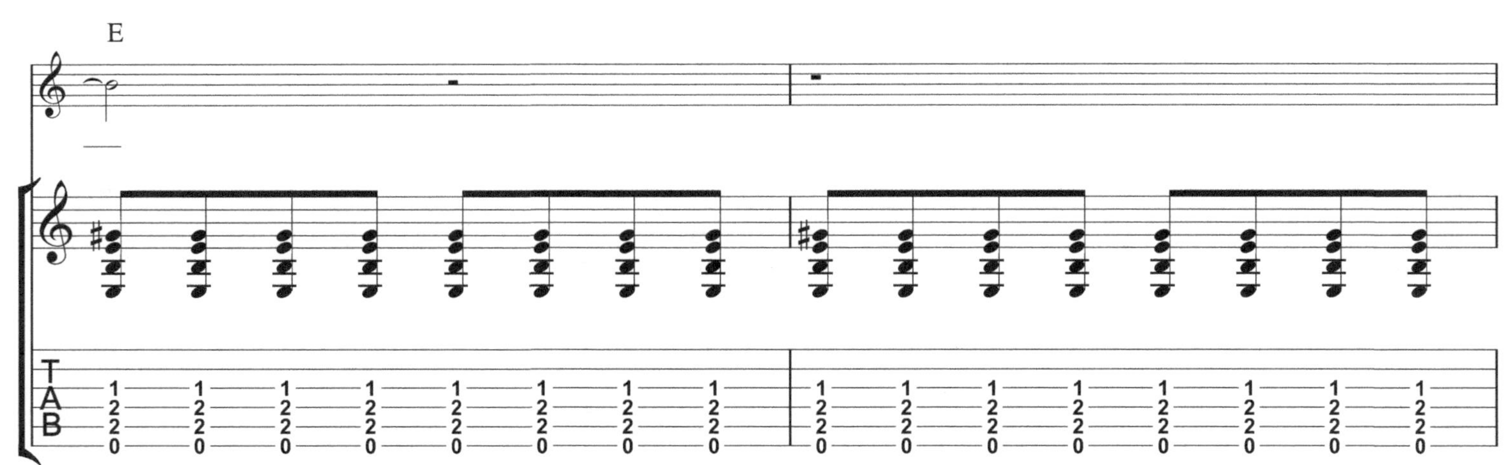

E
TAB

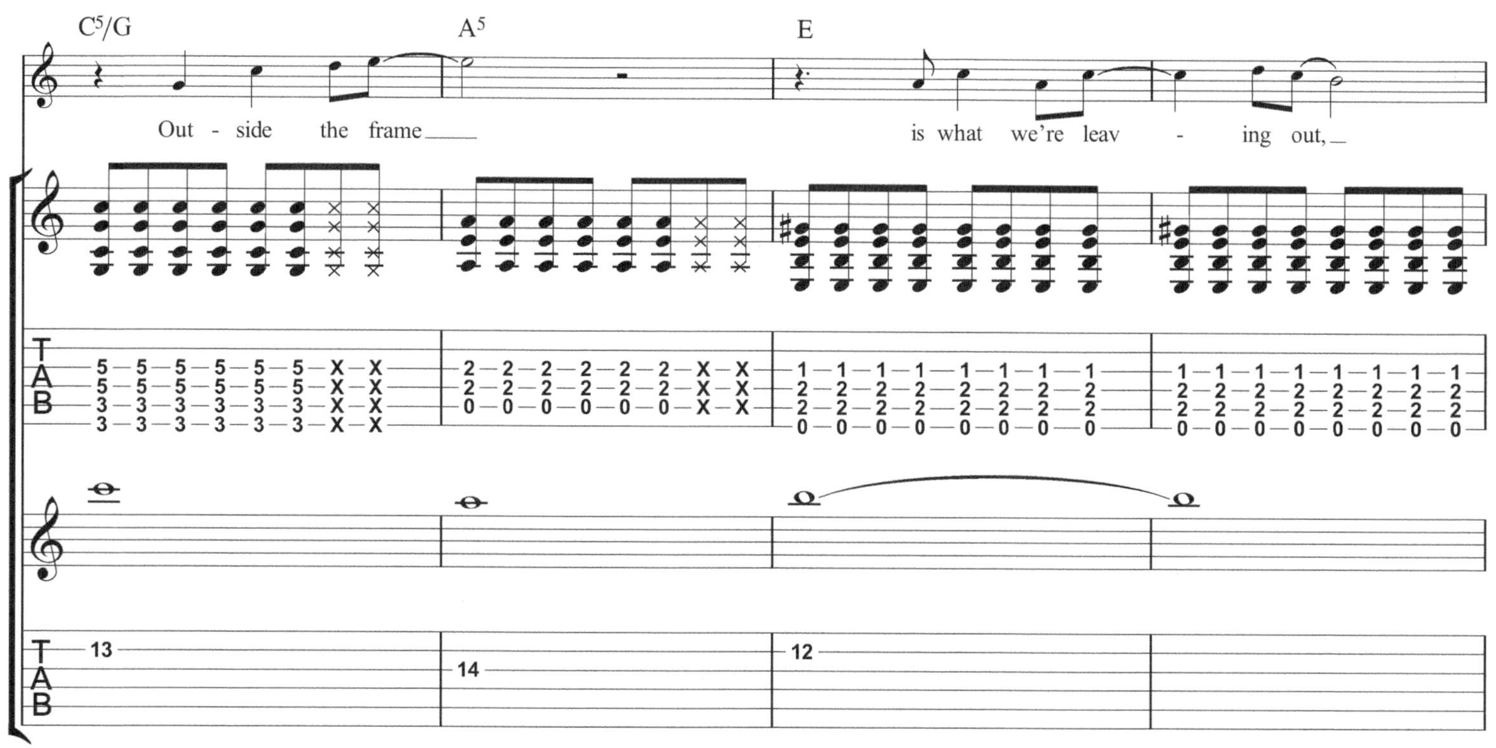

C5/G
A5
E
Out - side the frame___ is what we're leav - ing out,___
TAB

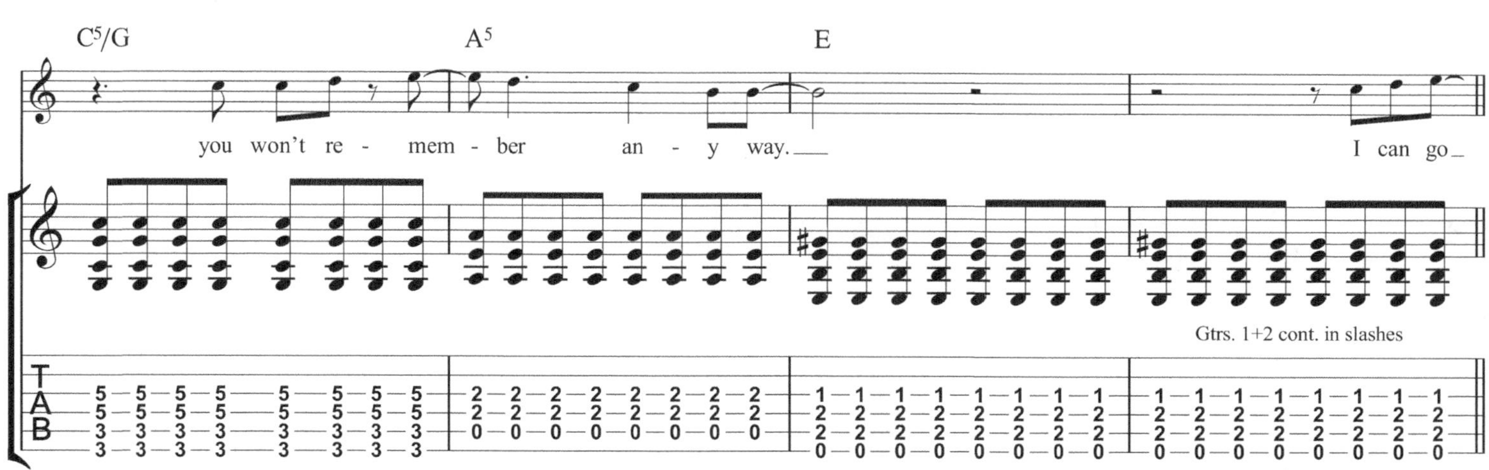

C5/G
A5
E
you won't re - mem - ber an - y way.___ I can go___
Gtrs. 1+2 cont. in slashes
TAB

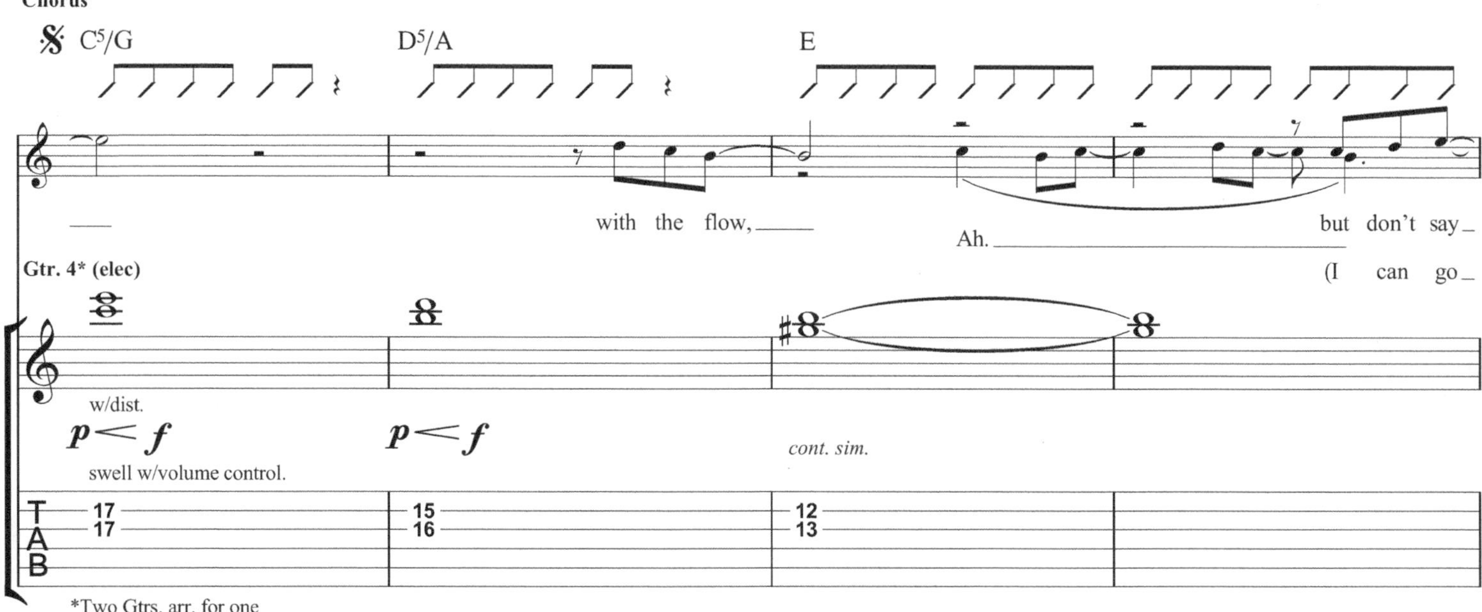

Chorus
C5/G
D5/A
E
with the flow,___ Ah.___ but don't say___
(I can go___
Gtr. 4* (elec)
w/dist.
p < f
p < f
cont. sim.
swell w/volume control.
TAB
*Two Gtrs. arr. for one

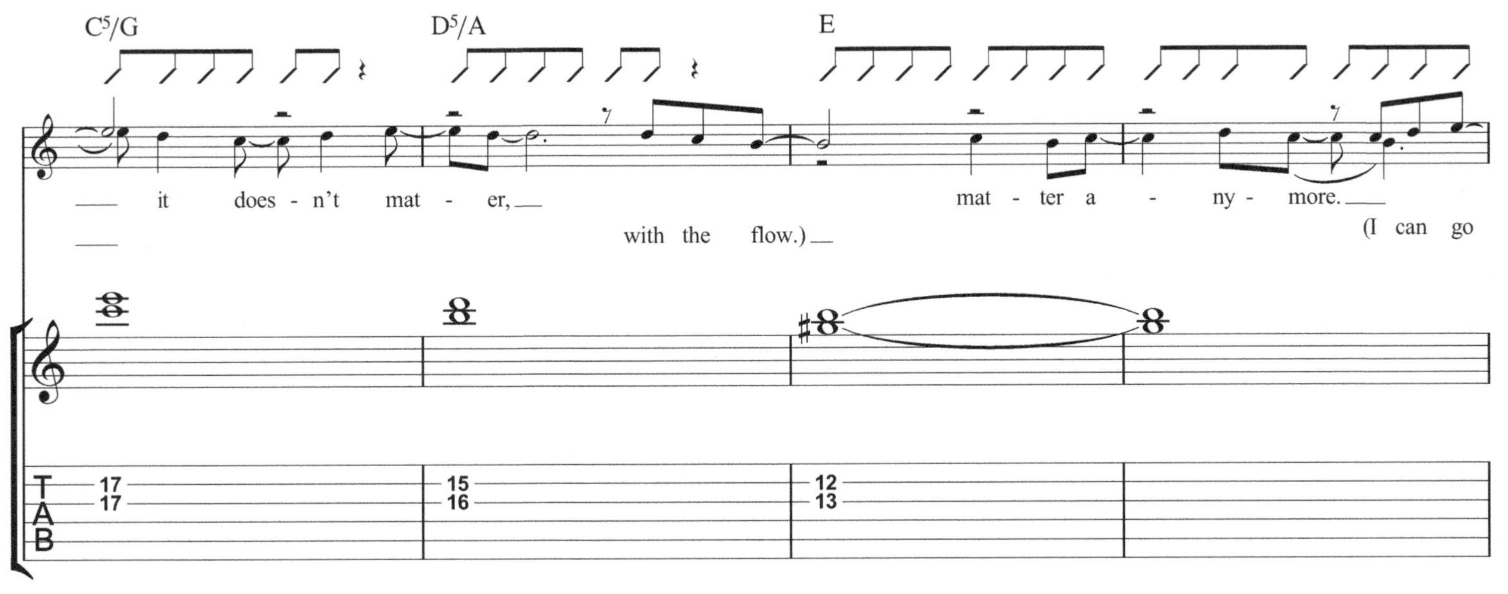

C5/G
D5/A
E
it does-n't mat - er,
with the flow.)
mat - ter a - ny - more.
(I can go
17
17
15
16
12
13

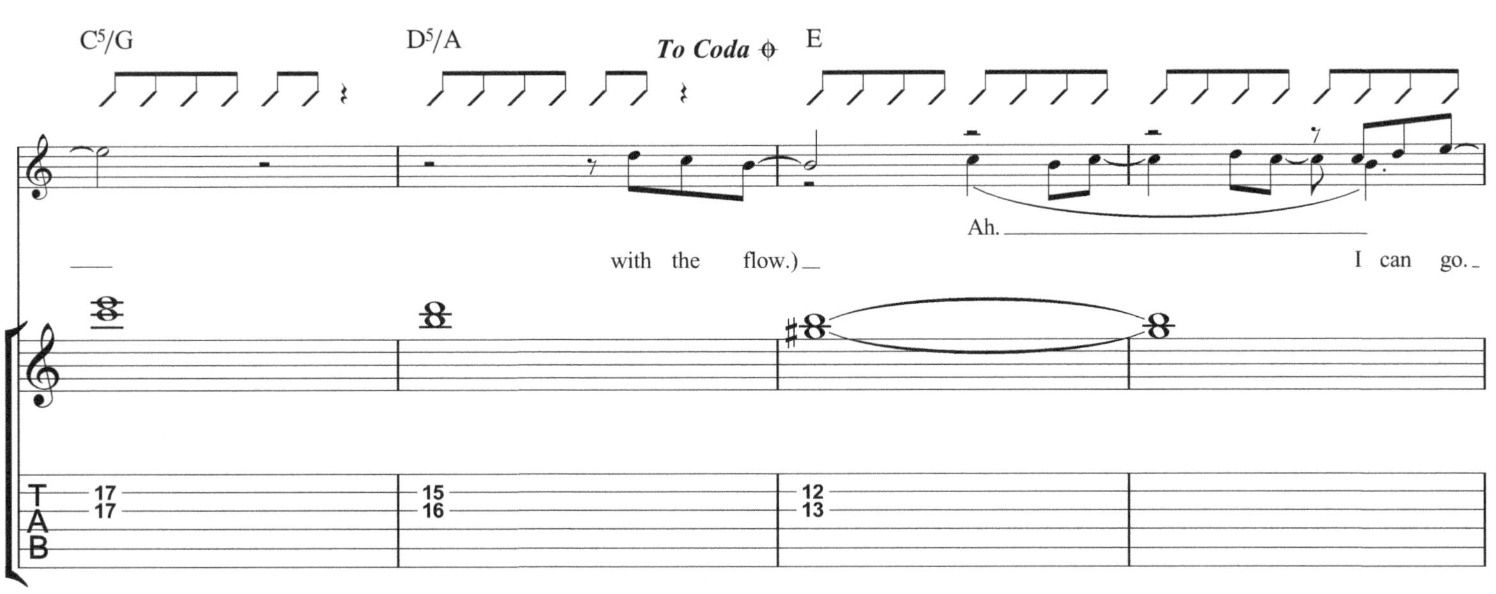

C5/G
D5/A
To Coda
E
with the flow.)
Ah.
I can go.
17
17
15
16
12
13

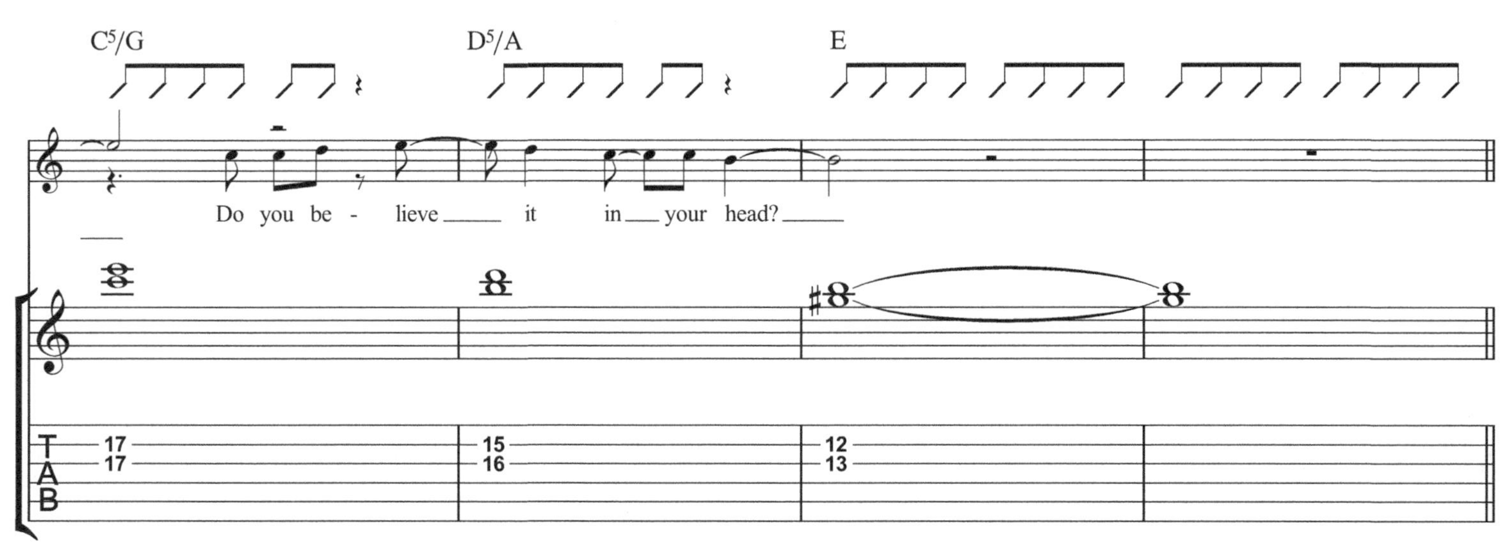

C5/G
D5/A
E
Do you be - lieve it in your head?
17
17
15
16
12
13

Verse
C5/G
A5
E
2. It's so safe to play a - long,
Gtr. 3
C5/G
A5
E
lit - tle sol - diers in a row.
C5/G
A5
E
Fall - ing in and out of love,
Ah,

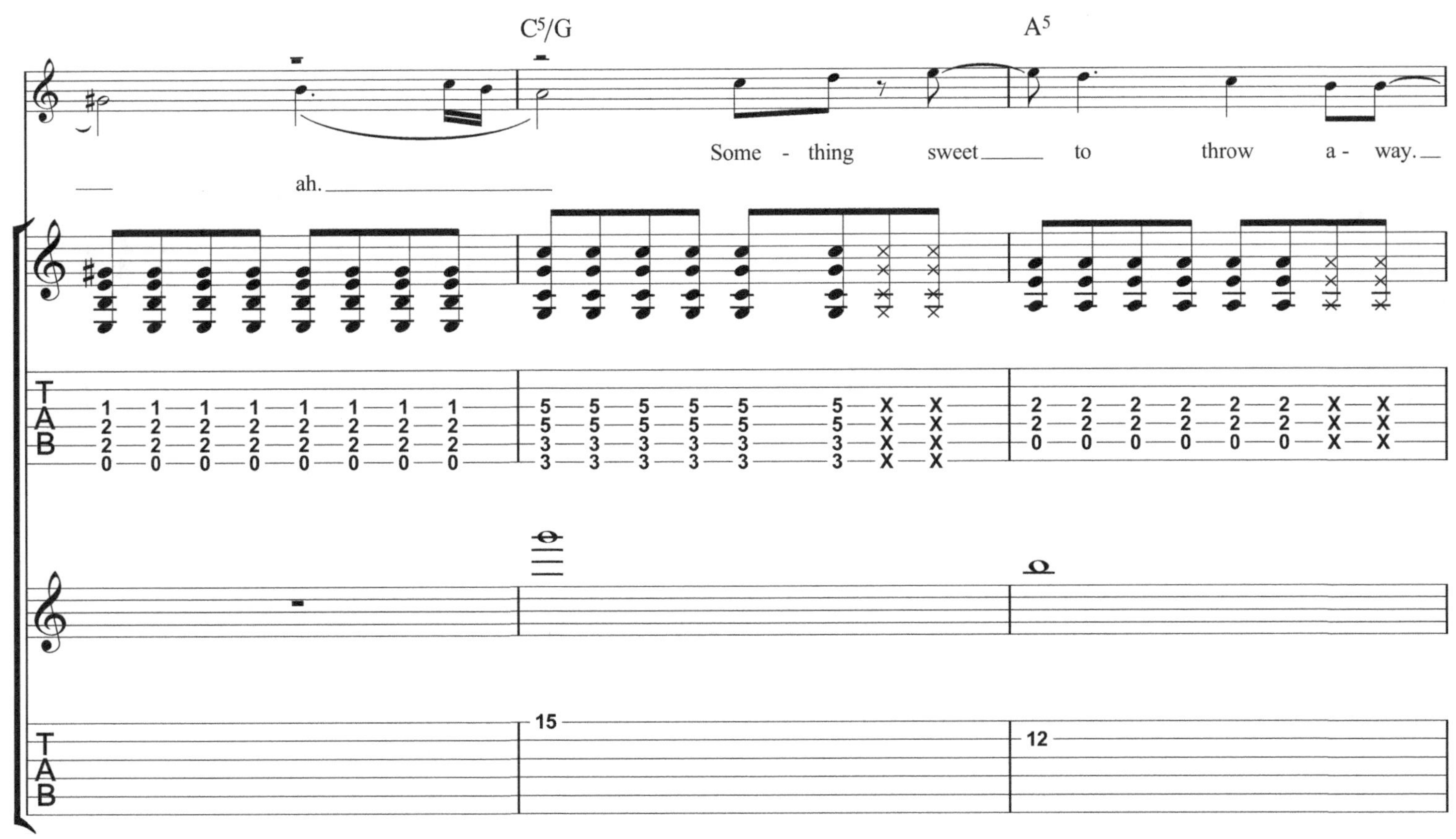

C5/G
A5
Some - thing sweet ___ to throw a - way. ___
ah. ___
15
12

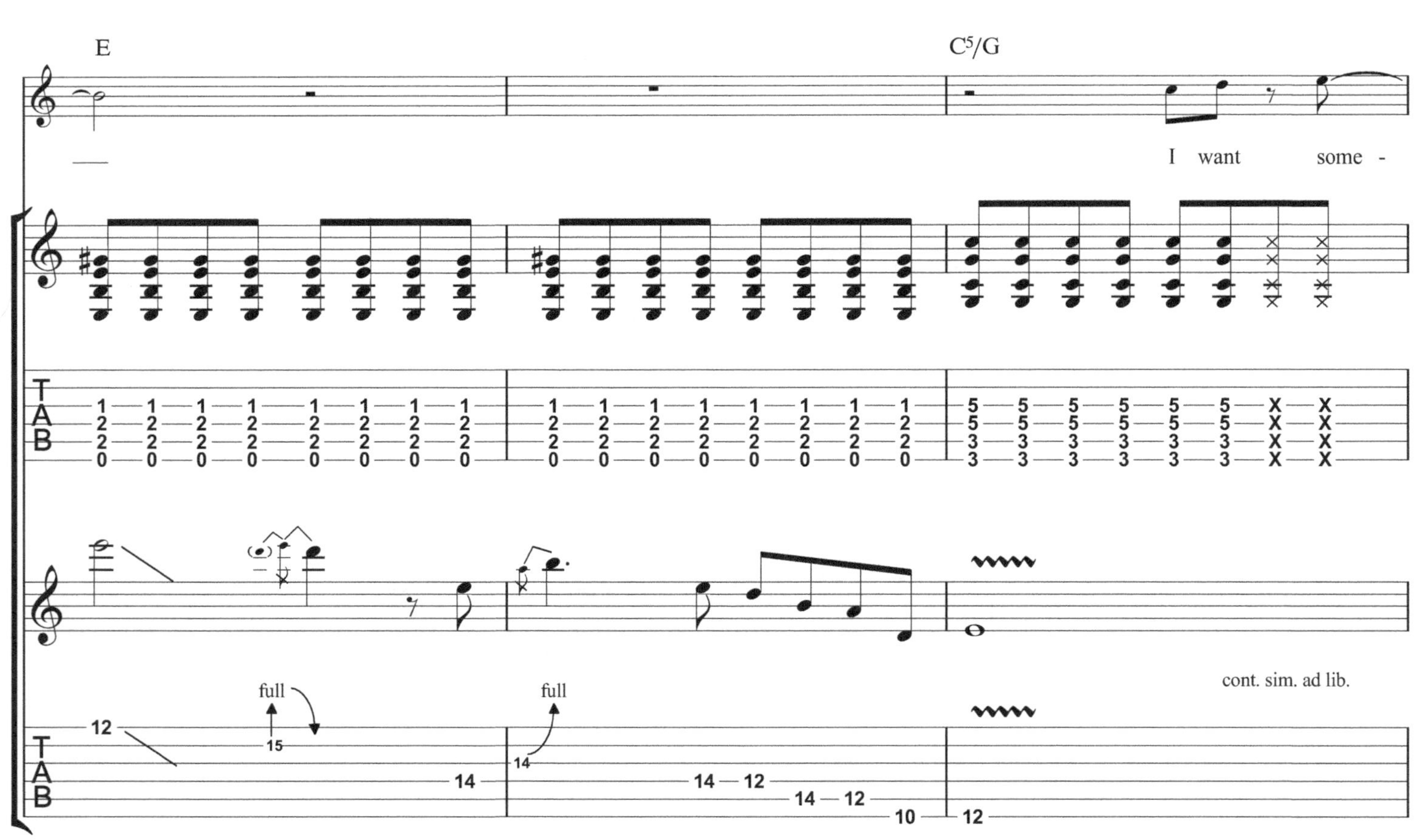

E
C5/G
I want some -
full
full
12
15
14
14
14 - 12
14 - 12
10
12
cont. sim. ad lib.

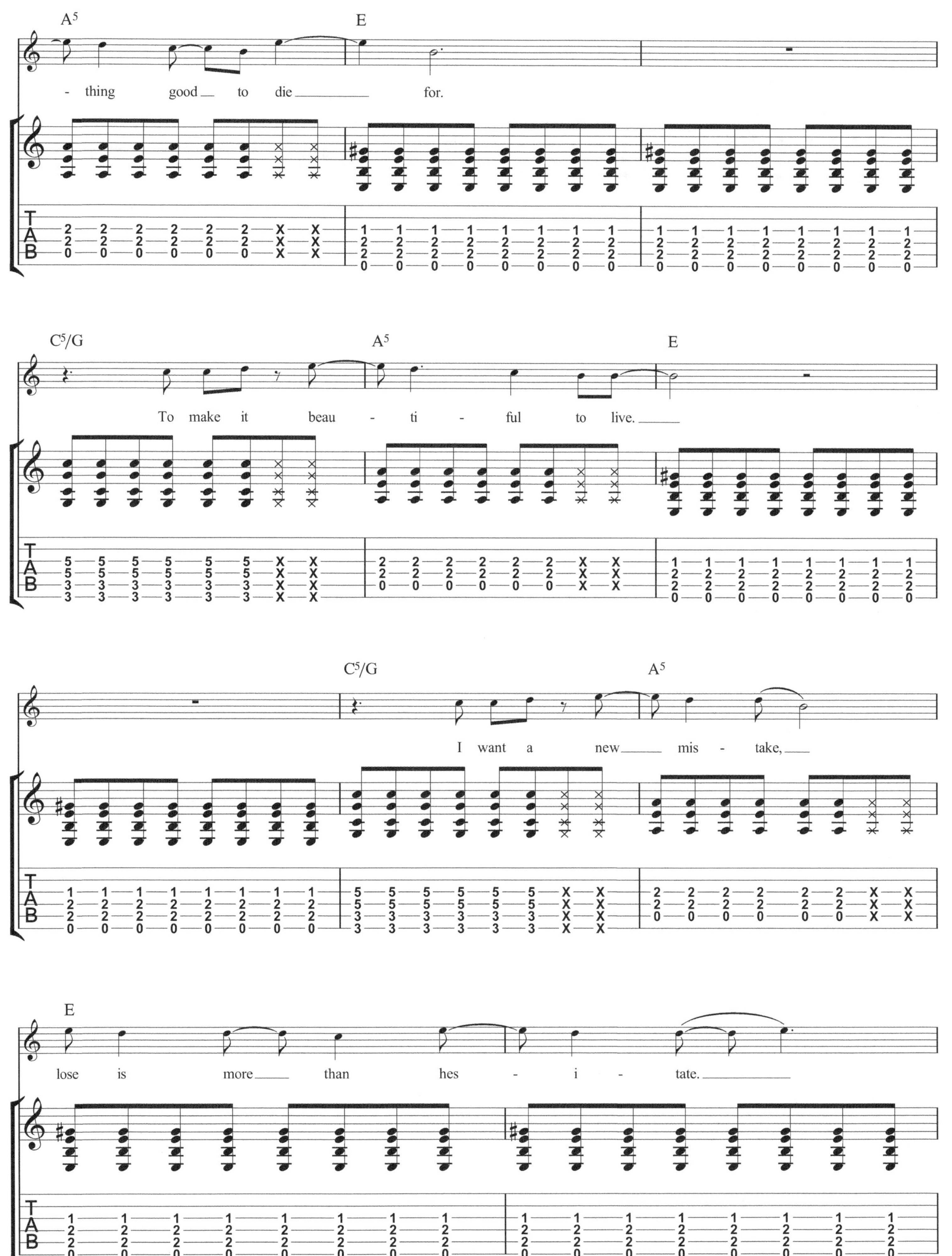

- thing good to die for.
To make it beau - ti - ful to live.
I want a new mis - take,
lose is more than hes - i - tate.

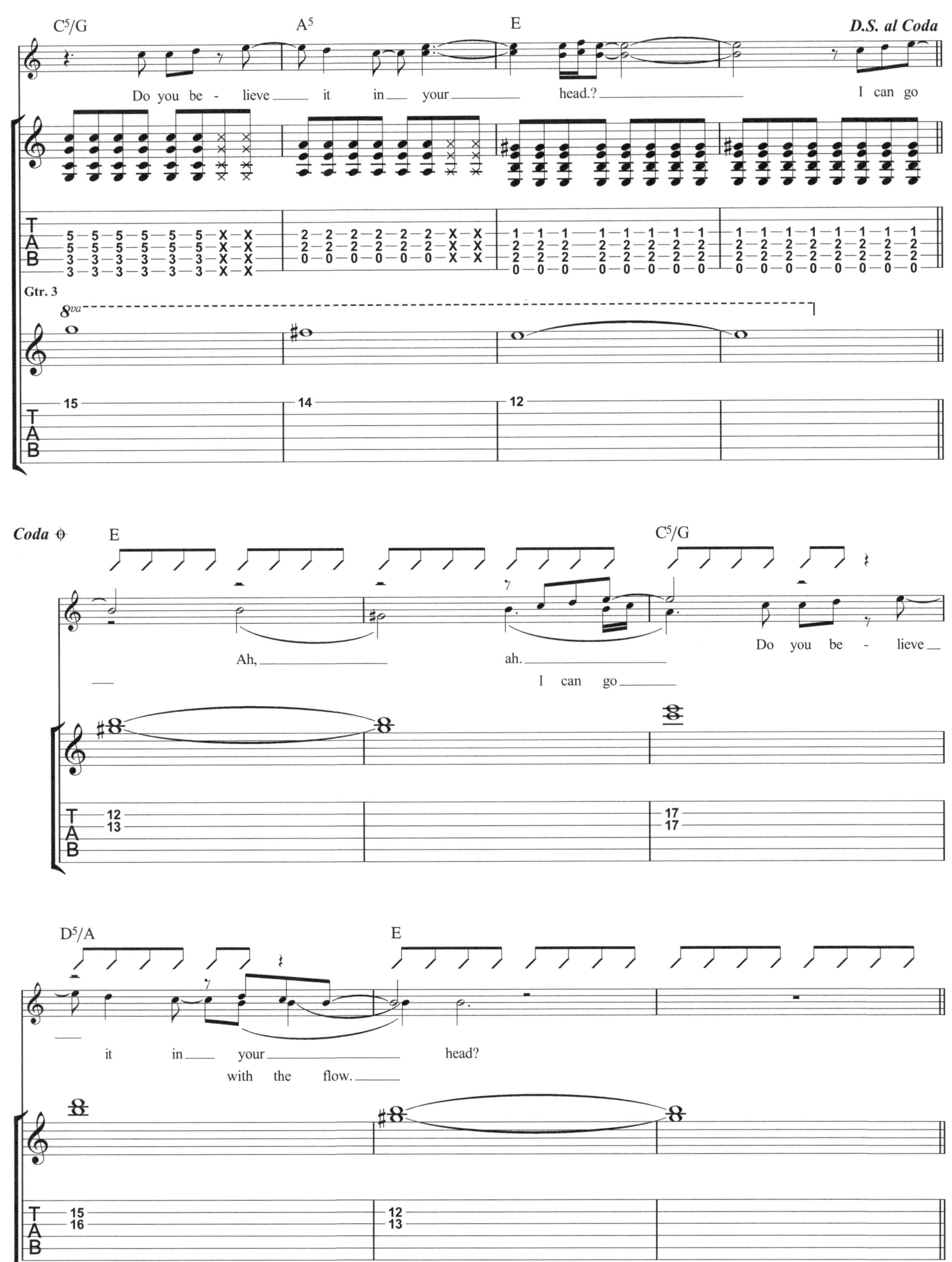

C5/G
A5
E
D.S. al Coda
Do you be - lieve it in your head.? I can go
Gtr. 3
8va
Coda
E
C5/G
Ah, ah.
I can go
Do you be - lieve
D5/A
E
it in your head?
with the flow.
68

C5/G
D5/A
E
Gtr. 3
8va
Do you be - lieve it in your head?
Gtr. 4 w/?????
15
12
12

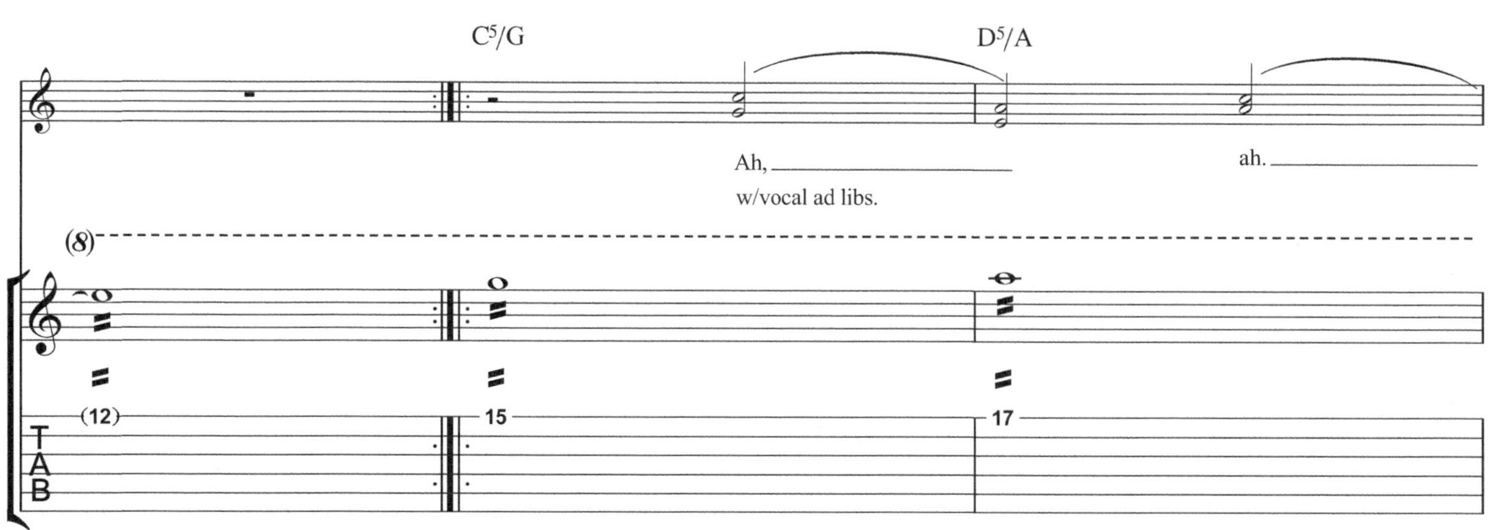

C5/G
D5/A
Ah,
w/vocal ad libs.
ah.
(8)
(12)
15
17

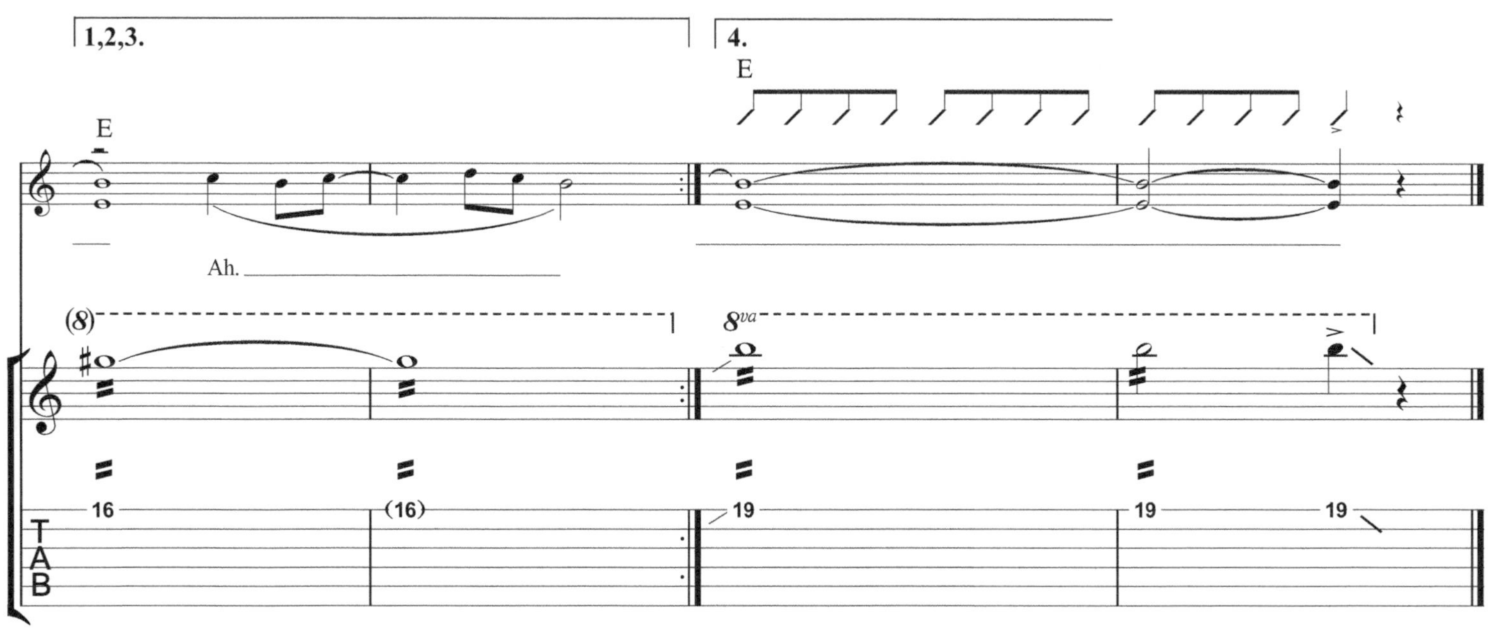

1,2,3.
4.
E
E
Ah.
(8)
8va
16
(16)
19
19
19

GONNA LEAVE YOU

Words & Music by Josh Homme & Nick Oliveri

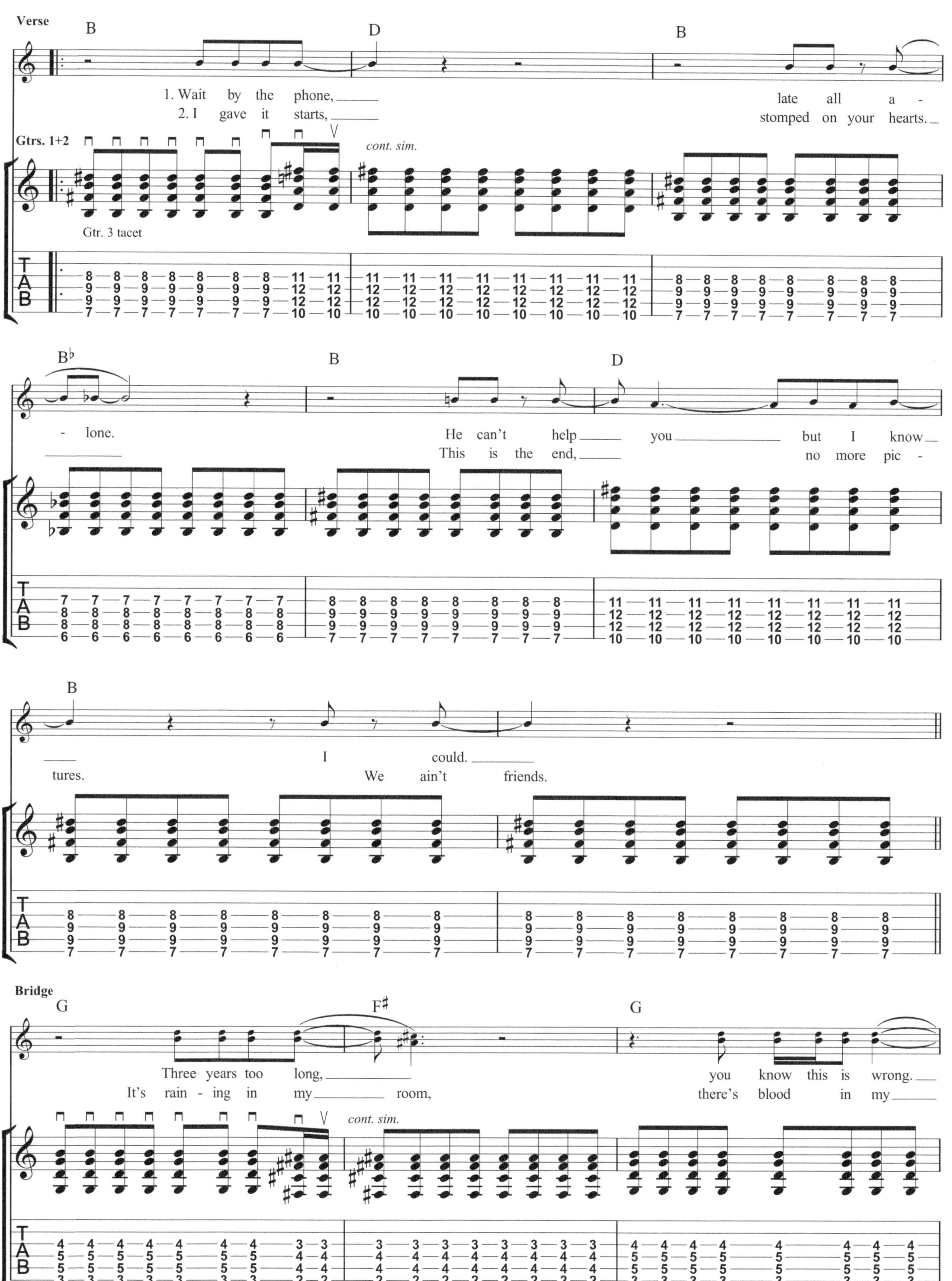

Verse
B
D
B
1. Wait by the phone,
2. I gave it starts,
late all a -
stomped on your hearts.
Gtrs. 1+2
cont. sim.
Gtr. 3 tacet
Bb
B
D
- lone.
He can't help you but I know
This is the end, no more pic -
B
I could.
tures.
We ain't friends.
Bridge
G
F#
G
Three years too long,
It's rain - ing in my room,
you know this is wrong.
there's blood in my

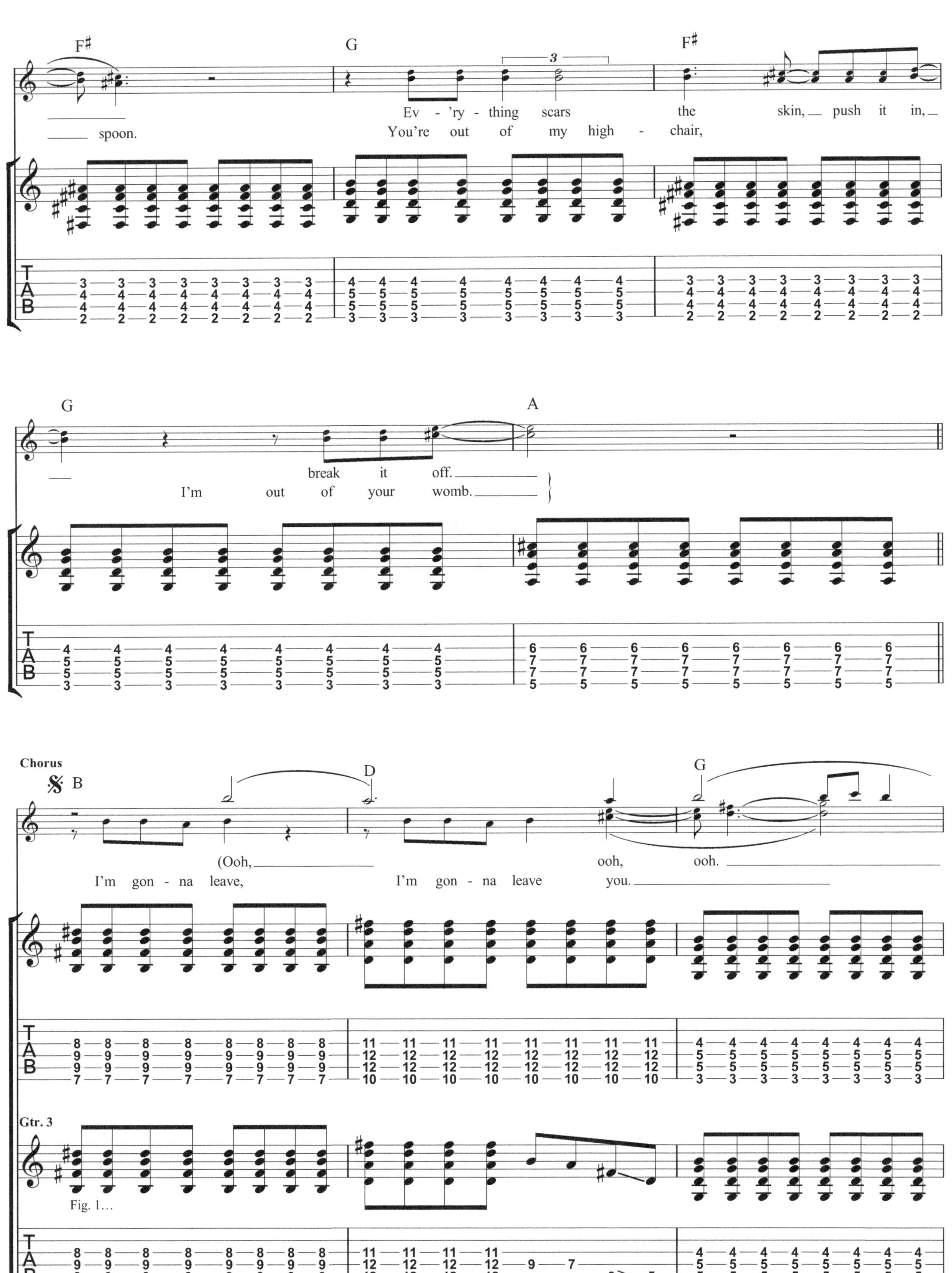

F#
G
F#
Ev - 'ry - thing scars the skin, push it in,
You're out of my high - chair,
spoon.
G
A
break it off.
I'm out of your womb.
Chorus
B
D
G
(Ooh,
ooh, ooh.
I'm gon - na leave,
I'm gon - na leave you.
Gtr. 3
Fig. 1...

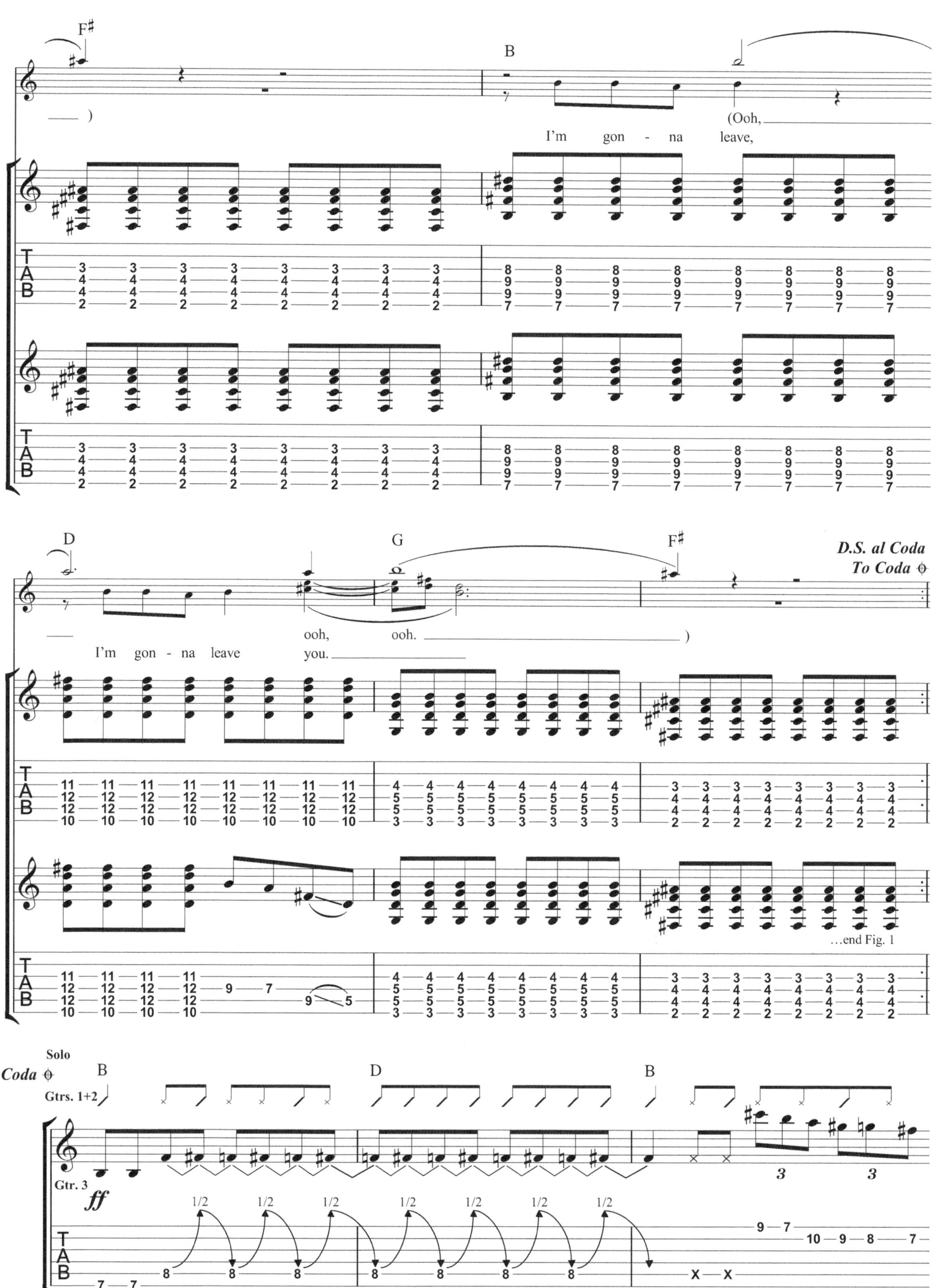

F#
B
(Ooh,
I'm gon - na leave,
TAB
D
G
F#
D.S. al Coda
To Coda
ooh, ooh.
)
I'm gon - na leave you.
...end Fig. 1
Coda
Solo
Gtrs. 1+2
B
D
B
Gtr. 3
ff
3
3
1/2
TAB

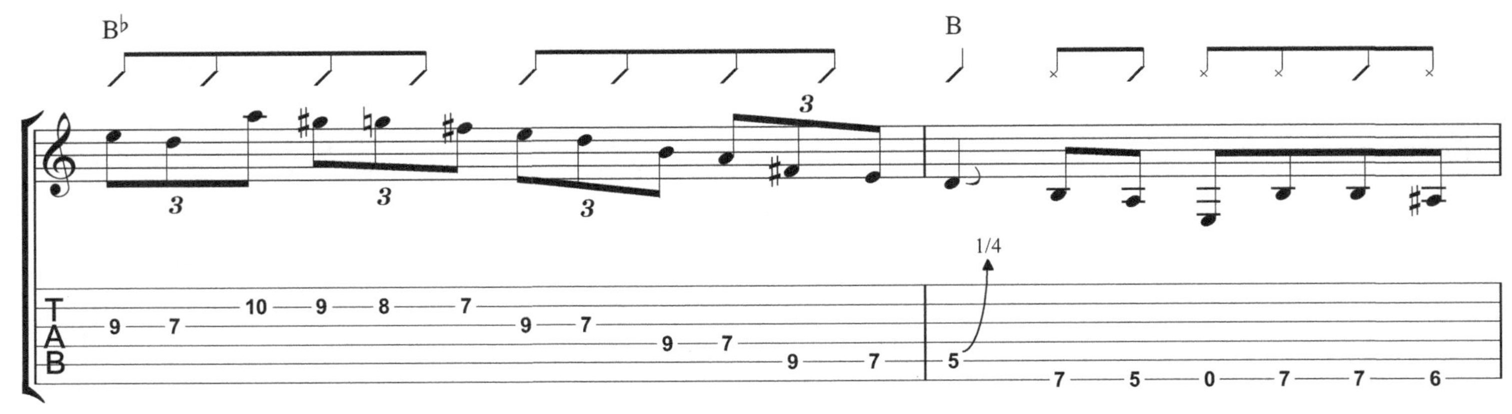

B♭
B
3
3
3
1/4

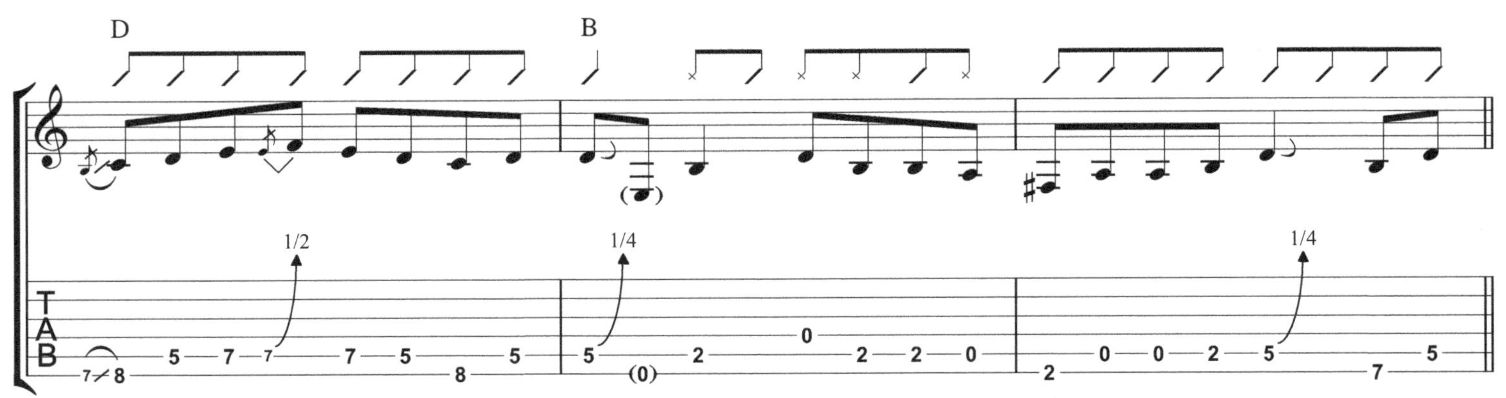

D
B
1/2
1/4
1/4
(0)

Bridge
G
F#
G
F#
cont. sim.
Three years too long,
you know this is wrong.
Hold bend then tap & release
full
T
full
T

G
F#
G
A
Ev -'ry - thing scars the skin, push it in, push it in, break it off.
Hold tap
full
T
full
T

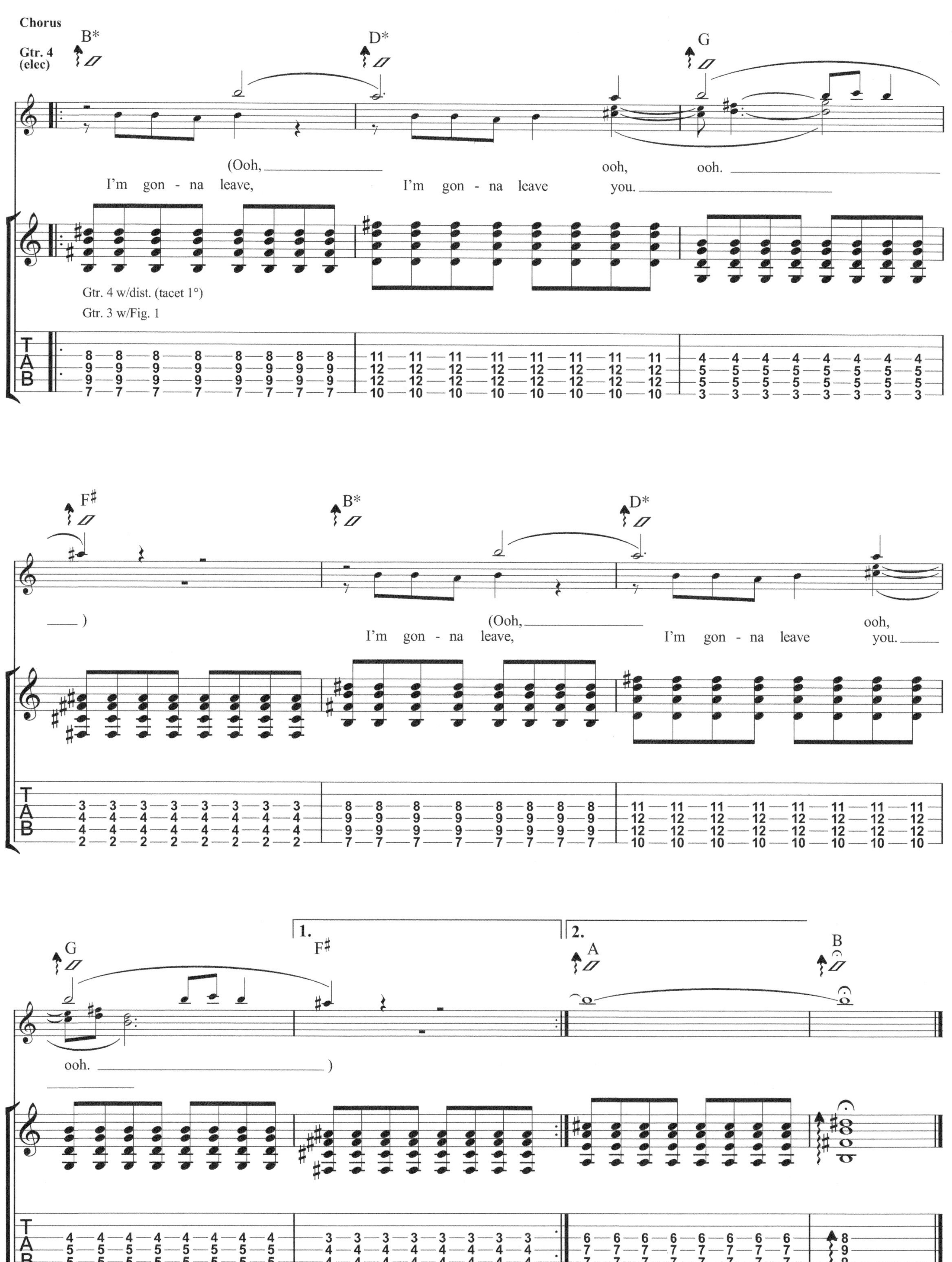

Chorus
Gtr. 4
(elec)
B*
D*
G
(Ooh, I'm gon-na leave, ooh, ooh.
I'm gon-na leave you.
Gtr. 4 w/dist. (tacet 1°)
Gtr. 3 w/Fig. 1
F#
B*
D*
_) (Ooh, I'm gon-na leave, ooh,
I'm gon-na leave you.
G
1.
F#
2.
A
B
ooh.)

DO IT AGAIN

Words & Music by Josh Homme & Nick Oliveri

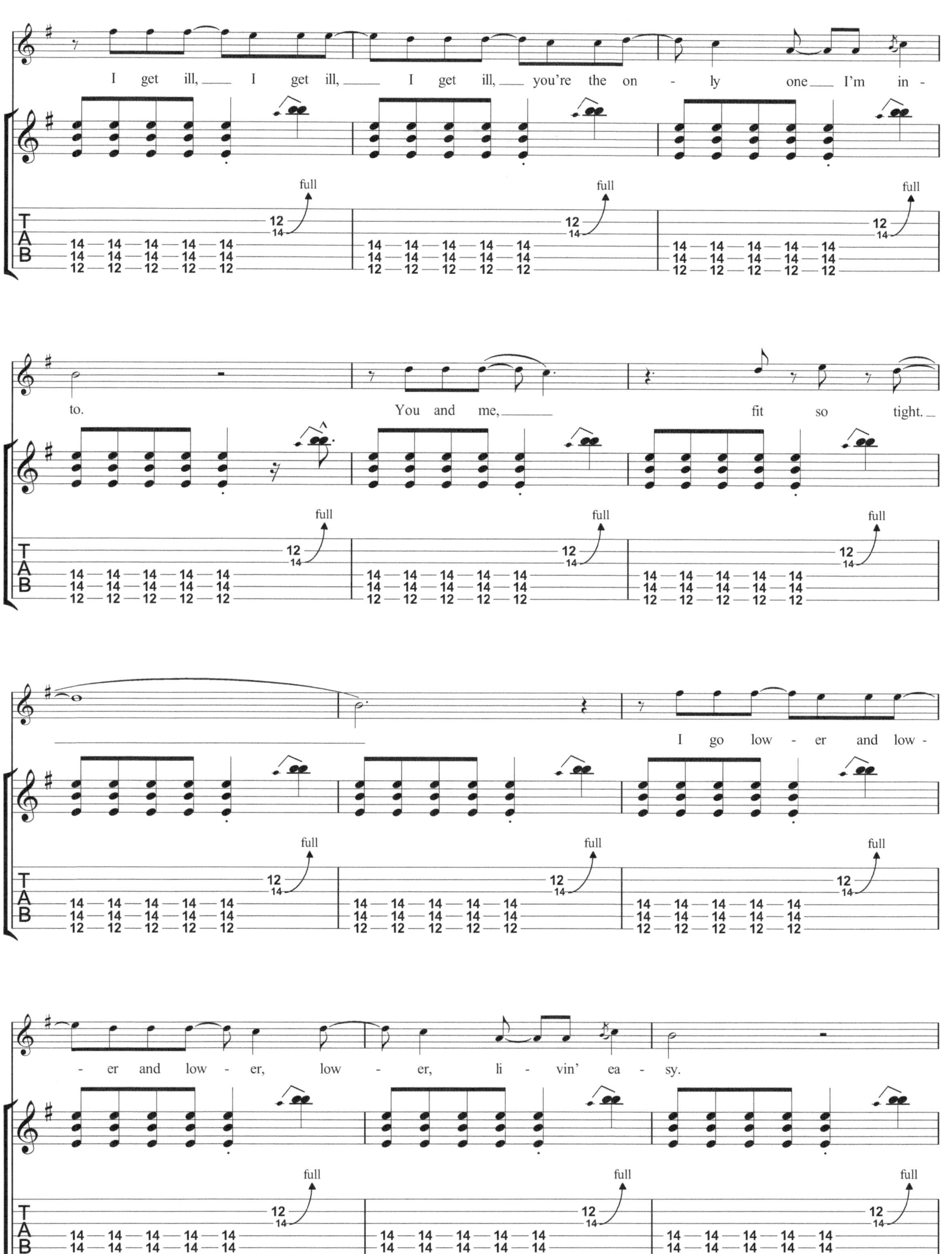

I get ill, I get ill, I get ill, you're the on - ly one I'm in -
to.
You and me, fit so tight.
I go low - er and low -
- er and low - er, low - er, li - vin' ea - sy.
full
full
full
12
14
14 14 14 14 14
14 14 14 14 14
12 12 12 12 12

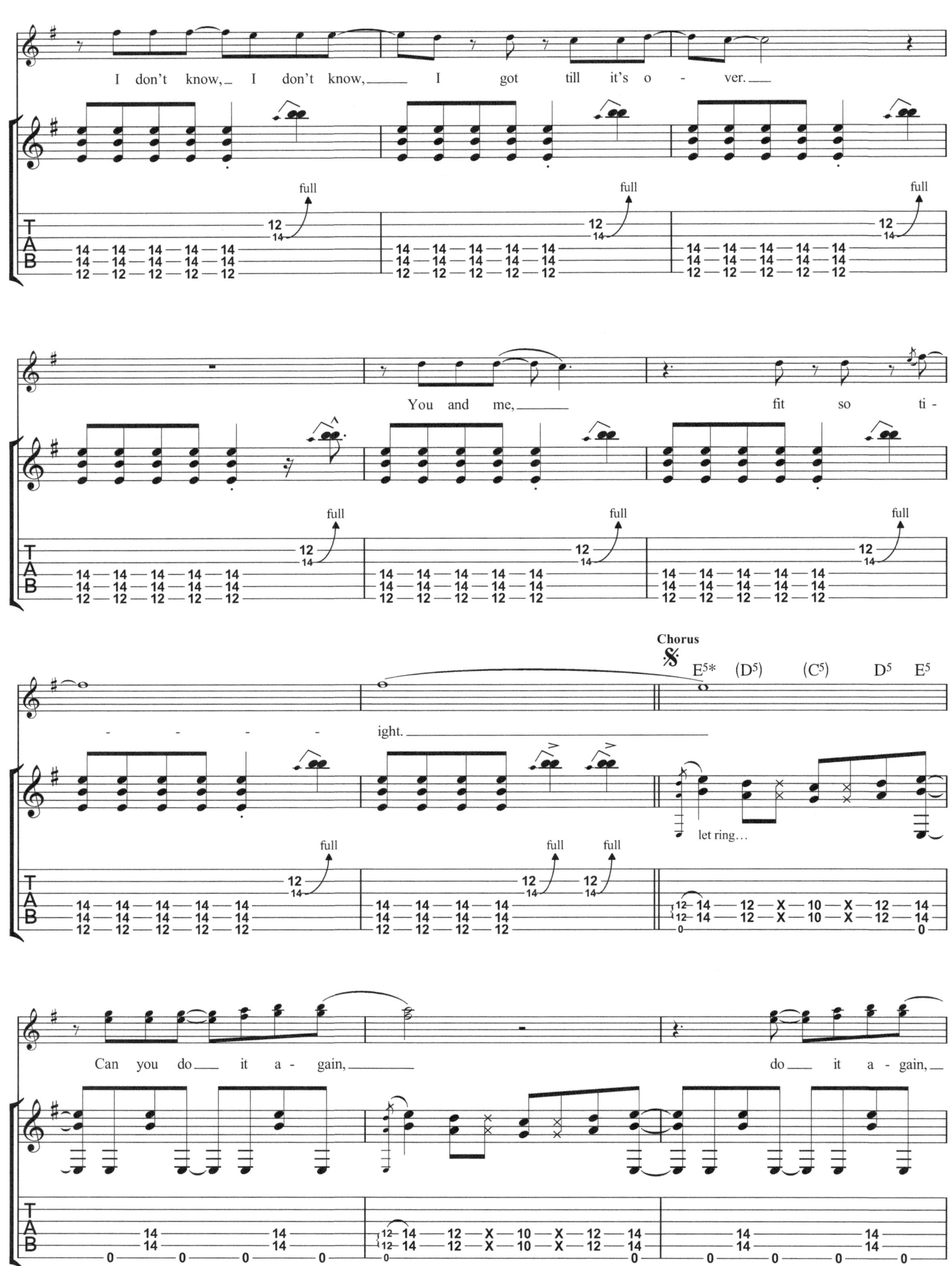

I don't know, I don't know, I got till it's o - ver.
full
12
14
14 — 14 — 14 — 14 — 14
14 — 14 — 14 — 14 — 14
12 — 12 — 12 — 12 — 12
full
12
14
14 — 14 — 14 — 14 — 14
14 — 14 — 14 — 14 — 14
12 — 12 — 12 — 12 — 12
full
12
14
14 — 14 — 14 — 14 — 14
14 — 14 — 14 — 14 — 14
12 — 12 — 12 — 12 — 12
You and me, fit so ti-
full
12
14
14 — 14 — 14 — 14 — 14
14 — 14 — 14 — 14 — 14
12 — 12 — 12 — 12 — 12
full
12
14
14 — 14 — 14 — 14 — 14
14 — 14 — 14 — 14 — 14
12 — 12 — 12 — 12 — 12
full
12
14
14 — 14 — 14 — 14 — 14
14 — 14 — 14 — 14 — 14
12 — 12 — 12 — 12 — 12
Chorus
E5* (D5) (C5) D5 E5
- ight.
full
12
14
14 — 14 — 14 — 14 — 14
14 — 14 — 14 — 14 — 14
12 — 12 — 12 — 12 — 12
full full
12 12
14 14
14 — 14 — 14 — 14
14 — 14 — 14 — 14
12 — 12 — 12 — 12
let ring…
12 — 14 — 12 — X — 10 — X — 12 — 14
12 — 14 — 12 — X — 10 — X — 12 — 14
0
Can you do it a - gain, do it a - gain,
14 14
14 14
0 0 0 0
12 — 14 — 12 — X — 10 — X — 12 — 14
12 — 14 — 12 — X — 10 — X — 12 — 14
0
14 14
14 14
0 0 0 0

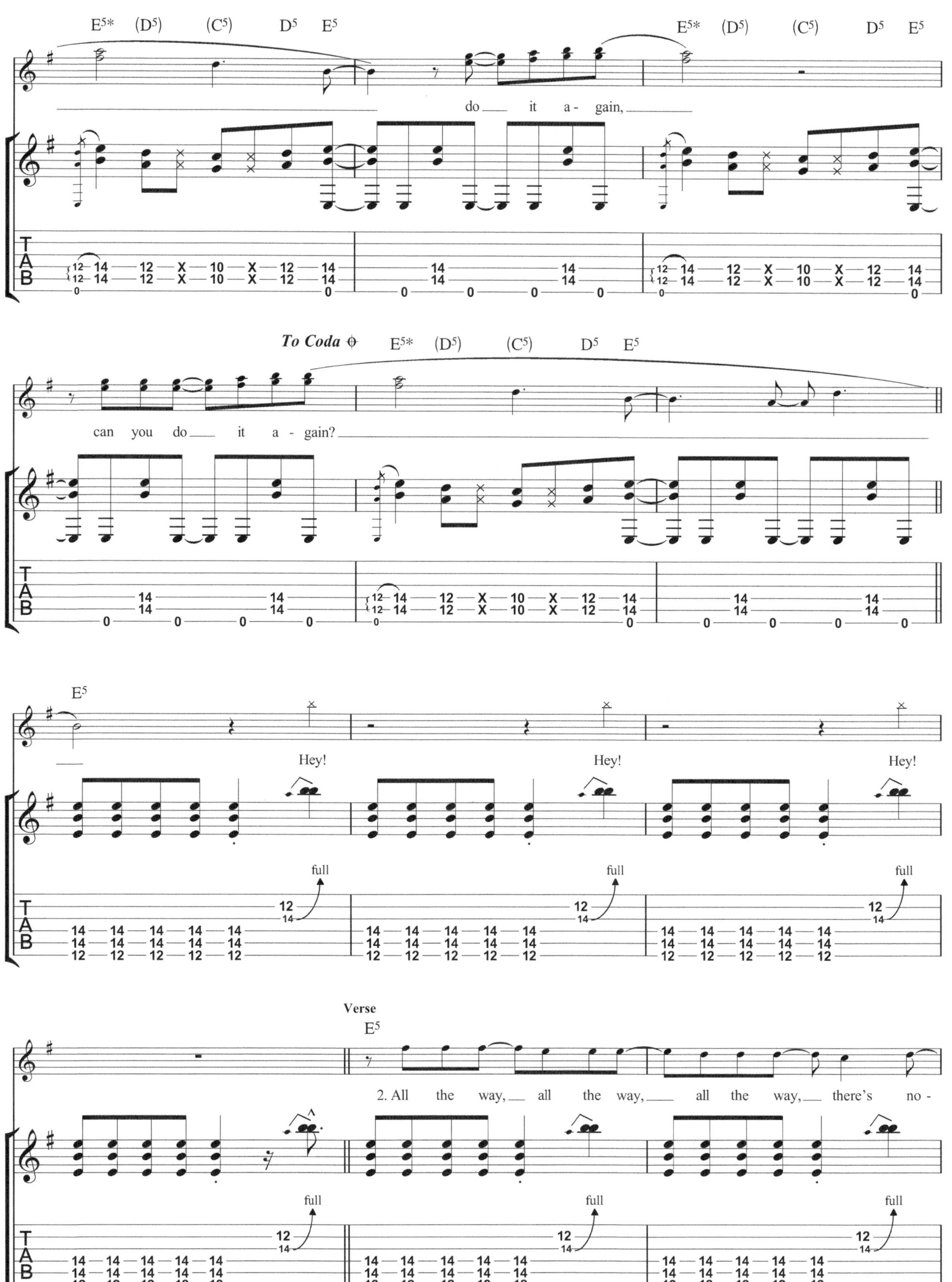

E5* (D5) (C5) D5 E5
do it a-gain,
To Coda
E5* (D5) (C5) D5 E5
can you do it a-gain?
E5
Hey!
Hey!
Hey!
full
full
full
Verse
E5
2. All the way, all the way, all the way, there's no-
full
full
full

- where left we can meet. I'm in - to what you do
but I leave you no - where.
You and me, fit so tight,
Hey! Hey! Hey!
all we need
Hey! Hey!
full
12
14
14 14 14 14 14
14 14 14 14 14
12 12 12 12 12

is one more time.
Hey!
full
full
full full
Coda
E5* (D5) (C5) D5 E5
do it a - gain,
E5* (D5) (C5) D5 E5
E5* (D5) (C5) D5 E5
do it a - gain,
can you do it a - gain?
E5* (D5) (C5) D5 E5

Bridge
C5* A5 G5 E5** C5* A5
On-ly get to live one life,___ won't pre-tend you're

G5 E5** C5* A5 G5 E5**
on-ly___ mine.___ Where will you go,___ where will you find___ the way?

C5* A5 G5 E5** Chorus C5* A5
So do it a-gain,___

G5 E5** G5 E5** E5 C5* A5 G5 E5** G5 E5** E5
do___ it a-gain,___ do___ it a-gain.__

C5*
A5
G5 E5** G5 E5**
E5
Do____ it a - gain,____
C5*
D5*
E5** E5
do____ it a - gain,____
C5*
D5*
E5** E5
do____ it a - gain.
C5*
D5*
E5** E5
full

GOD IS IN THE RADIO

Words & Music by Josh Homme, Nick Oliveri & Mark Lanegan

I know that God is in the ra - di - o, ch - ch - ch - check in the sta -
- tion. I'm glad I caught it from me to you,
just a call in the me - di - um. I know you hear it, I
hear it too, it's ev - 'ry - where that I go. You come
Fill 1.

Chorus
A5* G5 A5* F5
back an- oth- er day and do no wrong. You come
Gtr. 1
cont. sim.
Gtr. 2 tacet
A5 G5 C5/G A5 F5
back an- oth- er day. and do no wrong. You come
A5* G5 A5* F5
back an- oth- er day and do no wrong.
N.C.
1st open
(A5)
1st open
cont. sim.

Verse
A5
2. They say the de - vil is pa - ra - noid,   al - ways sign - in' the co -
Gtr. 3
(elec)
8va
Gtr. 1+2 w/Fig. 1 (x8)
Gtr. 3 w/dist.
T A B
17   17   17
15 - 17   15 - 17
14   14
17   15
15 - 16 - 17
15   14
17   17   17
15 - 17   15 - 17
14   14
- ver.   But God is leak - in' through the ste - re - o,
(8)
17   15
15 - 16 - 17
15   14
17   17   17
15 - 17   15 - 17
14   14
17   15
15 - 16 - 17
15   14
be - tween the sta - tion to stat - tion.   You be - lieve it,   I
(8)
17   17   17
15 - 17   15 - 17
14   14
17   15
15 - 16 - 17
15   14
17   17   17
15 - 17   15 - 17
14   14
know   you   do,   you won't ad - mit it or   say   so.
(8)
17   15
15 - 16 - 17
15   14
17   17   17
15 - 17   15 - 17
14   14
17   15
15 - 16 - 17
15   14

I know that God is in the ra-di-o just re-peat-ing a slo-
(8)
3 3 3 3 3
Chorus
A5* G5 A5*
-gan. You come back an-oth-er day
(8)
3
Gtr. 1 plays Fill 1.
Gtrs. 2+3 tacet
F5
and do no wrong. You come back an-oth-er day.
A5 G5 C5/G A5
F5
and do no wrong. You come
cont. sim.

88

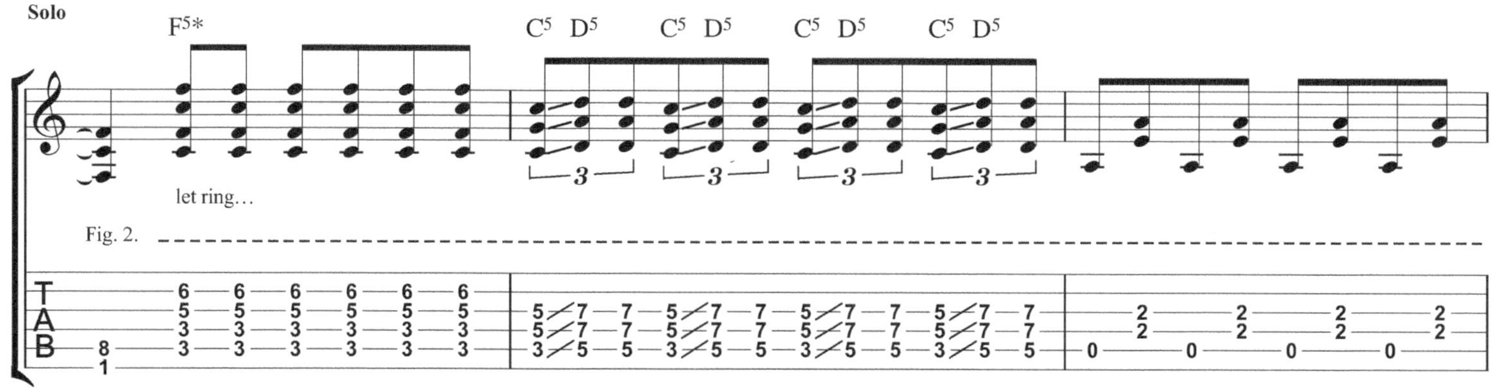

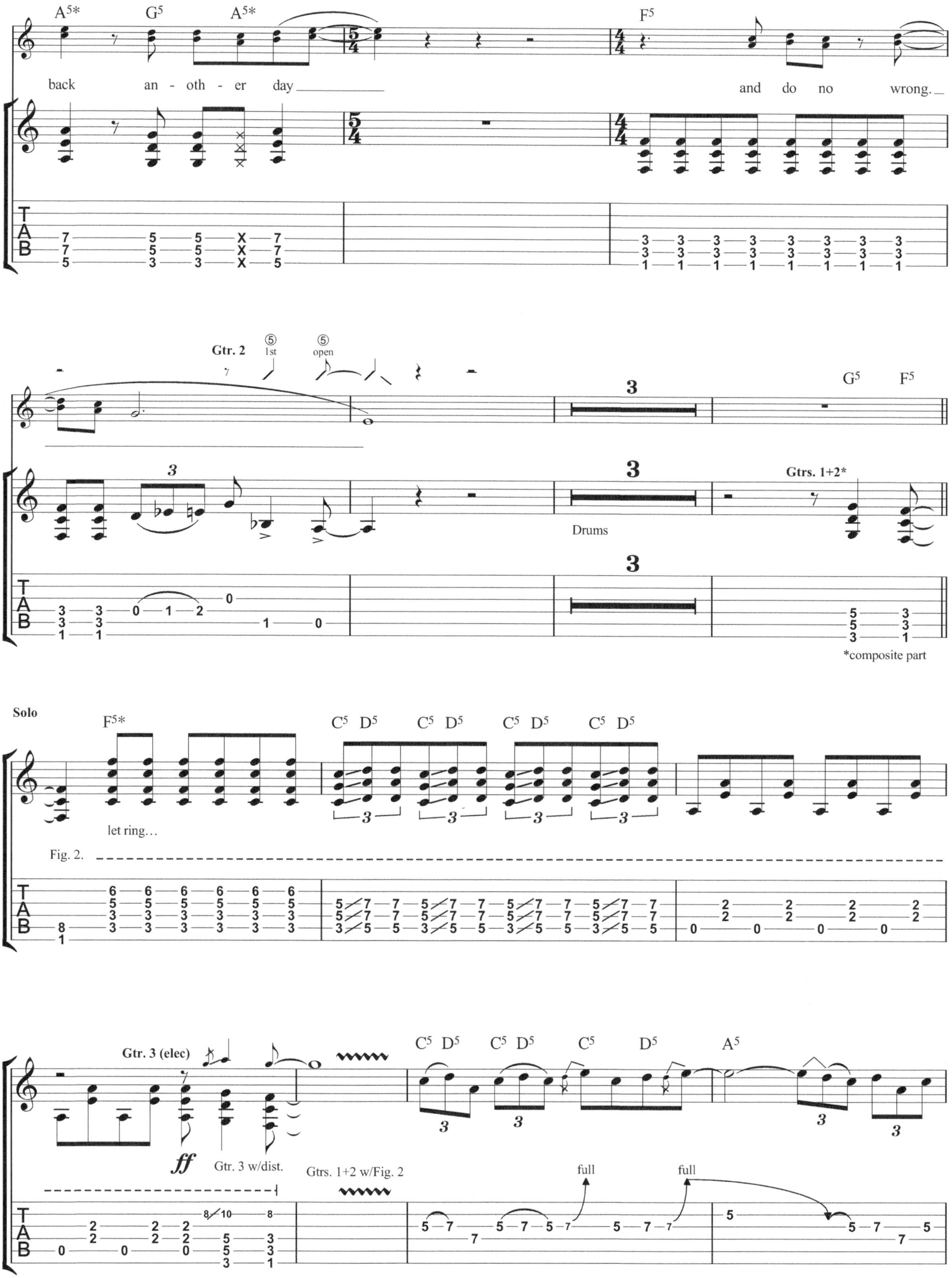

A5*   G5   A5*   F5
back   an - oth - er   day   and   do   no   wrong.
Gtr. 2
⑤ 1st   ⑤ open   G5   F5
Gtrs. 1+2*
Drums
*composite part
Solo
F5*   C5 D5   C5 D5   C5 D5   C5 D5   G5   F5
let ring...
Fig. 2.

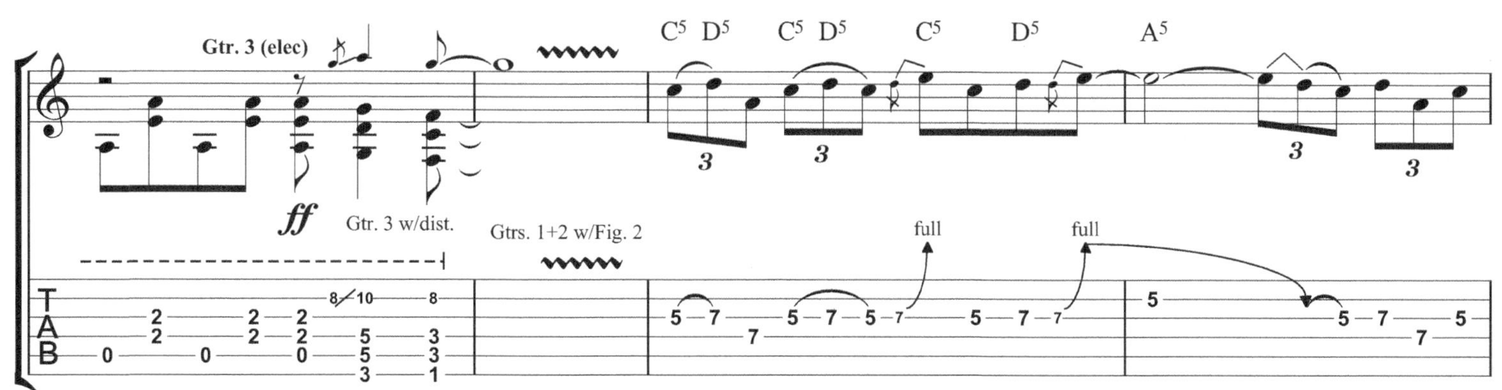

Gtr. 3 (elec)   C5 D5   C5 D5   C5   D5   A5
ff   Gtr. 3 w/dist.   Gtrs. 1+2 w/Fig. 2   full   full

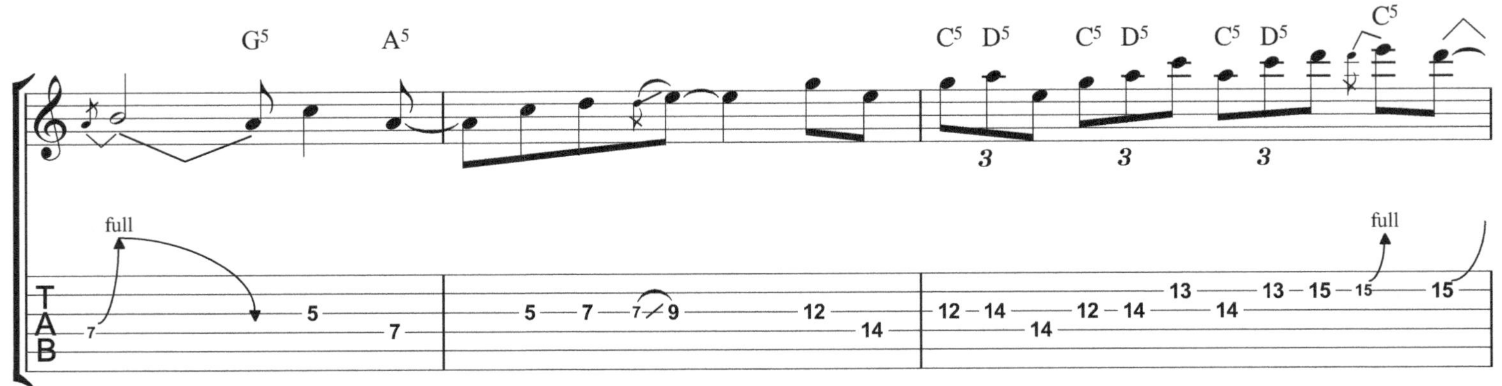

G5   A5   C5 D5   C5 D5   C5 D5   C5
full
full

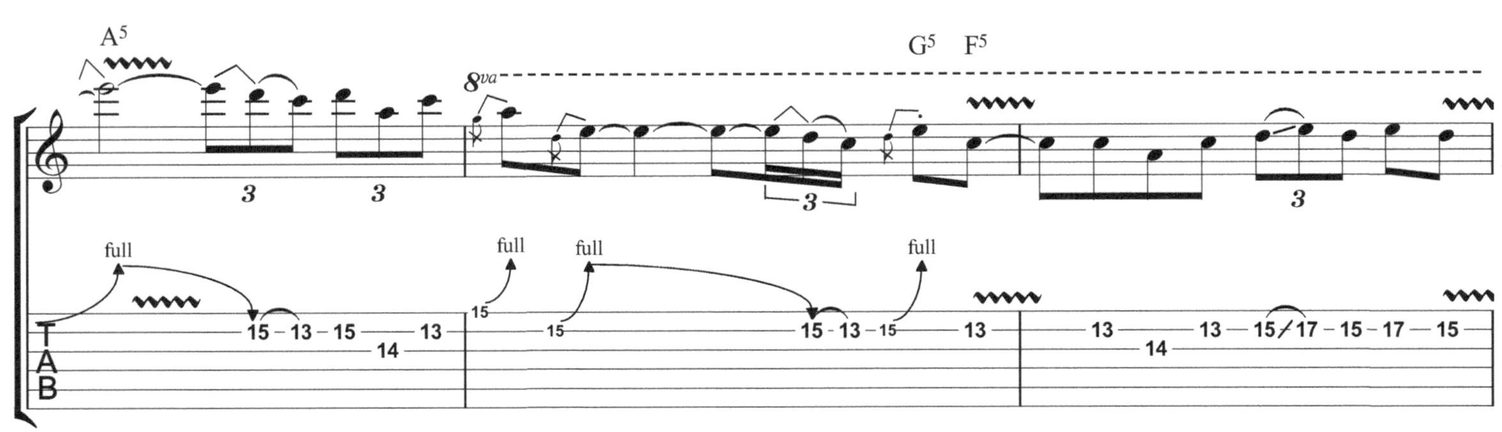

A5   G5 F5
8va
full
full   full   full

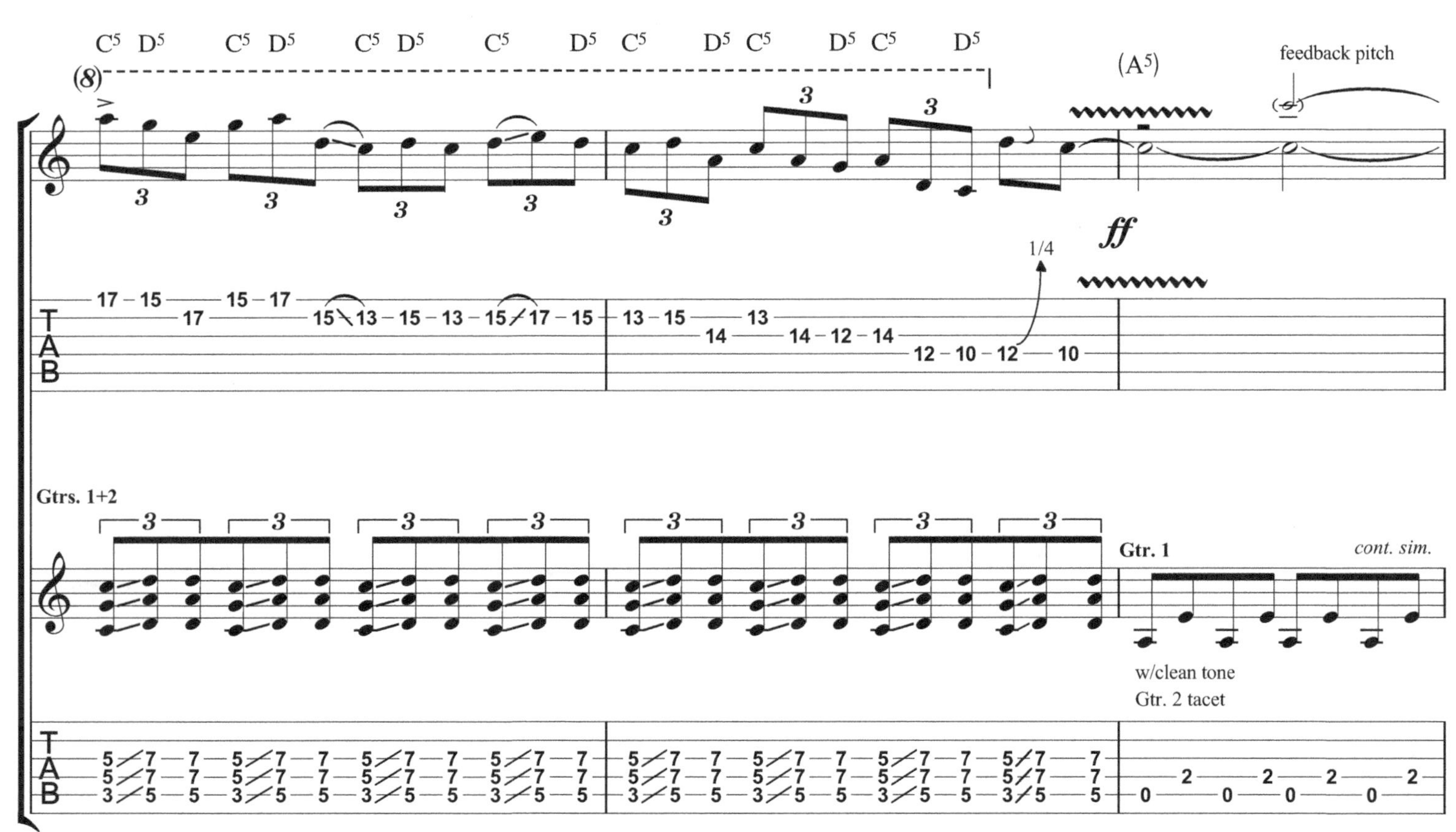

C5 D5   C5 D5   C5 D5   C5   D5 C5   D5 C5   D5 C5   D5
(8)
(A5)
feedback pitch
1/4
ff
Gtrs. 1+2
Gtr. 1
cont. sim.
w/clean tone
Gtr. 2 tacet

mf
6 — 5
6 — 5
3 — 5

Play 8 times
w/backward vocal effects
Gtrs. 1+3*
mp
p
Gtr. 2 w/ad libs.   Gradually decrease volume to silence over repeats
Fig. 3
0 — 1 — 2   0
1   0
2   2   2   2   2   2
0   0   0   0   0 — 1 — 0
*composite part

Outro

w/ad lib. vocals & effects
Gtr. 2
tr
p   w/clean tone
Gtr. 1 w/Fig. 3 & ad libs.
tr
(8) (10) 8   10 — 8   11 — 12 — 11 — 9   11 — 12 — 11
3   3   12

mp
full
3   3
5
tr
tr
4 — 5 — 4 — 2   2   4 — 5 — 4 — 2 — 4   5 7   7   5   (4) (5) 4   5 7

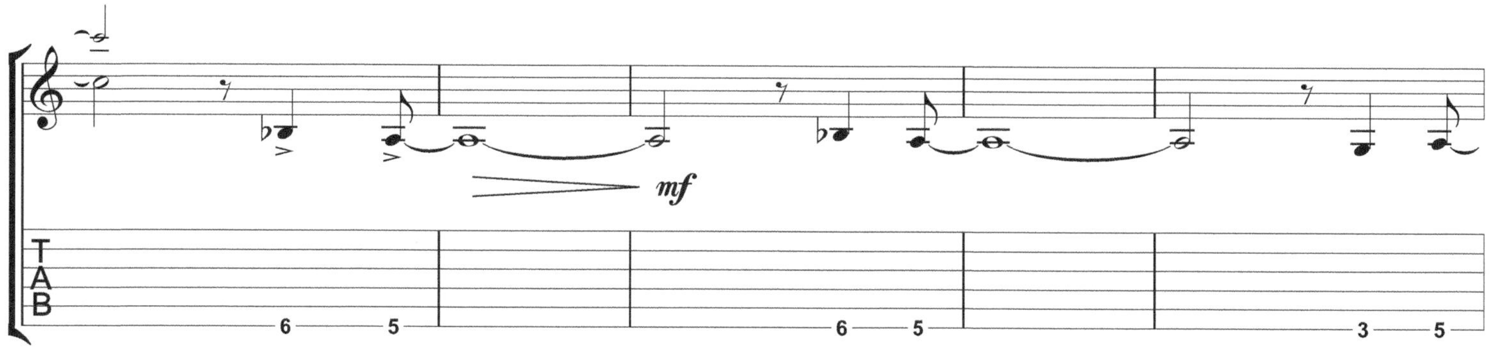

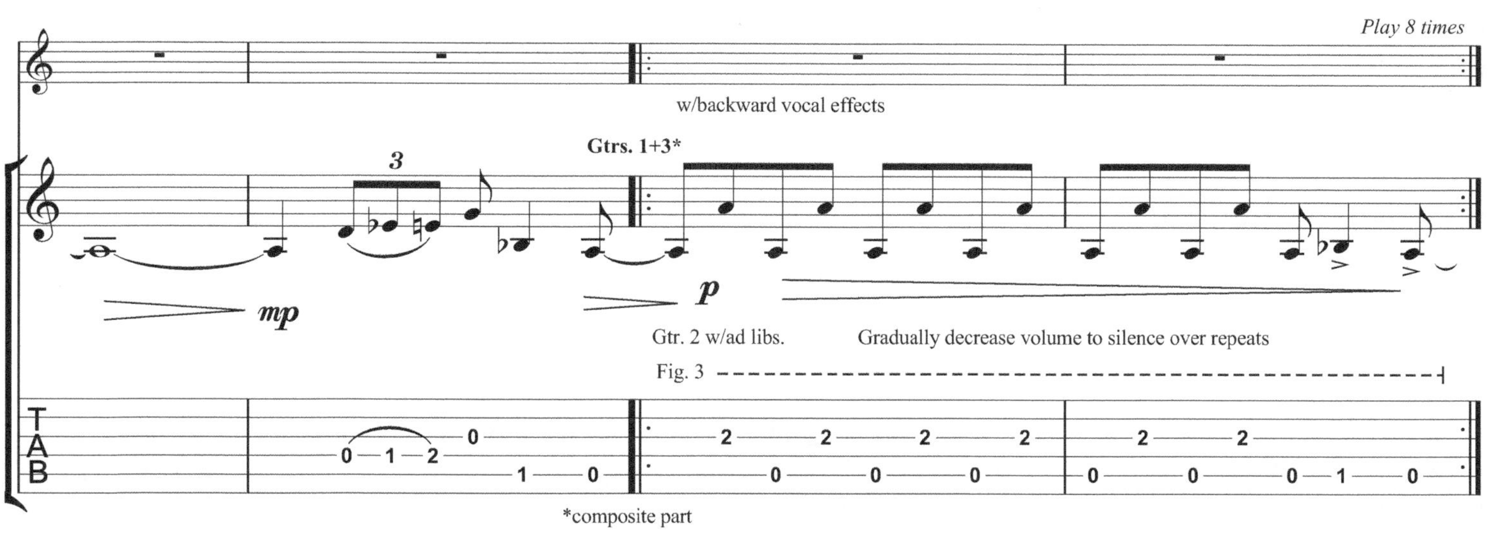

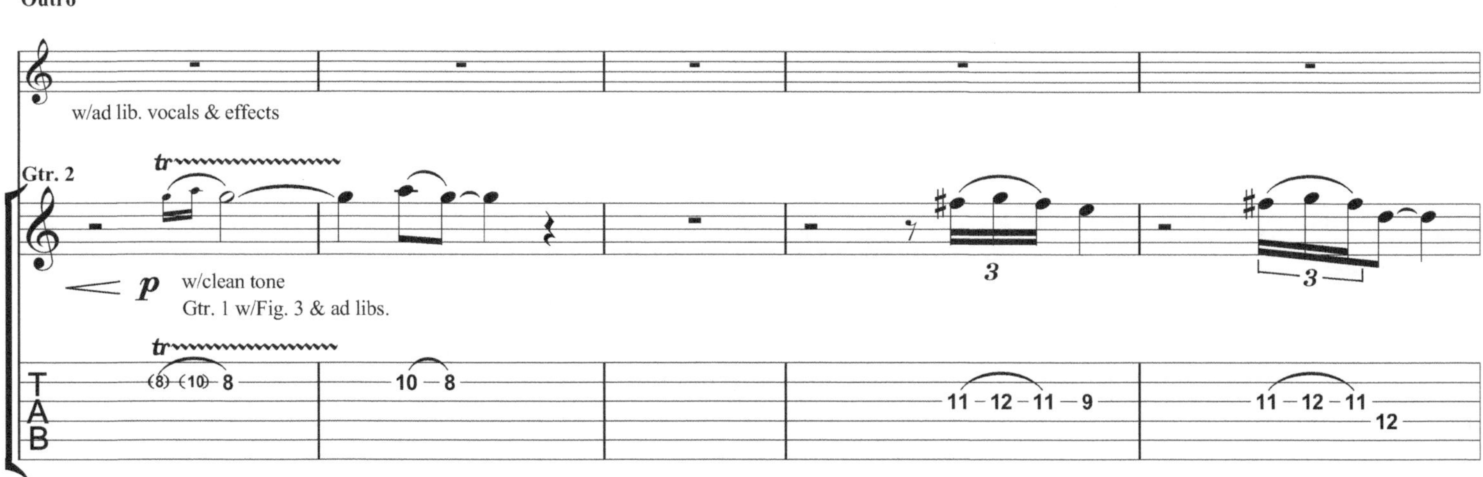

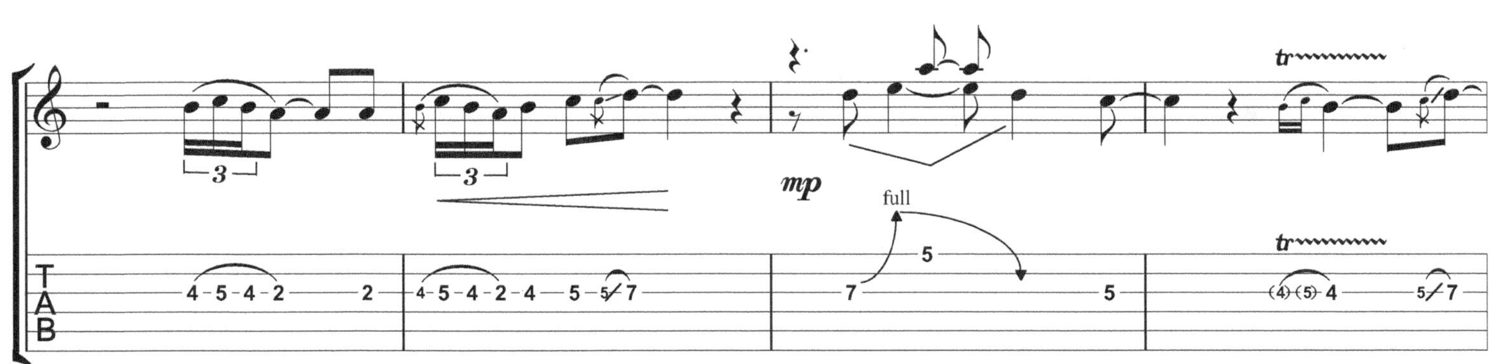

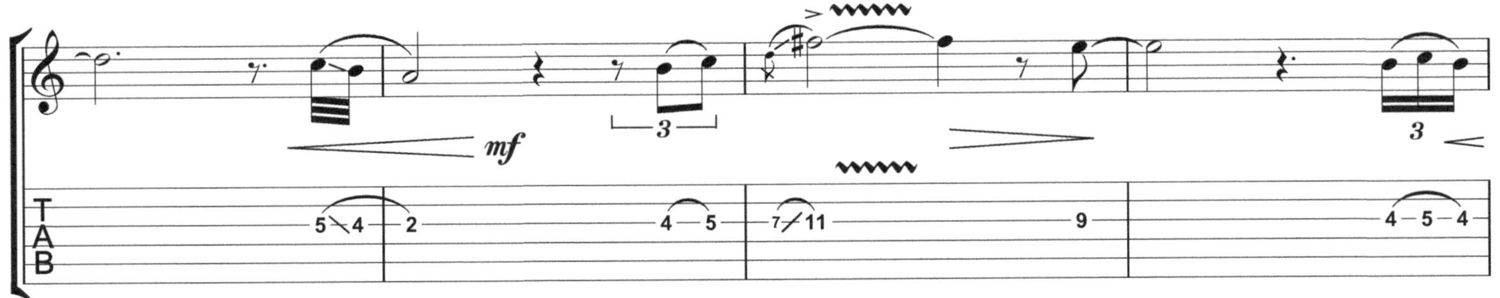

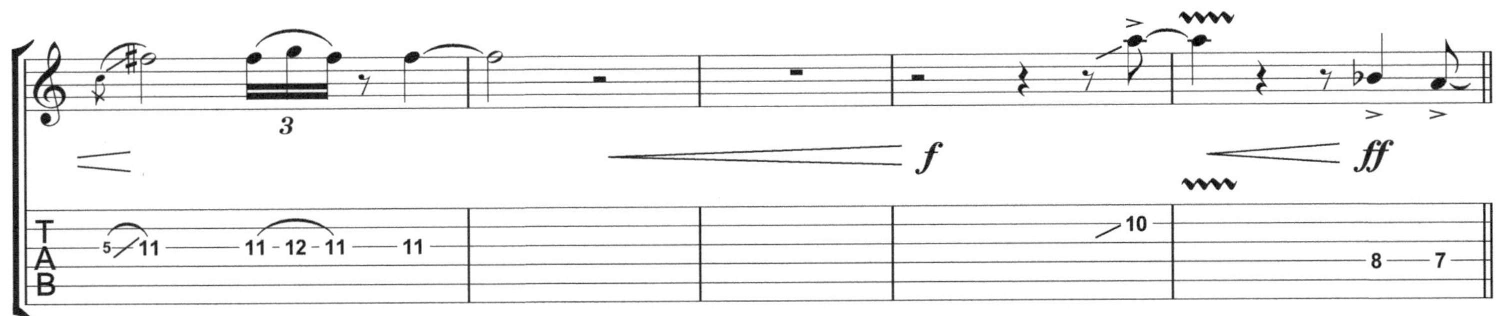

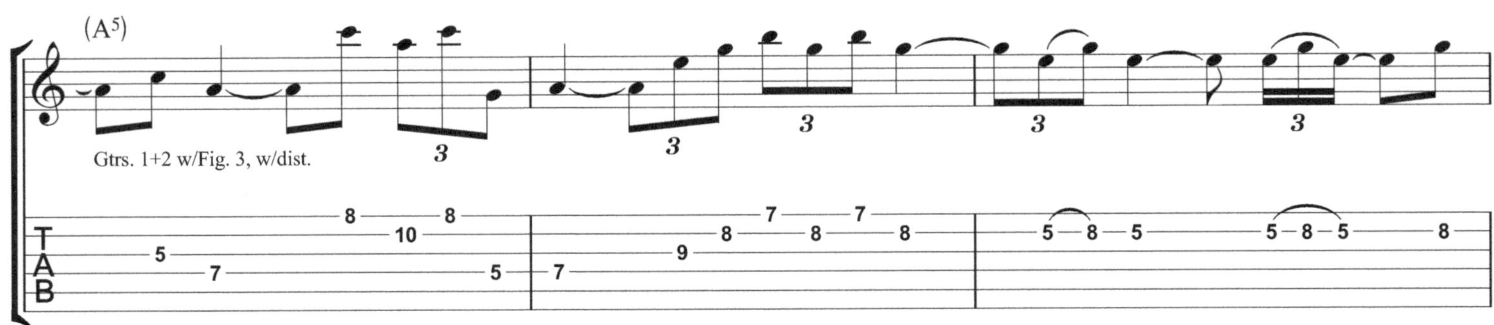
(A5)
Gtrs. 1+2 w/Fig. 3, w/dist.

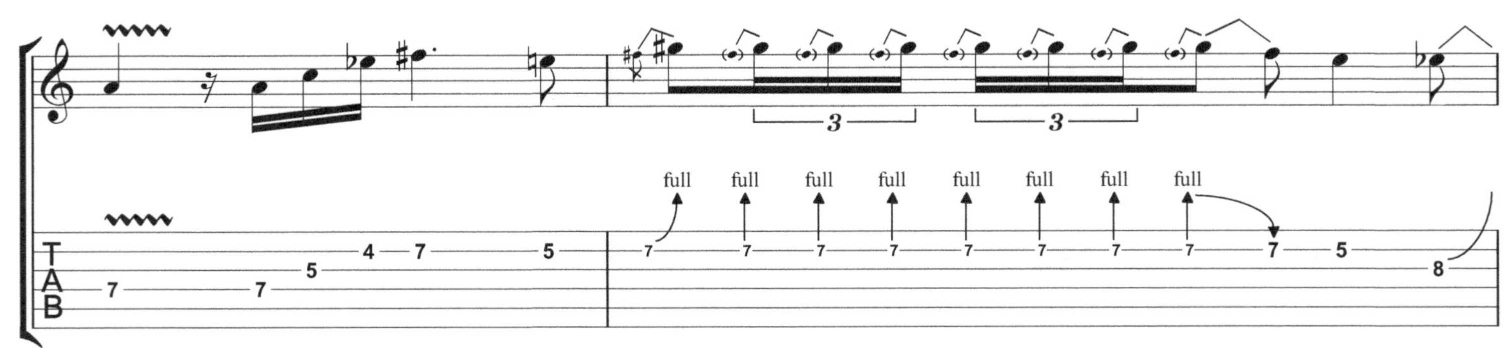

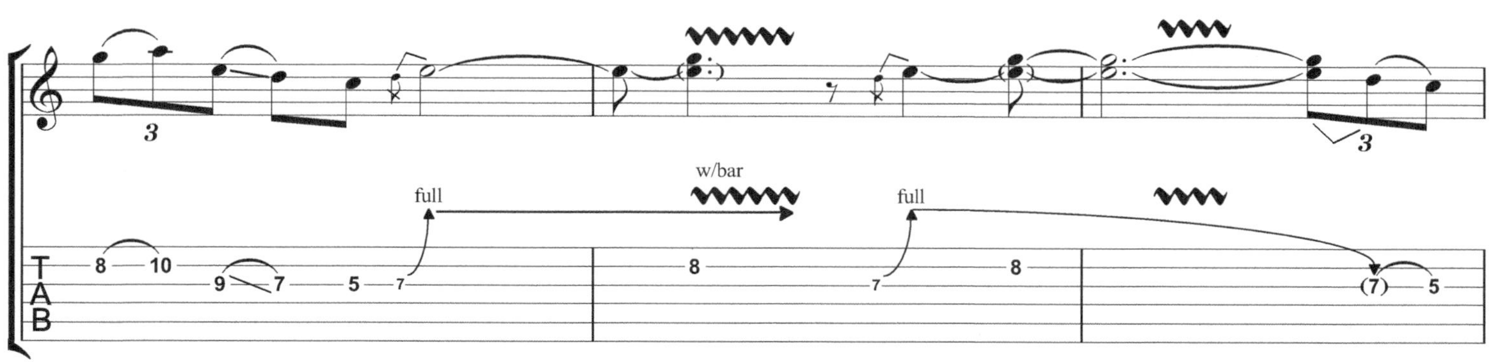
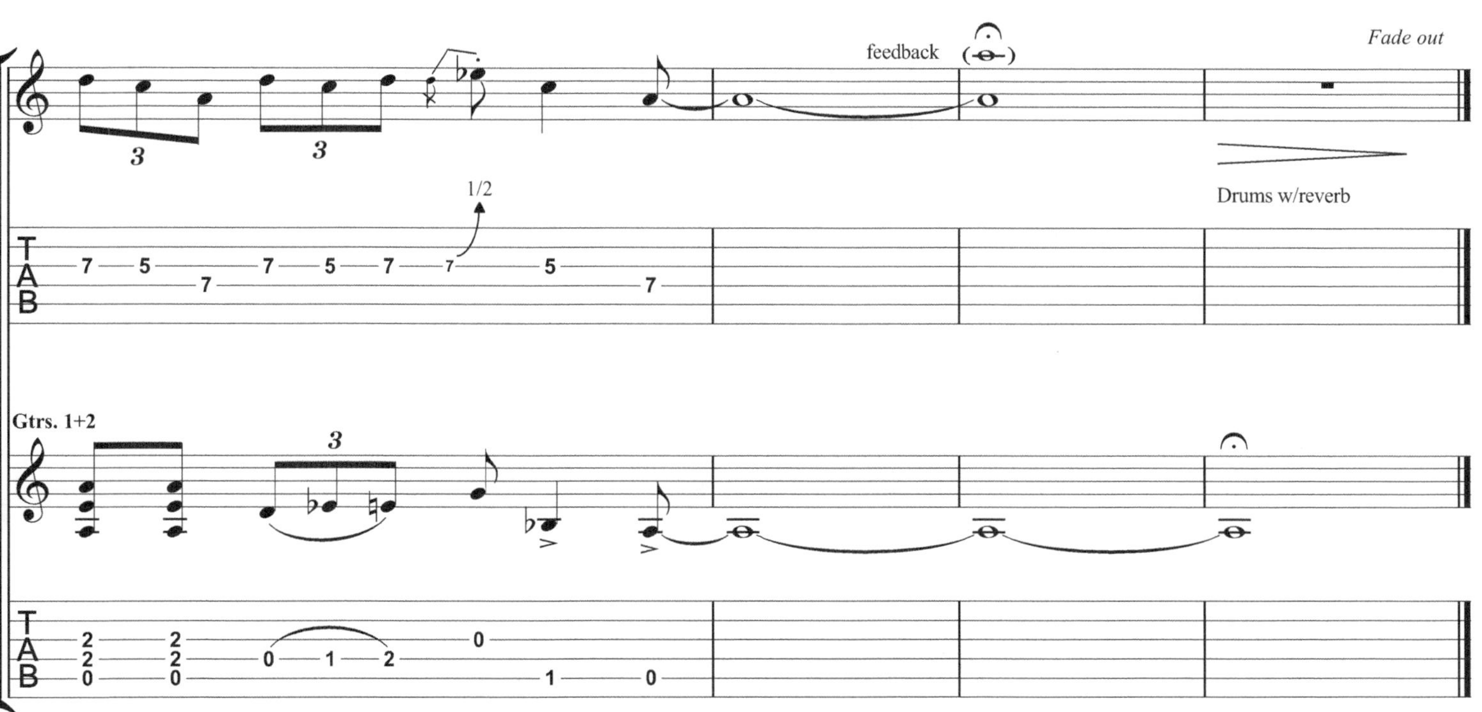

HANGIN' TREE

Words & Music by Josh Homme, Nick Oliveri, Alain Johannes & Mark Lanegan

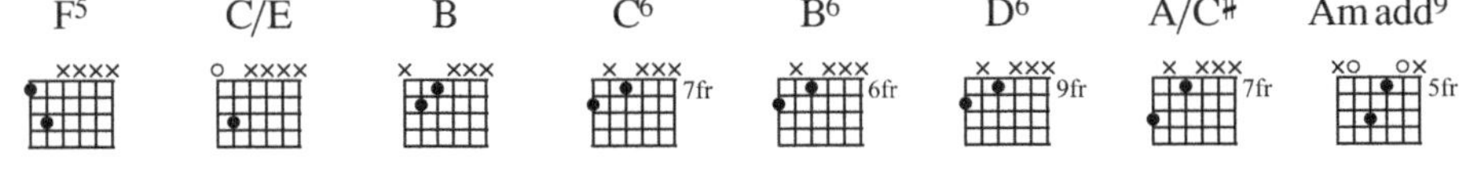

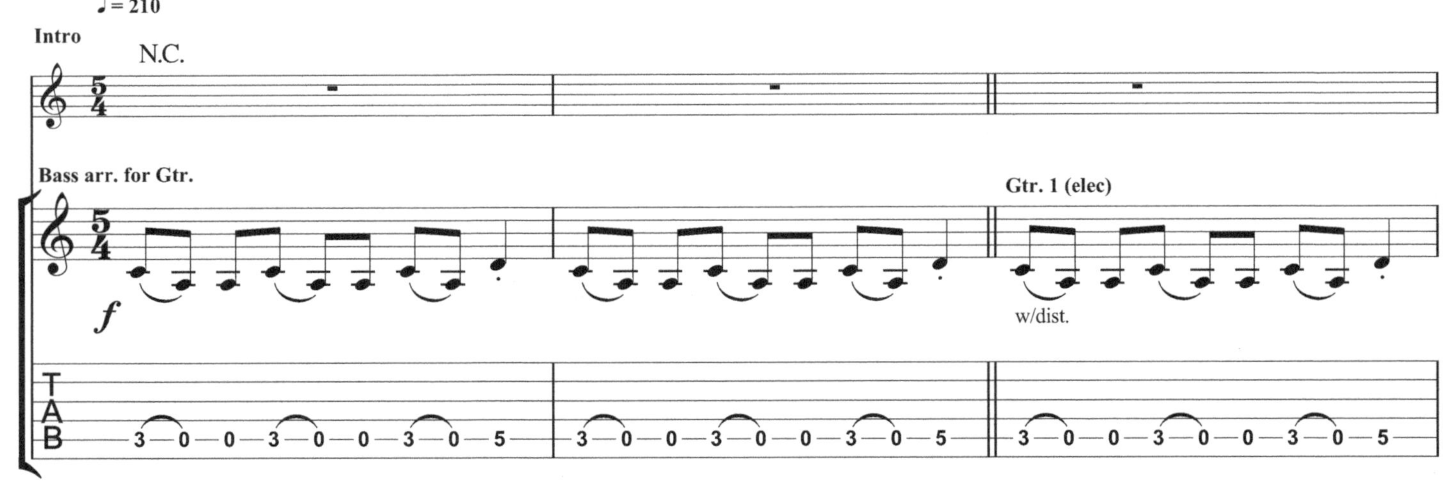

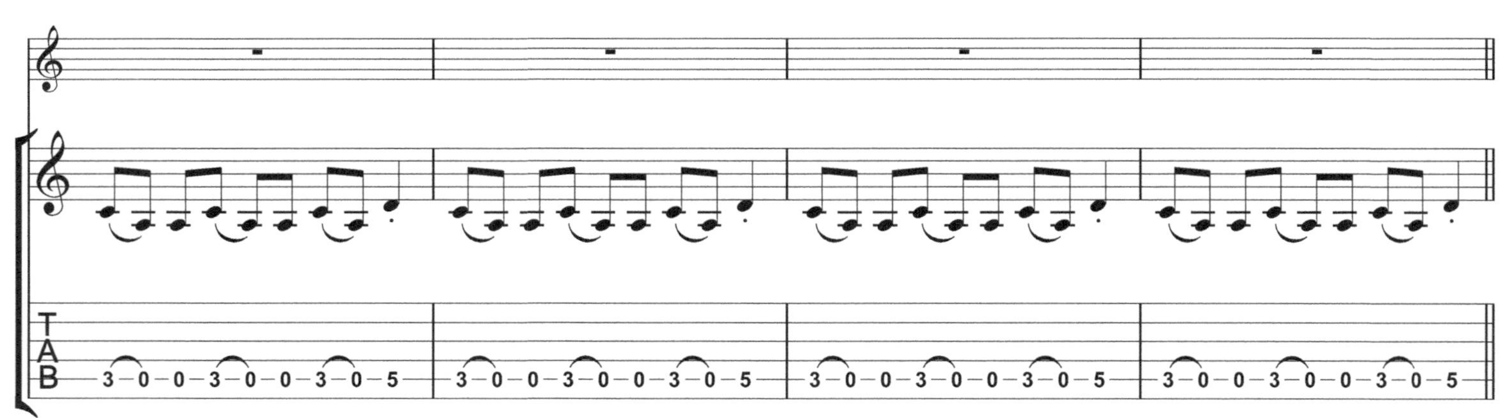

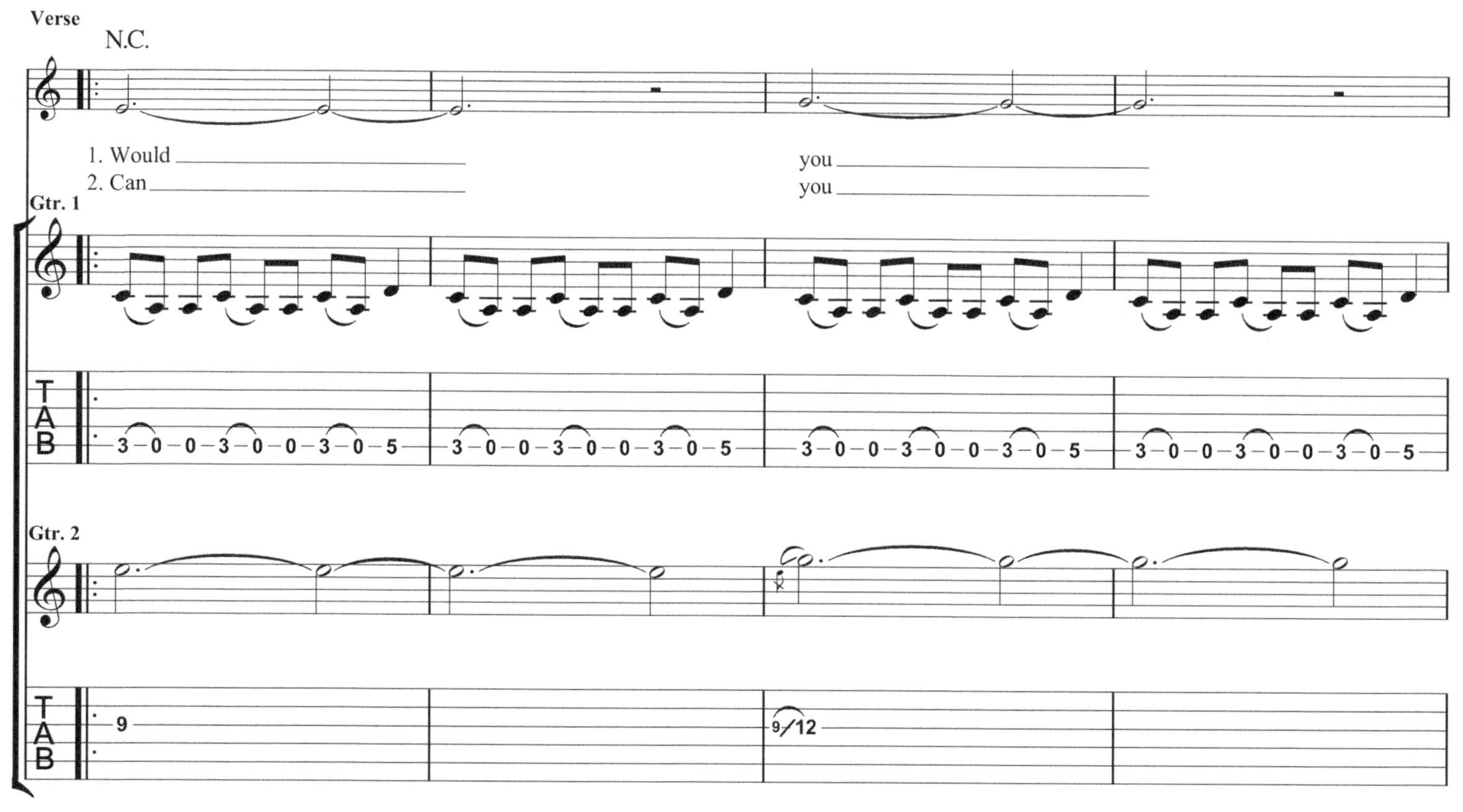

Verse
N.C.
1. Would you
2. Can you
Gtr. 1
T A B
3-0-0-3-0-0-3-0-5
3-0-0-3-0-0-3-0-5
3-0-0-3-0-0-3-0-5
3-0-0-3-0-0-3-0-5
Gtr. 2
T A B
9
9/12

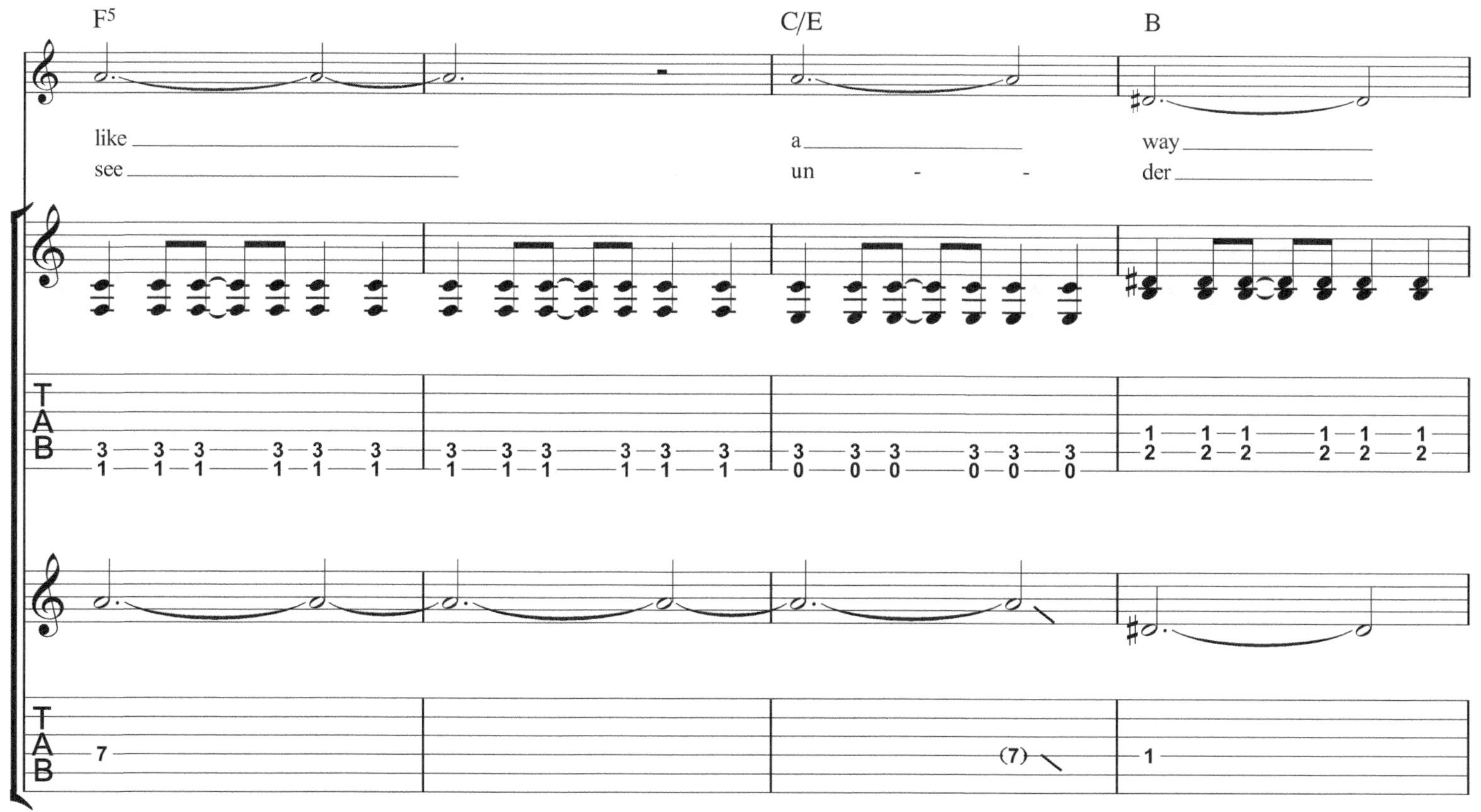

F5
C/E
B
like
see
a
un - - der
way
T A B
3-3-3 3-3 3
1-1-1 1-1-1
3-3-3 3-3 3
1-1-1 1-1-1
3-3-3 3-3 3
0-0-0 0-0-0
1-1-1 1-1-1
2-2-2 2-2-2
T A B
7
(7)
1

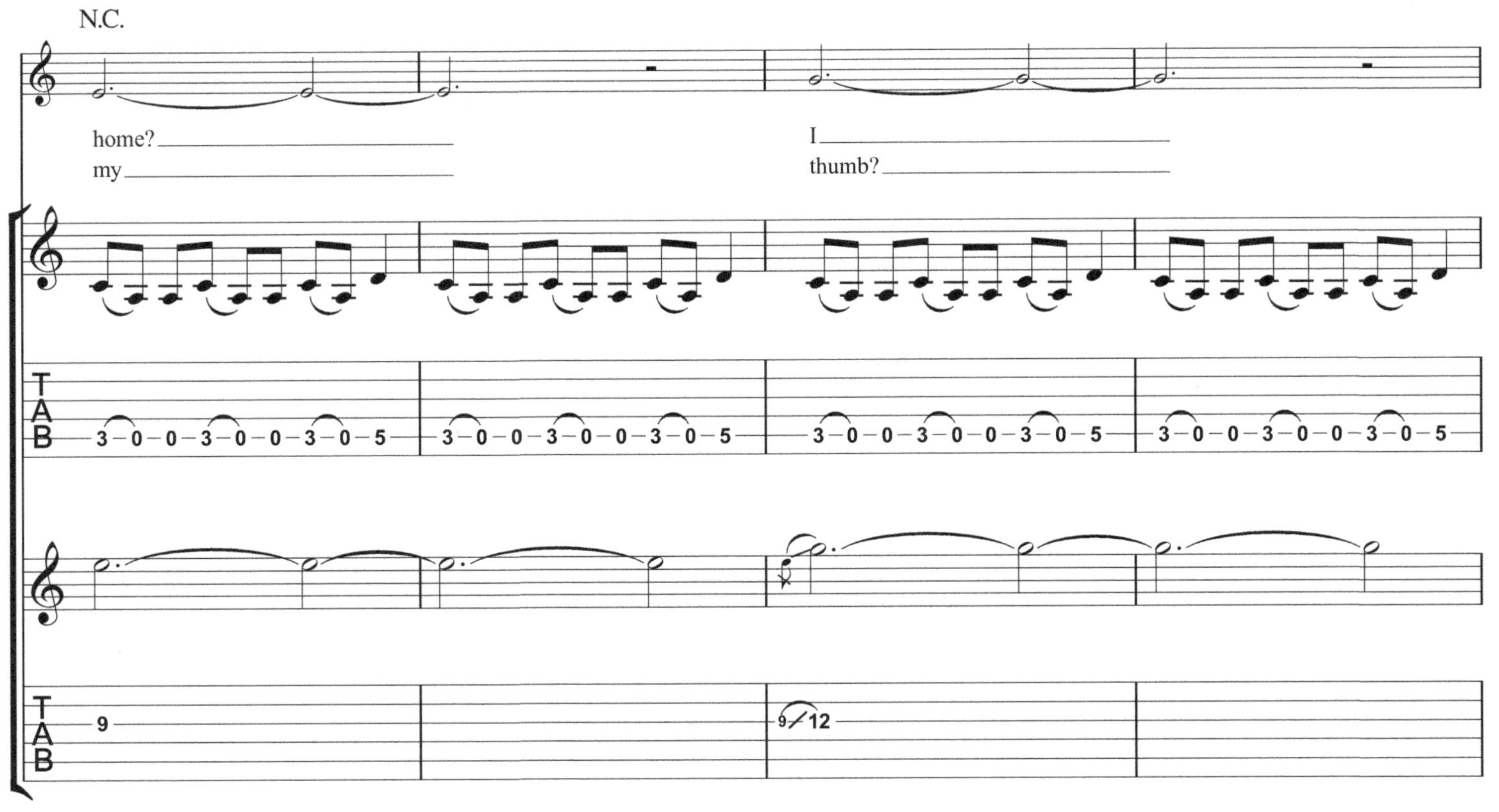

N.C.
home?
my
I
thumb?
9
9/12
3-0-0-3-0-0-3-0-5
3-0-0-3-0-0-3-0-5
3-0-0-3-0-0-3-0-5
3-0-0-3-0-0-3-0-5

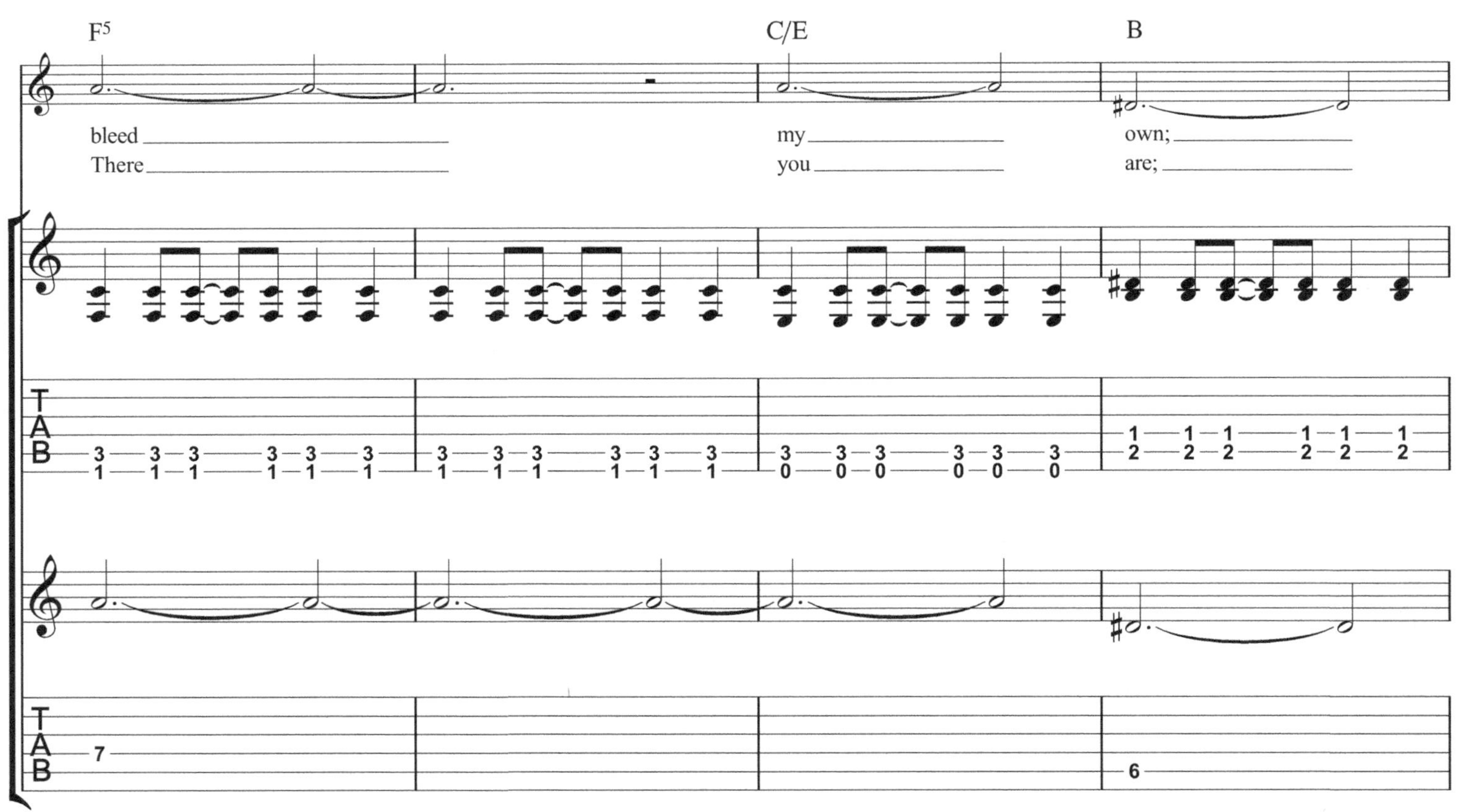

F5
C/E
B
bleed
There
my
you
own;
are;
3-3-3-3-3-3
1-1-1-1-1-1
3-3-3-3-3-3
1-1-1-1-1-1
3-3-3-3-3-3
0-0-0-0-0-0
1-1-1-1-1-1
2-2-2-2-2-2
7
6

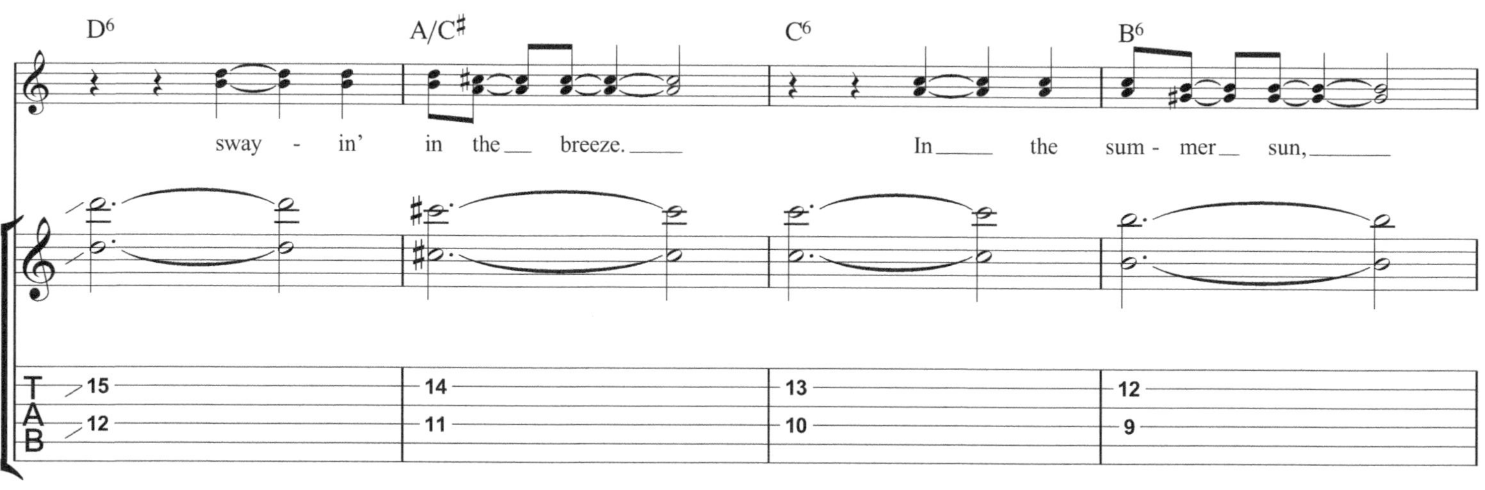

Am add9
Chorus
Gtr. 1
C6
B6
cont. sim.
Round the hang - in' tree,
Gtrs. 2+3 (elec)
Gtr. 3 w/dist.
Gtr. 1 cont. in slashes
D6
A/C#
C6
B6
sway - in' in the breeze. In the sum - mer sun,

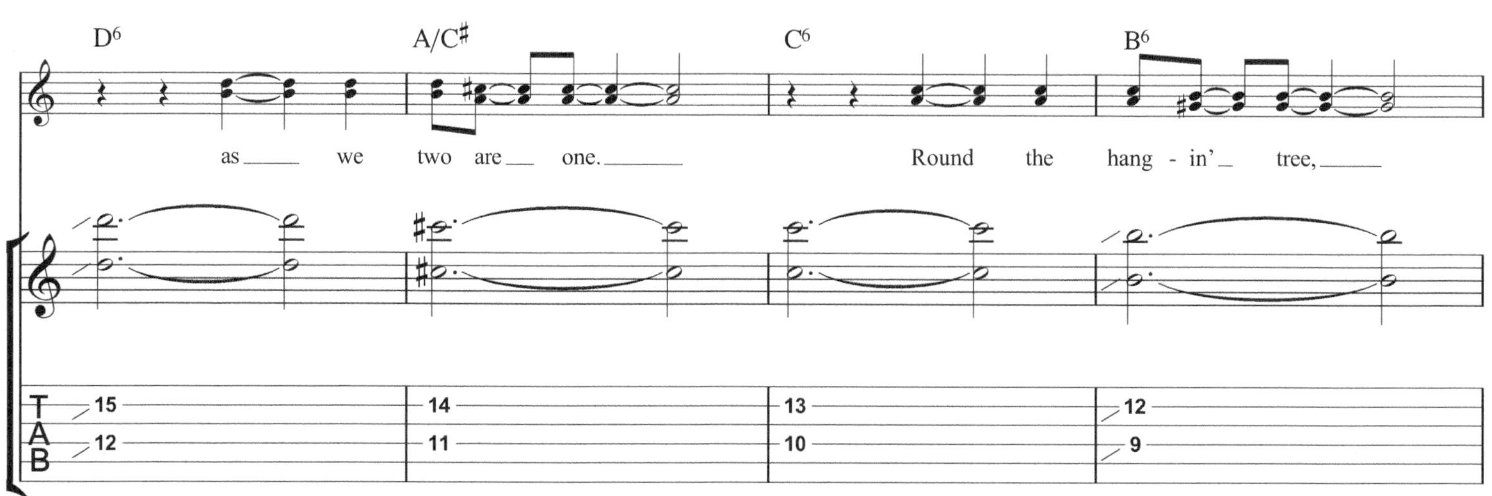

D6
A/C#
C6
B6
as we two are one. Round the hang - in' tree,

D6
A/C#
C6
B6
sway - in' in the breeze.
In the sum - mer sun,
TAB

D6
A/C#
C6
as we two are one.
Sway
TAB

B6
To Coda
N.C.
- ing.
Gtr. 1
Gtr. 3 tacet
Gtr. 2 w/ad lib. pitch shift fx
TAB

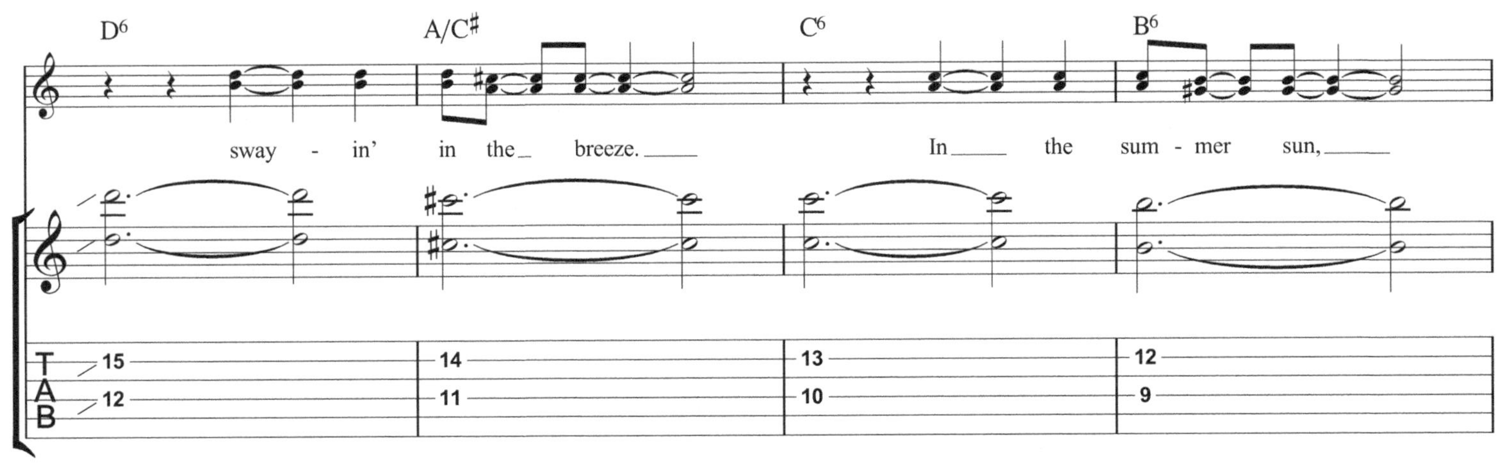

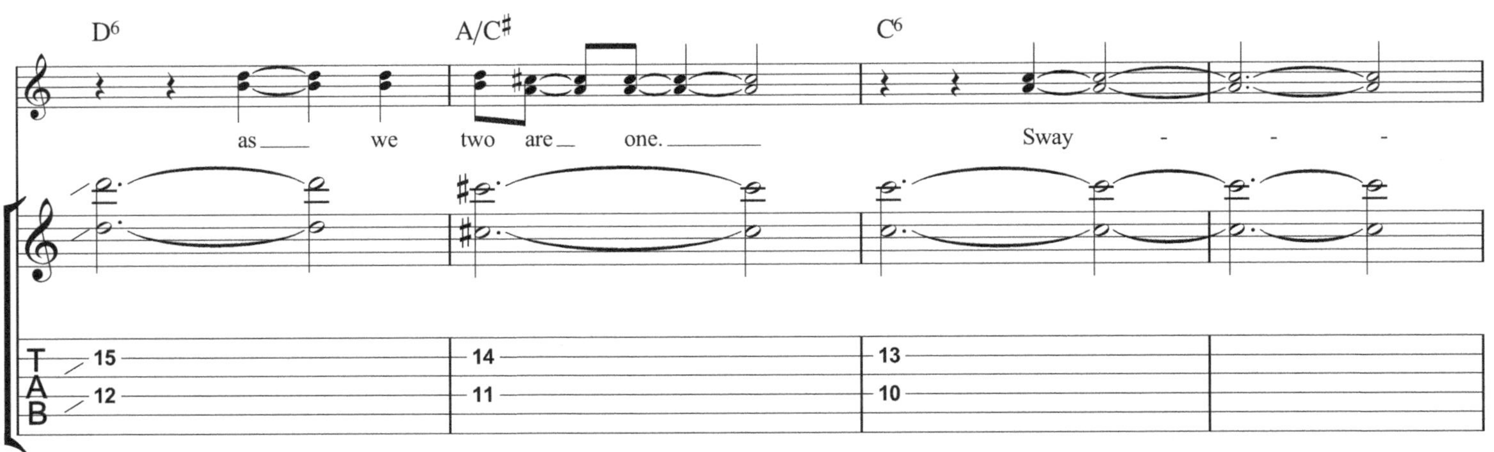

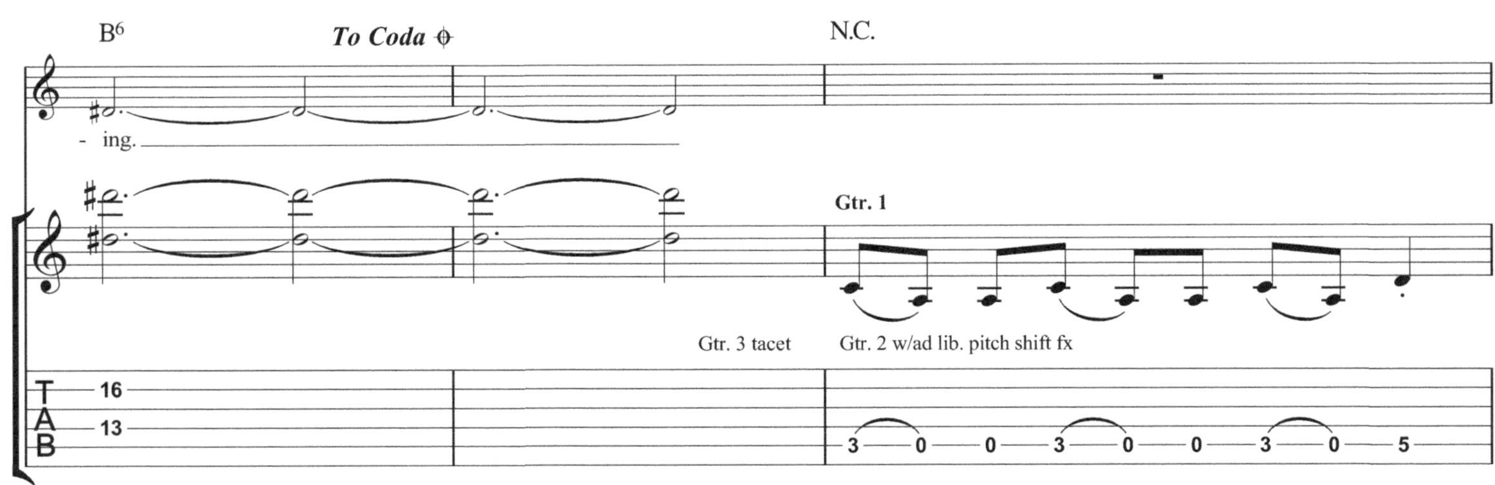

98

Solo
N.C.
Gtr. 1
T
A
B
Gtr. 2
T
A
B
99

Am add9
D.S. al Coda
Coda
B6
Gtr. 1
N.C.
Gtr. 2
Gtr. 1
100

ANOTHER LOVE SONG

Words & Music by Josh Homme & Nick Oliveri

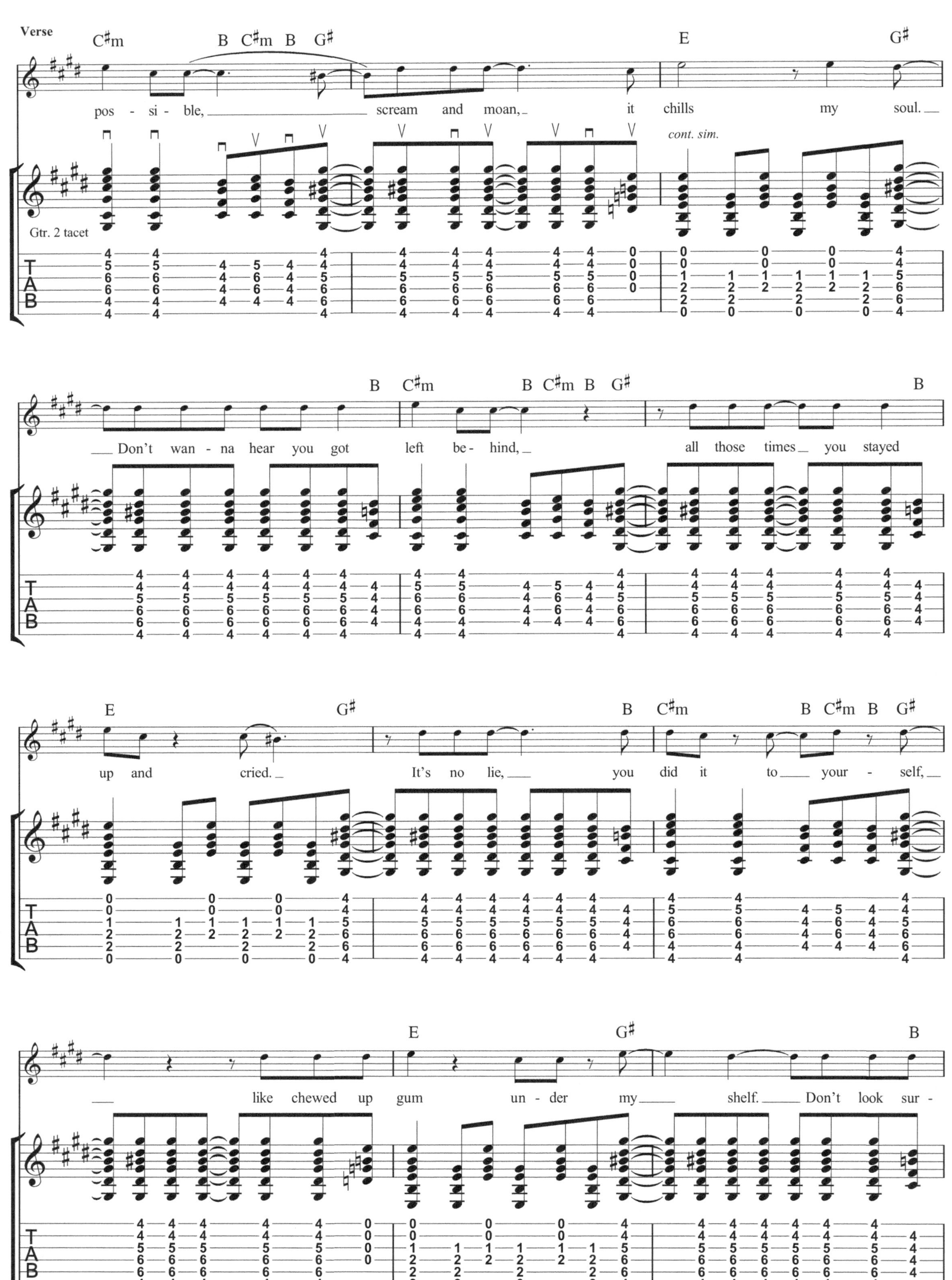

Verse
C#m   B C#m B G#   E   G#
pos - si - ble, _______ scream and moan, _ it chills my soul. _
Gtr. 2 tacet
cont. sim.

B C#m   B C#m B G#   B
_ Don't wan - na hear you got left be - hind, _ all those times _ you stayed

E   G#   B C#m   B C#m B G#
up and cried. _ It's no lie, _ you did it to _ your - self, _

E   G#   B
_ like chewed up gum un - der my _ shelf. _ Don't look sur -

C#m   B C#m B G#   Bm
prised, you must have known all a - long.
Gtr. 1 cont. in slashes

Chorus
C   D   C#m   B C#m B G#   B
cont. sim.
It's just an - oth - er love ___ song, ___ (a) - 'no - ther love __
Gtr. 2

C#m   B C#m B G#   B   C#m   B C#m B G#
song. __   2. It's ne - ver ea - sy,

B E   G#   B
it's not hard ___ when you've lost your mind. ___ With you it's

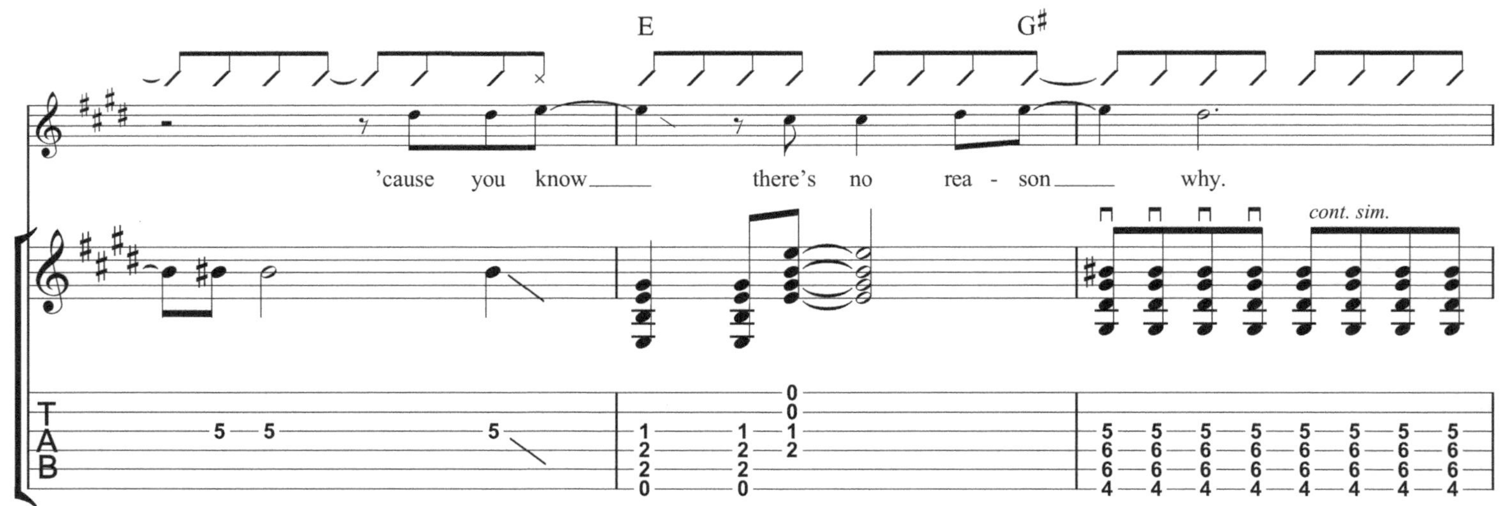

C#m   B C#m B G#   B C#m   B C#m B G#
slea - zy,   don't tell me your wor - ries. I'm sick,   I'll leave you   blind.

B   C#m   B C#m B G#
Now the time____ has   come,____   to leave this

E   G#   B   C#m   B C#m B G#
Gtr. 1
love   that's left you   dry.____   No need to work   this out   now,

E   G#
'cause you know______   there's no   rea - son______   why.
cont. sim.

Chorus
C#m   B C#m B G#
It's just an-oth-er love song,
B   C#m   B C#m B G#   B
(a)-no-ther love song,   (a)-no-ther love
cont.sim.
C#m   B C#m B G#   B   C#m   B C#m B G#
song,   it's just an-oth-er love song.
Solo
B   C#m   B C#m B G#   B
cont.sim.

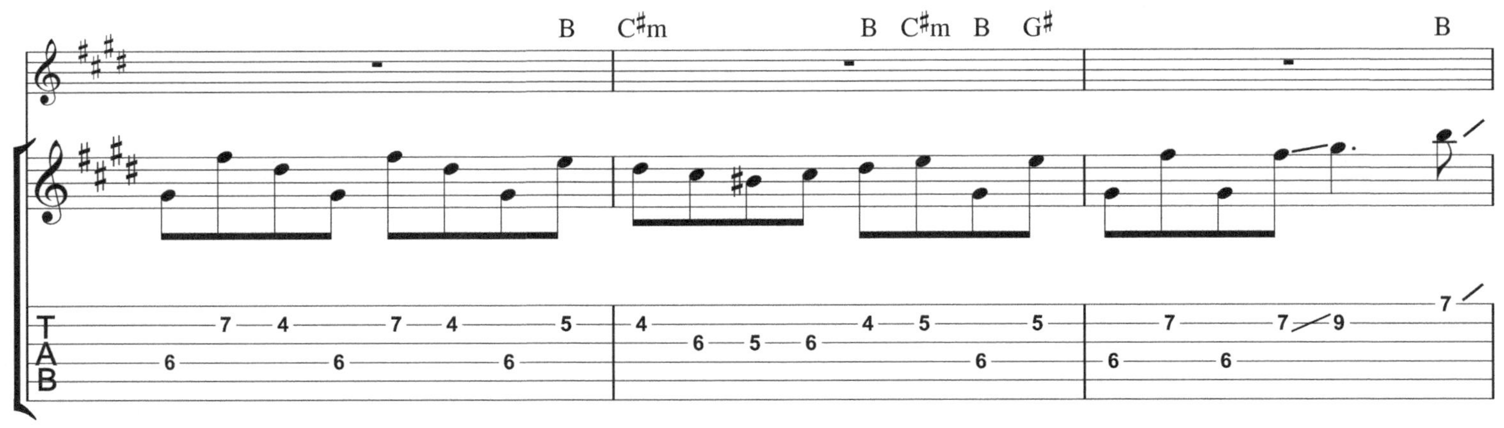
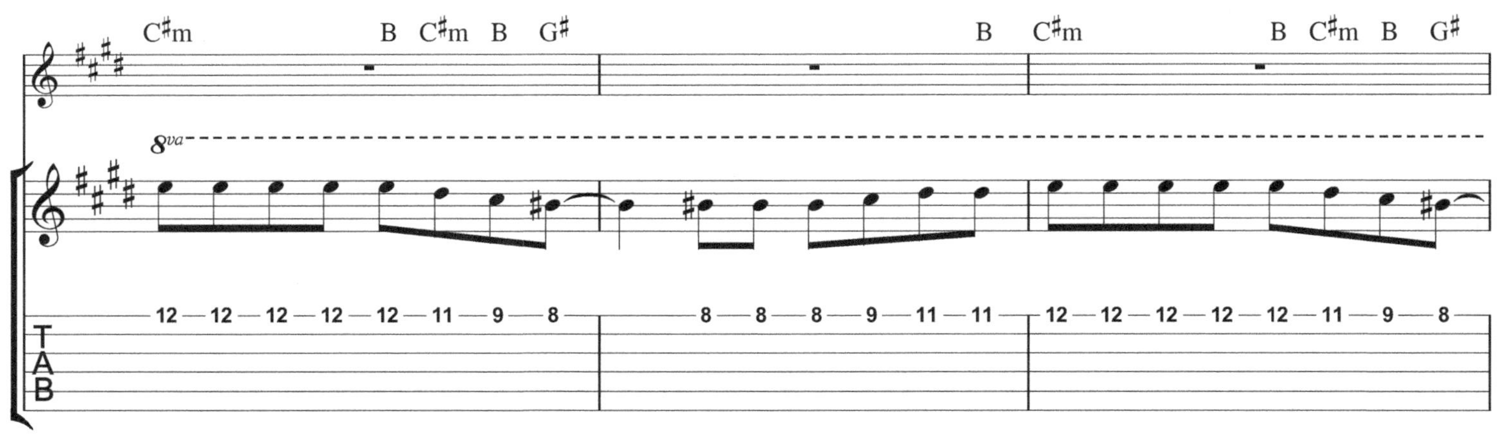
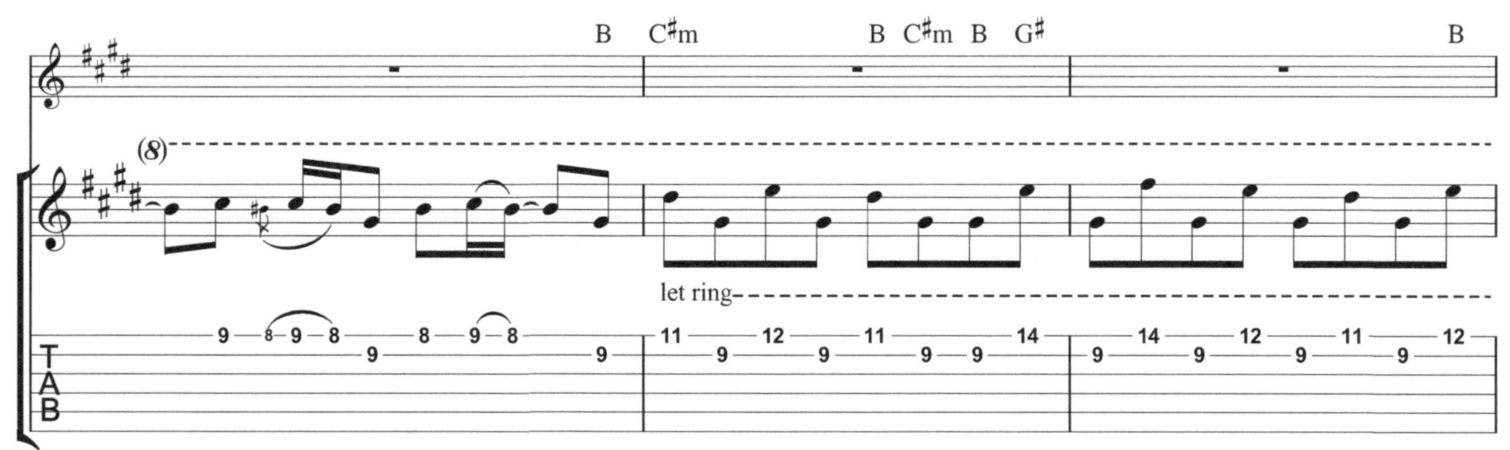

C#m   B C#m B G#   B   m
Bridge
C   D   C#m
I ne-ver told you it would last
B♭m   A   C#m
for e - ver, you can't hold
B♭m   A
this boy for long, dig it.
107

C#m
By the time you read my let-
B♭m
A
-ter,
C#m
ba - by, I'll be
B♭m
gone.
A
It's just an - oth - er love
Chorus
C#m
song,
B C#m B G#
(a) - 'no - ther love
B C#m
song.
B C#m B G#

B C#m   B C#m B G#   B
(a) -'no - ther love _____ song, _____ it's just an - oth - er love
C#m   B C#m B G#   B C#m   B C#m B G#
song.   It's just an - oth - er love _____ song, _____
B C#m   B C#m B G#   B
(a) -'no - ther love _____ song, _____ (a) -'no - ther love _
8va
C#m   B C#m B G#   B C#m   B G#
song,   it's just an - oth - er love song.
let ring...
(8)

A SONG FOR THE DEAF

Words & Music by Josh Homme, Nick Oliveri & Mark Lanegan

bo - dy _____ ech - oes in my head.
Bro - ken re - flec - tion _____ out - ta luck, _____ no -
bo - dy, _____ e - ver need - ed it. I
Chorus
A add9   B add11   G6
got   what was, _____   I
Gtrs. 1+2*
cont. sim.
*composite part

A add9
B add11
G6
8vb
want   to take   what's   left.
Rea - dy now!
N.C.
Gtr. 2
Gtr. 1
N.C.
Ah.
Gtr. 1
Gtr. 2

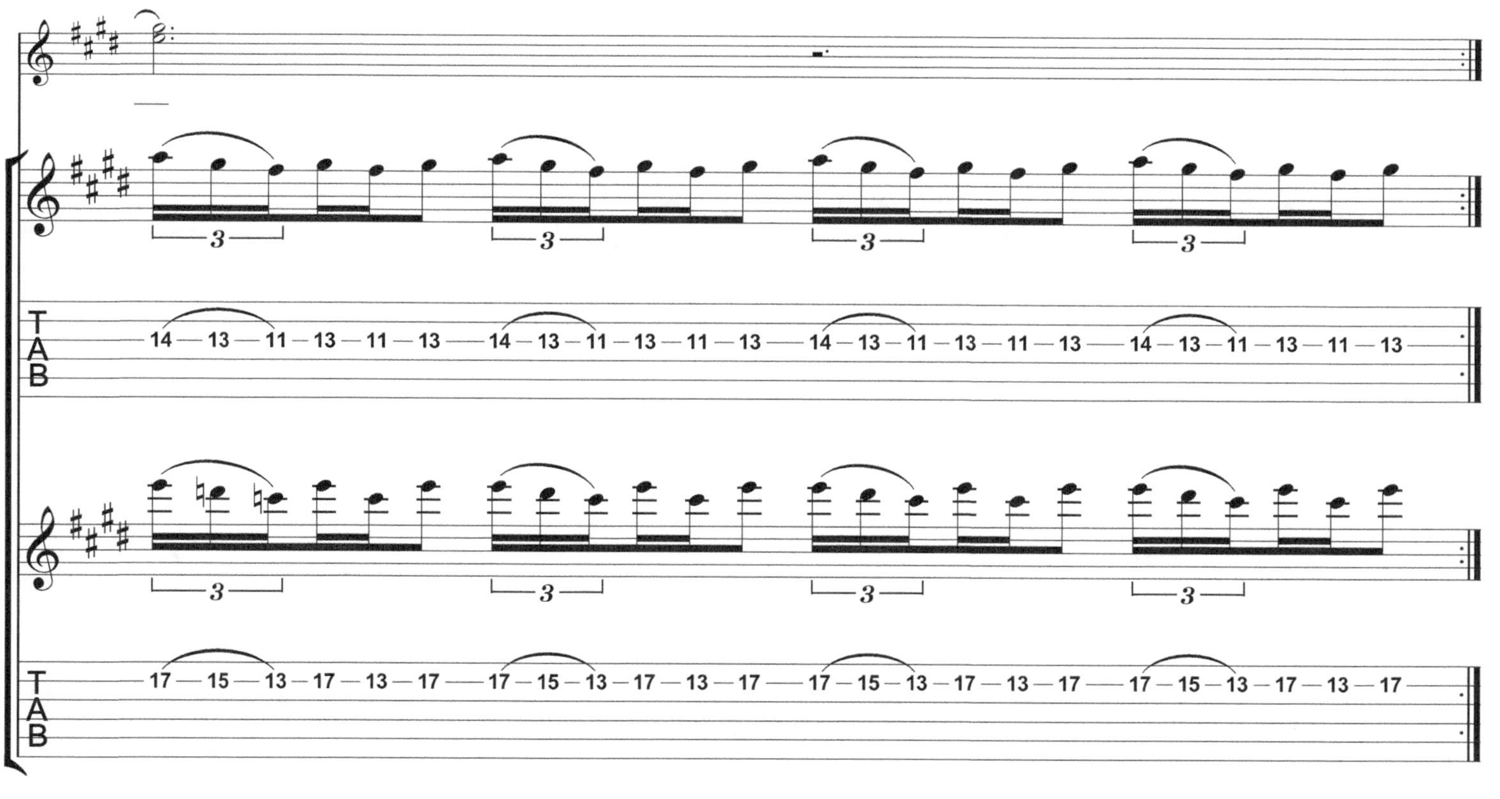

Verse
N.C.
2. Beau - ti - ful sen - ses____ are gone, ca -
Gtr. 1+2

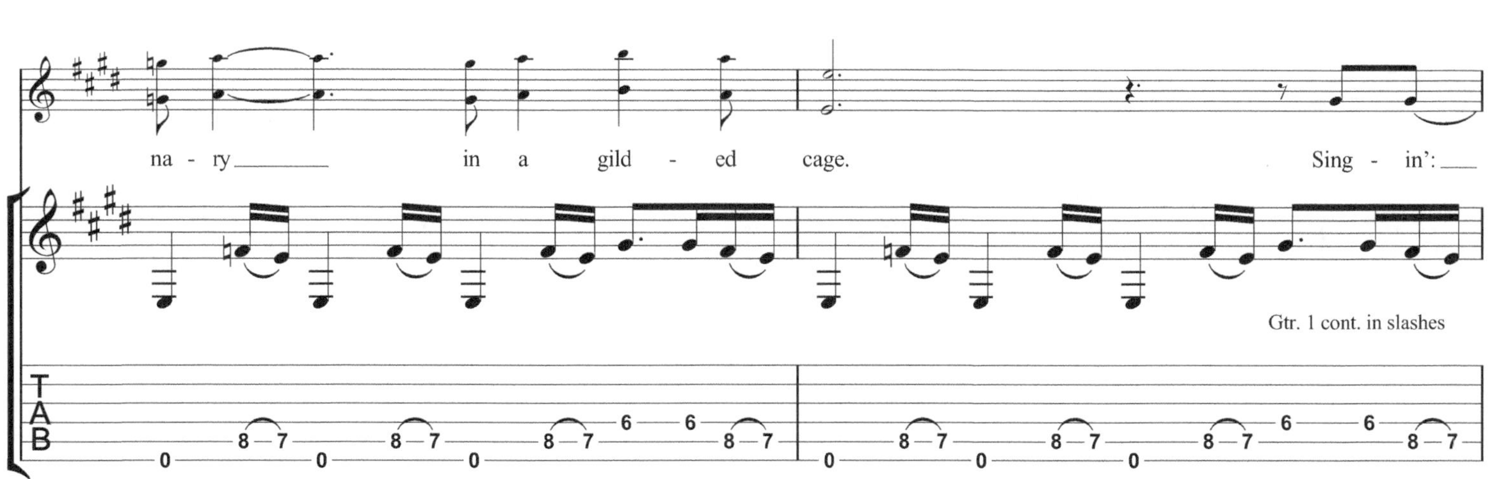
na - ry____ in a gild - ed cage. Sing - in':____
Gtr. 1 cont. in slashes

Gtr. 1
open
Gtr. 2
8va
Sweet, ____ soft and low, I will
poi - son you all, ___ come clo - ser ____ rac - ing to your
Chorus
A add9
B add11
cont. sim.
tongue. I got what was, ______
Gtr. 1 cont. in slashes
G6
A add9
B add11
I want to take ____ what's

G6
Aadd9
Badd11
left.
No talk will cure
G6
Aadd9
Badd11
To Coda
G6
what's lost,   or save   what's left   for the deaf.
8vb
3
3
3
Gtr. 2 tacet
E5
The blind can go get fucked, lie be-side the ditch, this ha-lo round my neck, has torn out ev-'ry stitch.

Gtr. 1
Ah.
3   3   3   3
T A B
17 — 16 — 14 — 16 — 14 — 16   17 — 16 — 14 — 16 — 14 — 16   17 — 16 — 14 — 16 — 14 — 16   17 — 16 — 14 — 16 — 14 — 16
Gtr. 2
3   3   3   3
T A B
17 — 15 — 13 — 15 — 13 — 15   17 — 15 — 13 — 15 — 13 — 15   17 — 15 — 13 — 15 — 13 — 15   17 — 15 — 13 — 15 — 13 — 15

3   3   3   3
T A B
14 — 13 — 11 — 13 — 11 — 13   14 — 13 — 11 — 13 — 11 — 13   14 — 13 — 11 — 13 — 11 — 13   14 — 13 — 11 — 13 — 11 — 13
3   3   3   3
T A B
17 — 15 — 13 — 17 — 13 — 17   17 — 15 — 13 — 17 — 13 — 17   17 — 15 — 13 — 17 — 13 — 17   17 — 15 — 13 — 17 — 13 — 17

Ah.
3
3
3
3
17 — 16 — 14 — 16 — 14 — 16   17 — 16 — 14 — 16 — 14 — 16   17 — 16 — 14 — 16 — 14 — 16   17 — 16 — 14 — 16 — 14 — 16
3
3
3
3
17 — 15 — 13 — 15 — 13 — 15   17 — 15 — 13 — 15 — 13 — 15   17 — 15 — 13 — 15 — 13 — 15   17 — 15 — 13 — 15 — 13 — 15

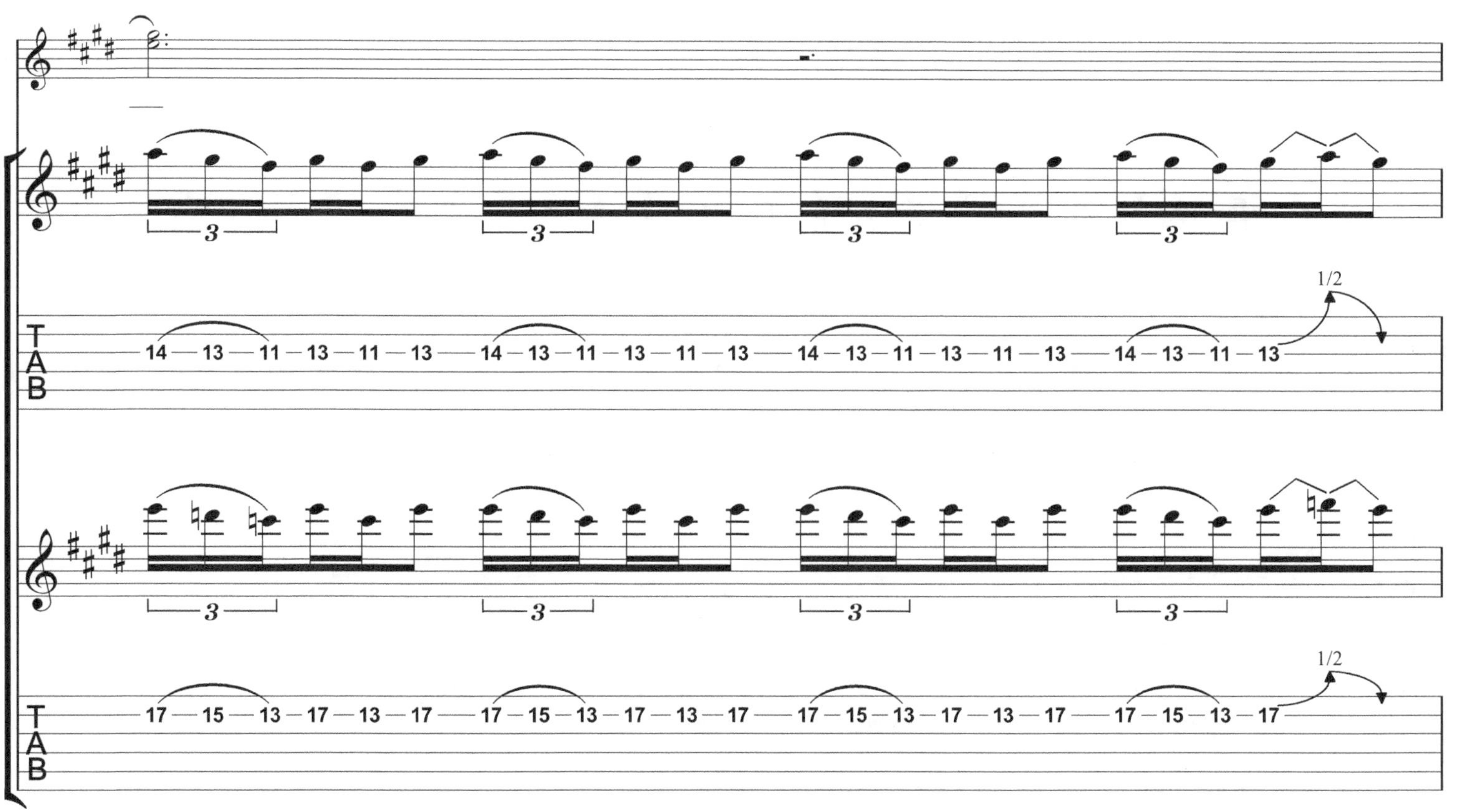

3
3
3
3
1/2
14 — 13 — 11 — 13 — 11 — 13   14 — 13 — 11 — 13 — 11 — 13   14 — 13 — 11 — 13 — 11 — 13   14 — 13 — 11 — 13
3
3
3
3
1/2
17 — 15 — 13 — 17 — 13 — 17   17 — 15 — 13 — 17 — 13 — 17   17 — 15 — 13 — 17 — 13 — 17   17 — 15 — 13 — 17

Ah.
3
1/2
full
3
Verse
N.C.
3. Who ___ are you hi - ding, ___ is it safe ___ for the deaf?
Gtrs. 1+2*
*composite part

Beau - ti - ful can - cer, in - fil - trate and for - get. And I

saw you com - ing, and I heard not a thing, a mis -

D.S. al Coda

take not to lis - ten when I knew where you'd been. And I

Coda

G6

E5

left for the deaf.

rit...

Gtr. 2

Volume swell w/feedback & sustain

119

MOSQUITO SONG

Words & Music by Josh Homme, Nick Oliveri & Michael Melchiondo

Am   C   E
skin   and   bone.
e - ver   taste.   (Taste,   taste.)

Am   C   E   Am
When   you   walk   a - mong   the   trees,   lis - ten - ing
So   you   scream,   whine   and   yell,   sup - ple   sounds   of

C   E   Am
to   the   leaves.   The   fur - ther   I   go   the
din - ner   bells.   We   all   will   feed   the

C   E   Am   C   E   To Coda
less   I   know,   the   less   I   know.
worms   and   trees,   so   don't   be   shy.

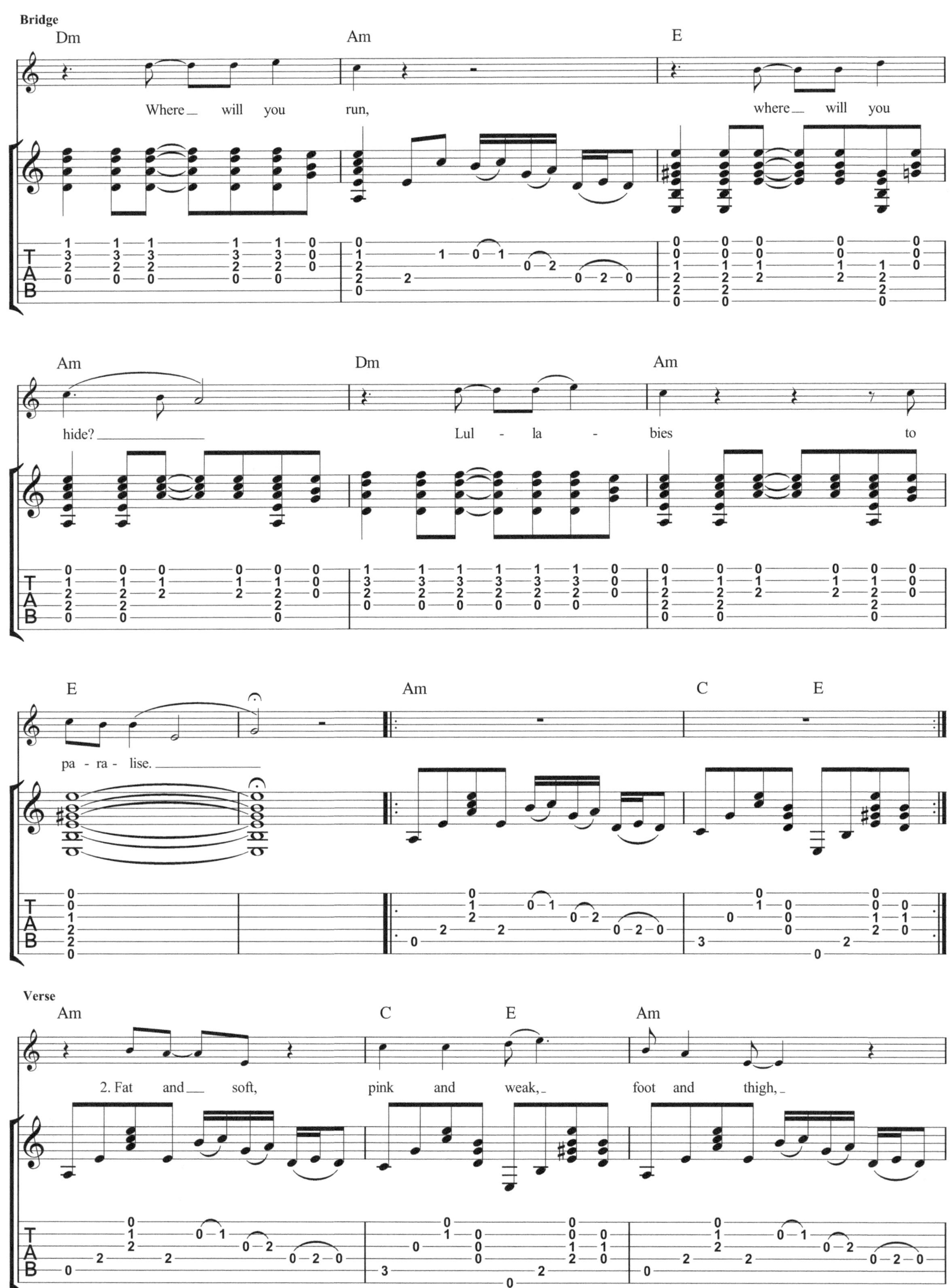

Bridge
Dm
Am
E
Where will you run, where will you
Am
Dm
Am
hide? Lul - la - bies to
E
Am
C
E
pa - ra - lise.
Verse
Am
C
E
Am
2. Fat and soft, pink and weak, foot and thigh,

C
E
Am
tongue   and   cheek. __   You   know,   I'm __ told   they
C
E
Am
C
E
swal - low you __ whole,   skin   and   bone. __
Am
C
E
Cut - ting __ boards   and   ha - ha - hang - ing   hooks,
Am
C
E
Am
blood - y   knives,   cook - ing   books.   Pro - mi - sing __   you

C   E   Am   C   E
won't feel a thing   at all.

Chorus
D   Am
Swal - low and   chew,

E   Am   D
eat___ you a - live. ___   All ___ of us

Am   E
food   that has - n't died. ___   And the light says:

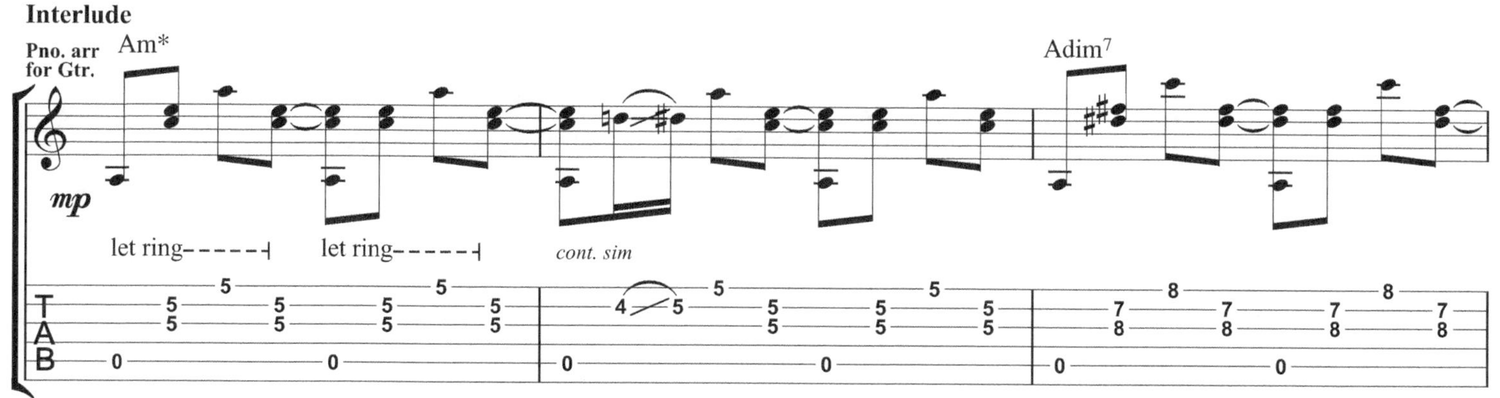

Interlude
Pno. arr
for Gtr.
Am*
Adim⁷
mp
let ring
let ring
cont. sim

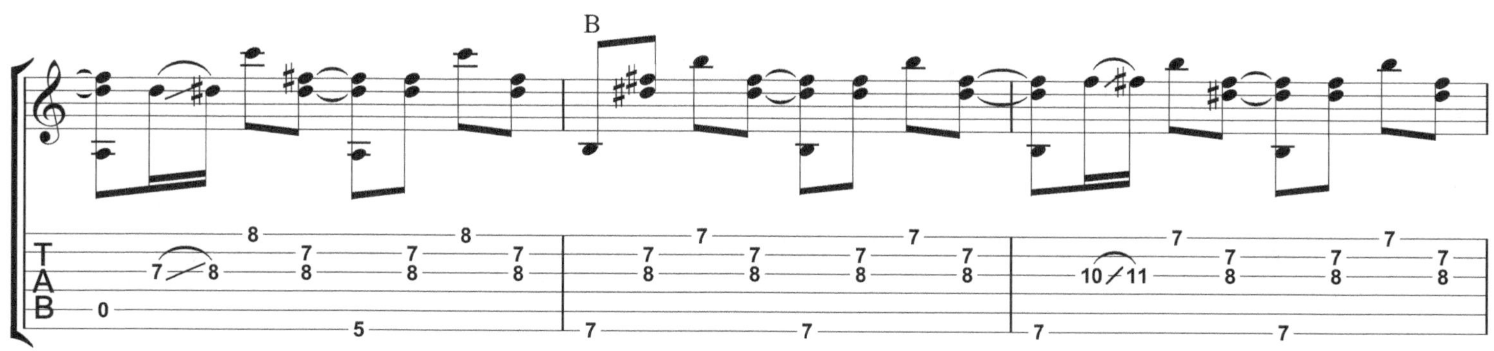

B

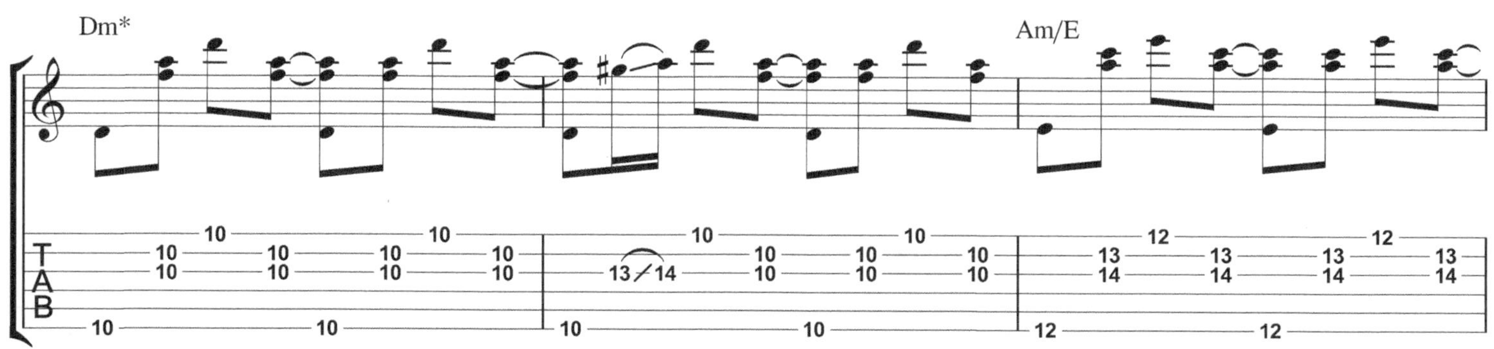

Dm*
Am/E

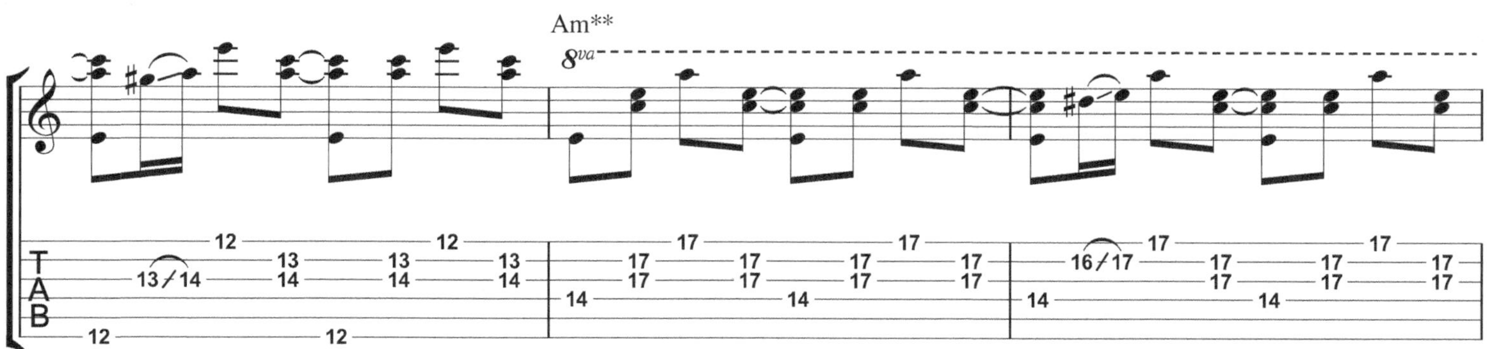

Am**
8va

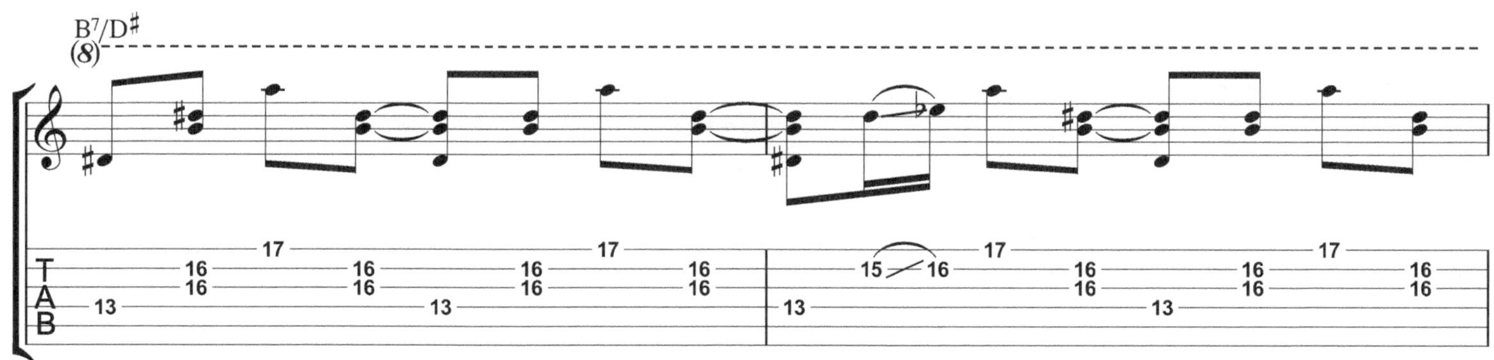

B⁷/D#
(8)

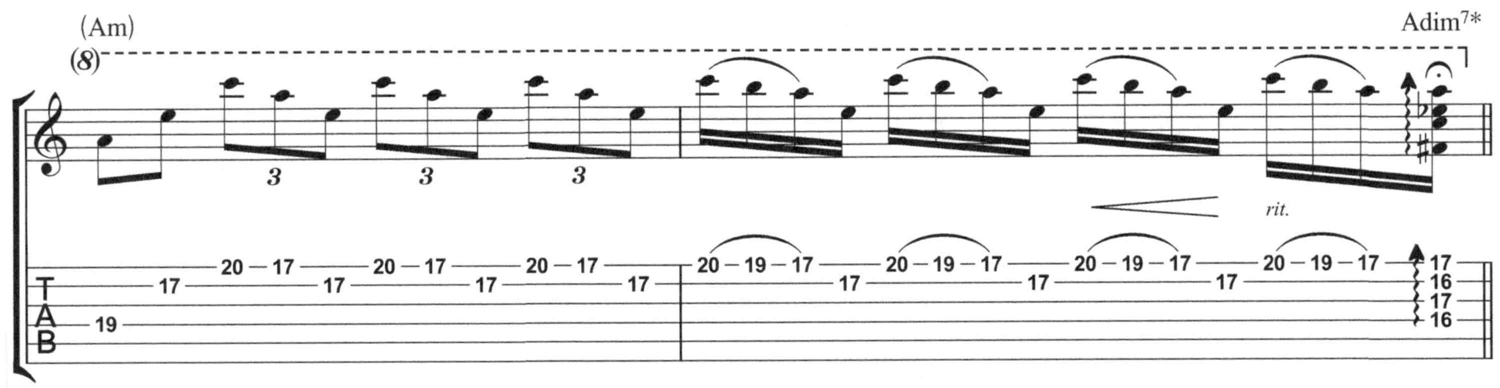
(Am)
(8)
Adim7*
3 3 3
rit.

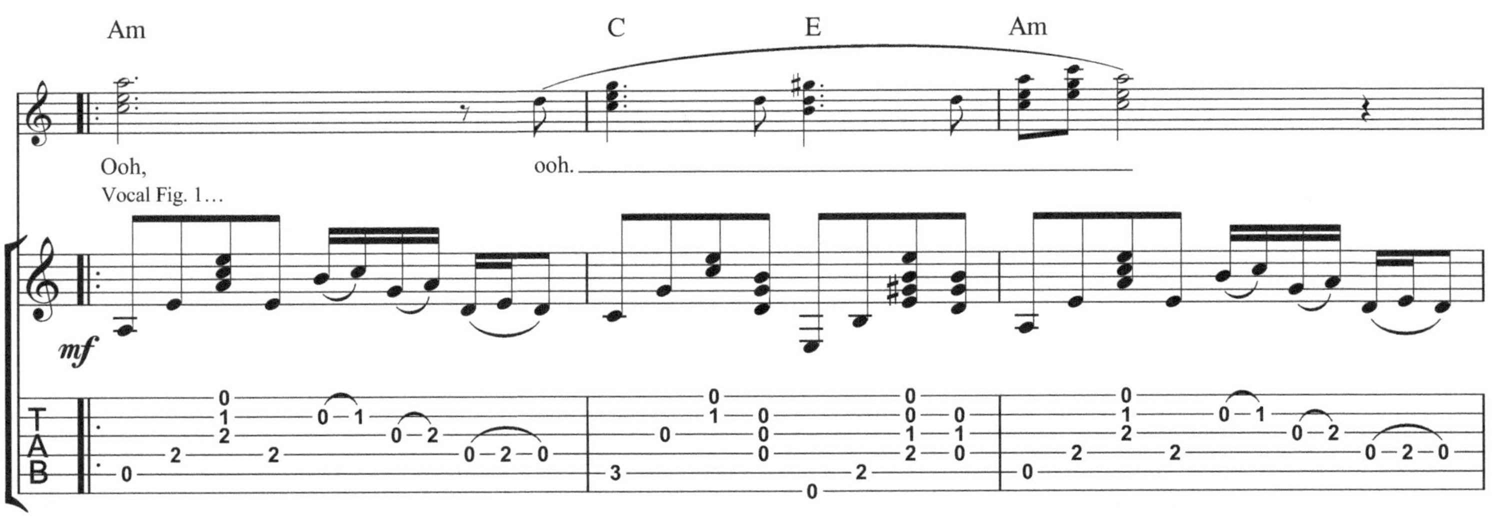
Am
C
E
Am
Ooh,
Vocal Fig. 1...
ooh.
mf

C
E
Am
C
E
Ooh.

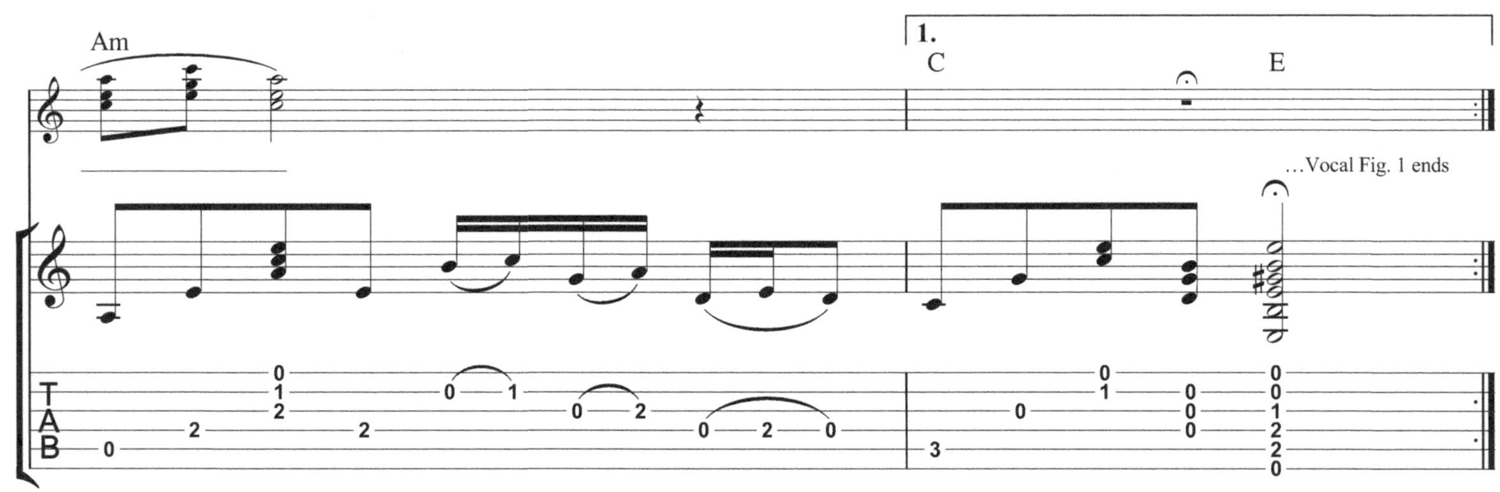
Am
1.
C
E
...Vocal Fig. 1 ends

Solo
2.
w/ Vocal Fig. 1 w/ad libs for 16 bars
Gtr. 2
Gtr. 1 w/Fig. 1 & ad libs (x8)
Harm.
127

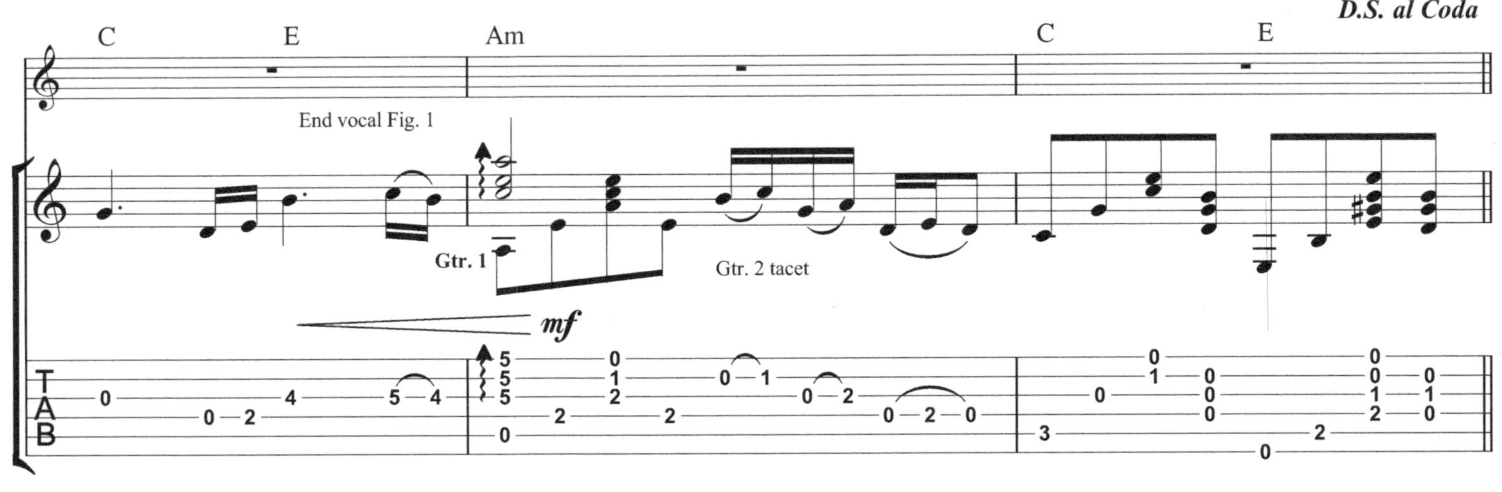
C
E
Am
C
E
End vocal Fig. 1
Gtr. 1
Gtr. 2 tacet
mf

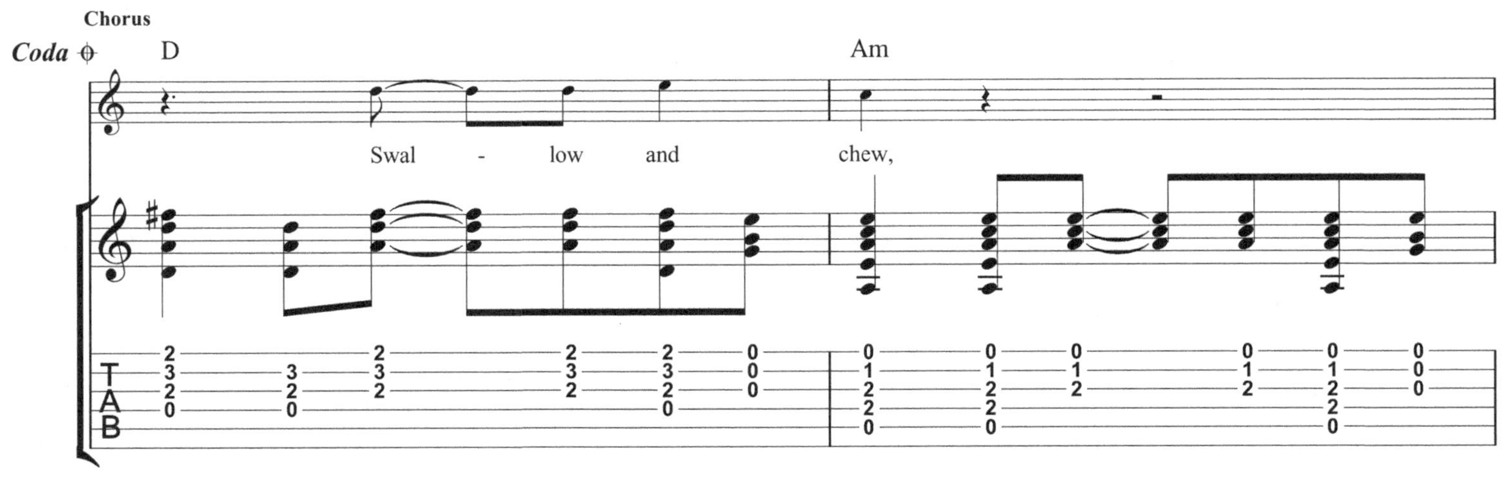
Chorus
Coda
D
Am
Swal - low and chew,

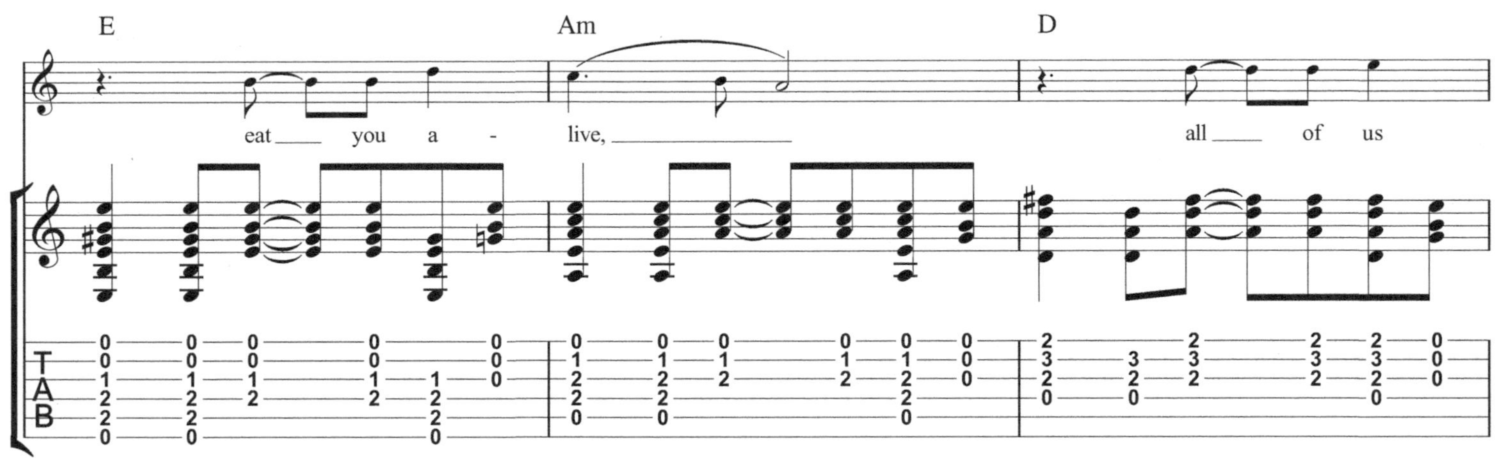
E
Am
D
eat you a - live, all of us

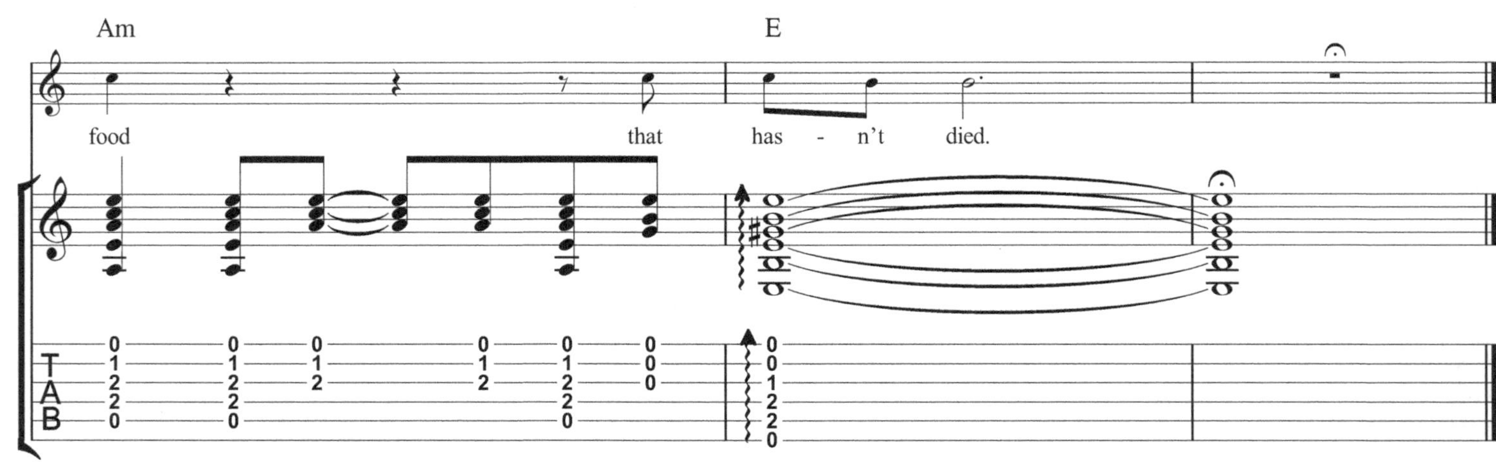
Am
E
food that has - n't died.